Action!
Acting Lessons
for CG Animators

Action!
Acting Lessons
for CG Animators

JOHN KUNDERT-GIBBS | KRISTIN KUNDERT-GIBBS

WILEY

Wiley Publishing, Inc.

Acquisitions Editor: Mariann Barsolo
Development Editor: Toni Ackley
Production Editor: Dassi Zeidel
Copy Editor: Liz Welch
Production Manager: Tim Tate
Vice President and Executive Group Publisher: Richard Swadley
Vice President and Publisher: Neil Edde
Book Designer: Caryl Gorska
Compositor: Chris Gillespie, Happenstance Type-O-Rama
Proofreader: Publication Services, Inc.
Indexer: Ted Laux
Cover Designer: Ryan Sneed
Cover Image: ©iStockPhoto
Project Coordinator/Cover: Lynsey Stanford

All photos, unless otherwise credited, are by John Kundert-Gibbs.

For general information on our other products and services or to obtain technical support, please contact our Customer Care Department within the U.S. at (877) 762-2974, outside the U.S. at (317) 572-3993 or fax (317) 572-4002.

Wiley also publishes its books in a variety of electronic formats. Some content that appears in print may not be available in electronic books.

Library of Congress Cataloging-in-Publication Data

Kundert-Gibbs, John L.

Action! : acting lessons for CG animators / John Kundert-Gibbs. — 1st ed.

  p. cm.

ISBN-13: 978-0-470-22743-5 (paper/DVD)

ISBN-10: 0-470-22743-5 (paper/DVD)

1. Computer animation. 2. Animation (Cinematography) 3. Motion picture acting. 4. Motion pictures—Production and direction. I. Title.

TR897.7.K82 2009

006.6'96—dc22

                    2008052149

10 9 8 7 6 5 4 3 2 1

Dear Reader

Thank you for choosing *Action! Acting Lessons for CG Animators*. This book is part of a family of premium-quality Sybex books, all written by outstanding authors who combine practical experience with a gift for teaching.

Sybex was founded in 1976. More than 30 years later, we're still committed to producing consistently exceptional books. With each of our books, we're working hard to set a new standard for the industry. From the authors we work with to the paper we print on, our goal is to bring you the best books available.

I hope you see all that reflected in these pages. I'd be very interested to hear your comments and get your feedback on how we're doing. Feel free to let me know what you think about this or any other Sybex book by sending me an email at `nedde@wiley.com`; if you think you've found a technical error in this book, please visit `http://sybex.custhelp.com`. Customer feedback is critical to our efforts at Sybex.

Best regards,

Neil Edde
Vice President and Publisher
Sybex, an Imprint of Wiley

For our boys:
Josh and Kenlee.

Acknowledgments

This book would not have been possible without generous support from the University of Georgia. The Department of Theatre and Film Studies provided space and equipment as well as many talented students. We wish to thank, in particular, David Saltz, head of the department, and Garnett Stokes, dean of the Franklin College of Arts and Sciences, for their enduring support. The Master of Fine Arts (MFA) and undergraduate students in acting, media, and design all contributed time and energy to this project. The MFA performance class of 2009 was instrumental in our work. Their members include Jacqueline Carey, Ruth Crews, Norman Ferguson, Koqunia Forté, Scotty Gannon, Rob Glidden, Jonathan Phipps, Amy Roeder, Brandon Wentz, and Shana Youngblood. In addition, James Orara, David Floyd, and Lena Gieseke contributed countless hours modeling and rigging the characters included on the DVD.

The people at Sybex have been amazing partners in this journey. We thank them all, especially Mariann Barsolo, Toni Zuccarini Ackley, Dassi Zeidel, Ryan Sneed, Liz Welch, and Publication Services.

About the Authors

John Kundert-Gibbs is an associate professor of animation in the Theatre and Film Studies Department at the University of Georgia. John is an author of the popular *Mastering Maya* series, and also edited the two volumes in the *Maya: Secrets of the Pros* series. In addition to his books on Maya and 3D animation, John writes, designs, and directs for the theater.

Kristin Kundert-Gibbs has worked as a producer, director, vocal coach, and actress in theaters such as 7 Stages, the North Carolina Shakespeare Festival, the Kingsmen Shakespeare Festival, the Warehouse Theatre, and others. She is an assistant professor of acting and voice in the Department of Theatre and Film Studies at the University of Georgia, and has also taught at Duke, William and Mary, and Indiana State University.

CONTENTS AT A GLANCE

Contents

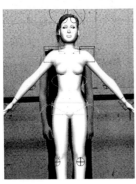

Introduction

As an animator, you are basically doing the job of an actor—just very slowly. You are creating a living, breathing character that tells a story, shares an experience, and moves an audience. Your character becomes "animated" with the body, voice, and emotions you breathe into it. This process is similar to what an actor goes through when creating a role, so you need to understand the process of creating a realistic character on the screen from the actor's perspective as well as from the perspective of the CG artist in order to create the most compelling characters possible.

This book is a synthesis of the fields of acting and animation, a guidebook for you, the animator, who most likely has more training in the technique of animating (motion, keyframing, solid drawing, and the like) than in the process of developing a character with emotion, intent, and a through line (a driving desire that the character has). Within these pages you will discover secrets actors spend years (and often lots and lots of money) learning—and how to apply these secrets directly to animation. Rather than having to read a number of books on acting and animating and figuring out how to put them together yourself, this book is purpose-built just for you: the animator who wants to understand how to create more powerful, compelling characters utilizing the advanced techniques stage and screen actors have perfected over the years.

In a sense, your process in creating character animation is twofold. First, you must create the character, and then you must transfer it to the computer. Perhaps you could argue that you are creating the character directly on the screen, but in any case your artistic medium is not the same as an actor, who uses their own body, voice, and emotions as the final output. Instead, your instrument is the hardware and software available to you. Nevertheless, your character still has a body, voice, and emotions, just as the actor's character does, so understanding and employing the techniques of an actor is essential to bettering your artistry.

What is most important for you to take away from this book is the understanding of the process an actor goes through when creating a character, along with the knowledge of how to transfer or use one or more acting techniques in a given animation. The techniques presented in this book are designed to broaden your storehouse of knowledge and increase your "toolbox" for developing a character. This book is not intended to turn you into an actor; we would venture to say that no book could turn someone into an actor. As with becoming an accomplished character animator, only years of hard work can do that. Sanford Meisner, one of the greatest acting teachers of the 20th century, said that it takes 20 years to make an actor, to gain the experience and technique necessary to truly act. Rather than send you out on a 20-year quest to become an actor, we present numerous proven (and sometimes private) techniques that help actors create character, communicate emotion and intent, and connect with the audience. These techniques provide an excellent complement to the technical knowledge of 3D software (or 2D software, or drawing) that animators learn.

We believe it is virtually impossible to understand and internalize the work and process of an actor without participating in this process. Reading about it will only increase your intellectual understanding, while doing it will allow you to viscerally experience the creation of a new life. In most theater programs across the country, acting is a required element of a degree in theater. Even if an individual never intends to set foot on the stage—instead planning to design, write, or direct—he or she must fully participate in an acting class to understand the art of acting, which is central to the creation of character. In similar fashion, you are creating character through animation, and there is no substitute for experience in creating animation to learn the process and master the technique. To facilitate the need to practice what you learn, a large percentage of this book involves both acting and animation exercises, where you can apply the knowledge you learn in these pages directly to your own and your virtual character's bodies. Take your time, have patience with yourself, participate in the exercises fully, and your skills as an animator (and actor for that matter) will grow immensely.

What You'll Learn

Character animation is far more than simply moving body parts around and hoping everything looks good when you get done. It is a blending of technical, artistic, and acting skills that come together to create a performance, by pixels on a screen (or lines on paper), that connects with and moves an audience. This combination of skills is a complex alchemy, but all too often books and classes focus only on the technical aspect of animation. Knowing how to work in a 3D package is crucial to being able to animate, but it is not sufficient for creating the memorable performances any animator wants to make.

This book is our answer to filling in what many animators miss in their reading or classroom training: the artistic and especially acting part of animation. While not as easily quantifiable as the technical skills, we feel it is imperative that animators have a solid understanding of acting techniques and methodologies. Although taking a basic acting class is great and we highly recommend it, there are many techniques that only advanced acting students have access to—techniques that are ideally suited to animators as well as actors—and we have gathered these techniques together in this book to present to you, the animator.

This book is designed for you, with a special emphasis placed on external acting techniques. These techniques create the body or outside of the character, so they will translate more closely to your work of graphically creating a character. Working through this book will provide you with a solid knowledge of how these advanced acting techniques work, as well as how to apply them to your character animation work. From utilizing Commedia lazzi (or "takes"), to breathing in patterns that create emotion, to analyzing energy blocks within one's body, to many others, you will have a veritable smorgasbord from which to choose when creating your next character animation.

In addition to intellectual knowledge, this book presents numerous exercises designed to help you incorporate character and acting into your own body—and then transfer this knowledge to practice in animation exercises. You will thus practice what you learn with immediate, precisely focused exercises to help you internalize and master the skills and knowledge presented.

What You Should Already Know

This book is for people with some experience with a 3D animation package. Although we cover the basics quickly in Chapter 2, we assume you already know how to open a scene, what animation is, how to create keyframes, and all the other fundamentals of working in a 3D package. Additionally, any experience you have doing character animation will be very useful. If you feel you need some help on the basics, try a book to get you started, such as Dariush Derakhshani's *Introducing Maya 2009* (Sybex 2009).

This book focuses on 3D animation, particularly using Autodesk's Maya 3D animation package. However, we have presented the techniques and exercises in these pages in as platform-agnostic a fashion as we can, and thus you should be able to follow along using any 3D package, any 2D animation package, or even if your preferred animation "package" is a pencil and paper: the knowledge presented here is for all animators.

How the Book Is Organized

The book begins with a basic introduction to the history of acting and of animation. It then progresses to discuss the Stanislavski system of acting, which is the foundation of almost all modern acting theory. Chapters 4 through 9 form the heart of the book, presenting different external acting techniques, their theories and practice. Chapters 10 and 11 discuss creating character voices and working with recorded voiceovers when creating verbal character animation.

In each chapter is a series of exercises designed to help you understand and incorporate the work discussed in the chapter. We present acting exercises for the given technique first, and then progress to animation exercises designed to help you transfer the techniques from your own body to the virtual one on your computer screen.

The acting exercises are divided into two kinds: solo exercises and group exercises. If you are working through this book with a class, or at least a group of friends and colleagues, you will find the group exercises to be invaluable additions to the solo exercises. Acting is always best learned with others, as most acting work on the stage, on the screen, and in the animated world is centered on the communication between characters. Thus, if possible, find colleagues or other partners to play with in the group exercises. If not, you will still make progress and understand the techniques by performing the solo exercises. In the best-case scenario, you will be able to do them both.

Using the DVD

The DVD included with this book is chock-full of invaluable resources to help you discover the power of applying acting techniques to your character animation work. We have two fully functional character rigs created in Autodesk's Maya (one male, one female) that not only allow for easy animation, but also provide built-in advanced features like squash and stretch. These powerful character rigs will allow you to follow along with the book's exercises as well as to further explore the techniques on your own.

In addition to the character rigs, we have example Maya files for most of the animation exercises, allowing you to explore exactly how we created the animations we present in our exercises. (Of note, many exercises contain working versions of the character rigs, so you will sometimes notice differences between these exercise samples and the final rigs.) We also include a vast amount of video footage of actors performing the techniques described in these pages. This footage lets you see exactly how trained actors apply the work described in the pages—a massive benefit to both the acting and animation exercises.

The painstakingly collected material on this DVD is, we believe, a unique collection of acting technique, animation examples, and character rigs. Nowhere else will you find such extensive, highly focused assets all collected in one convenient place for your educational benefit.

Feedback

Both Kristin and John are educators as well as practitioners of their art. They are always happy to answer questions or to listen to your feedback concerning the book. Feel free to contact them:

Kristin Kundert-Gibbs: kkundert@uga.edu

John Kundert-Gibbs: jkundert@uga.edu

CHAPTER 1

What Is Acting?

Acting is defined as the art or practice of representing a character on a stage or before cameras and derives from the Latin word *agere*, meaning "to do." When someone is acting, they are performing an action: thus, something is being done as a character. Generally an actor is someone who takes on another character by altering parts of their body, voice, or personality in order to share a story with an audience. Ironically, or perhaps appropriately for this book, an obsolete meaning for the word acting is *to animate*.

In regard to CG animation and your work in this book, the definition seems perfect: If actors are animating a character, then CG animators are acting as they create. What exactly actors do and how they do it has changed over time. What was acceptable and what was preferred has varied radically throughout history.

This chapter discusses:

- **A brief history of acting**
- **How acting has changed over time**
- **The work of an actor**
- **How an actor trains**
- **How acting relates to the animator**
- **Exercises to begin your journey of exploring the training of an actor**

A Brief History of Acting

Similar to many noted animated tales, the history of acting begins with a legend. During the sixth century in ancient Greece, a man named Thespis stepped out of a chorus of performers to utter several solo lines, and thus acting was born. Prior to this time, if you went to a dramatic festival in Greece you would see a group of 50 performers singing or chanting in unison the tales of Greek gods or heroes. When Thespis first spoke, he assumed a character and told the story from the character's point of view, not from a third person as was done by the chorus. Although this is only a legend, Thespis has been granted a special place in the history of acting, and to this day actors are called thespians.

> Jon Lovitz brought the word thespian to the forefront of popular culture with his character, Master Thespian, on *Saturday Night Live*.

Eventually, in ancient Greece the number of actors grew to three and were accompanied by a chorus. Although often more than three characters took part in a play, only three of the characters could appear on the stage at any one time, as there were only three actors. Thus one actor would often play more than one role in any given production. They would change characters with a change of costume and mask.

Given the nature of the large, outdoor amphitheatres that the Greeks performed in, and the emphasis placed on the ritual of theatre, the work of the first actors was predominately voice and gesture work (see Figure 1.1). The actors, all men, were dressed in large robes that covered their bodies and oversized masks that hid their faces so that the actor/character could be seen at a great distance. They communicated character and emotion through changes in the voice and in the physical stature of their bodies.

Unlike actors in ancient Greece, who were revered, it is believed the actors in ancient Rome were slaves owned by company managers. The performances were still outdoors and masks were still used, so much of the work of actors remained focused on the voice and gesture. There was no restriction on the numbers of actors in Roman theatre, but they still were all men. The dramatic material also went through a great transformation in Rome. The stories of the Greeks were of their heroes and gods. The stories of ancient Rome were often of everyday life and could be quite licentious.

The late Roman empire was the first period where Christianity began to target theater, and actors in particular. Theater was associated with pagan festivals and could often be vulgar. Mimes of the time even went so far as ridiculing Christian practices such as baptism and communion. By AD 300, Christians were told not to attend the theater, and any Christian who went to the theater instead of the church on a holy day was excommunicated. Actors were not allowed to partake of the sacraments or be buried in church cemeteries. During the rise of the Christian period, theaters declined and almost completely disappeared. Traveling jugglers, mimes, storytellers, and acrobats who could be seen at fairs carried on the performance traditions.

Figure 1.1

Amy Roeder plays Hecuba in a scene from *Trojan Women* at the University of Georgia Department of Theatre and Film Studies, directed by George Contini

The Middle Ages

It is ironic that after all the opposition by the church to theater, the church is the very place where theater was revived during the Middle Ages. During an Easter service in AD 925, a performance that was probably sung depicted the three Marys looking for Jesus at his tomb and encountering angels that proclaim him to be risen from the dead. This was the beginning of liturgical drama where clergy and choirboys performed biblical stories and moral lessons as part of the church services. There was no real emphasis on acting here; the importance of the event was the didactic lessons that were learned, not artistic merit.

Eventually the popularity of these performances led to the development of theater outside the church. Although the scripts were still approved by the church, trade and craft guilds took over the production of plays. Actors for these productions were local townspeople. Sometimes they received their roles by auditioning, and sometimes they merely volunteered. The scripts were stereotypical with one-dimensional characters and thus did not require any subtlety of acting. Once again the most important aspect of the performance was the voice and stylized gesture.

Commedia dell'Arte

During the Renaissance, most theatrical productions moved to the court and were performed by courtiers. This theater was more for showing off than any real acting. The development of a professional, public theater happened in Italy with the rise of Commedia dell'Arte, an improvised form of theater based on stock characters and scenarios. Each member of an acting troupe had a specific character they performed. The scripts were completely improvised from plot synopses developed by the troupe in rehearsal. Commedia was at its height between 1570 and 1650.

A Commedia actor would take on a character and perform this character for her or his entire life. All of the stock characters had masks that were specifically designed to show the qualities of the character, and the performers had certain physical gestures or comic bits called lazzi that were associated with the mask and character (see Figure 1.2). The work was highly physical and demanded a great deal of vocal and physical control, power, and stamina. Commedia also introduced women to the stage. However, the characters were stock types and the situations were stereotypical, so there still was no need for subtly of acting. Instead, the emphasis was placed on the physical and vocal work as well as a quick wit to be able to improvise the scenarios.

Figure 1.2

The University of Georgia Commedia troupe

Commedia laid the groundwork for characters that we still use today in theater, film, and animation. The "dirty old man," the "braggart solider," the "sneaky servant," the "empty-headed young lover," and the "licentious servant" are all character types that we recognize in our comedies. These and almost all stock types can be traced back to Commedia. (For more on Commedia, see Chapter 4, "Commedia dell'Arte.")

Acting in Shakespeare's Day

In 1570, the Queen of England sanctioned daily theatrical performances, and consequently many acting troupes were formed in England. Actors were shareholders in their companies and were paid by a member of the royal family who served as their patron. A shareholding actor had to invest a sum of money in the company and then shared in any profits that were made from the performances. One of the most famous troupes was The King's Men— William Shakespeare himself was a member of this company. (See Figure 1.3.)

Figure 1.3

Drawing of the stage of Shakespeare's Globe Theatre

BY JASON ALLEN

There are many different opinions concerning the acting style of the Elizabethan performer. Some descriptions of performances have called them realistic. Hamlet's advice to the players would suggest that the Elizabethan actors understood the ground rules for producing a psychologically realistic character on the stage. On the other hand, men playing women, stylized stage backgrounds, and the unrealistic nature of many of the scripts suggest that the actor was still focused on the external voice and gesture of the character. In either case, audience members have written accounts of the actors moving audiences emotionally by the power of their performances.

Hamlet: Speak the speech, I pray you, as I pronounc'd it to you, trippingly on the tongue. But if you mouth it, as many of our players do, I had as lief the town crier spoke my lines. Nor do not saw the air too much with your hand, thus, but use all gently; for in the very torrent, tempest, and (as I may say) whirlwind of your passion, you must acquire and beget a temperance that may give it smoothness. O, it offends me to the soul to hear a robustious periwig-pated fellow tear a passion to tatters, to very rags, to split the ears of the groundlings…, Suit the action to the word, the word to the action; with this special observance, that you o'erstep not the modesty of nature: for anything so overdone is from the purpose of playing, whose end, both at the first and now, was and is, to hold, as 't were, the mirror up to nature; to show Virtue her own feature, scorn her own image, and the very age and body of the time his form and pressure.

— HAMLET ACT III, SCENE II

During the 1640s, England was embroiled in a civil war between the Royalists and the Puritans. The Puritans attempted to end all theatrical activity because they had returned to the early Christians' beliefs concerning the theater and actors. In 1642, a law was passed suspending all performances, and five years later another law was passed that ordered all actors to be apprehended as rogues. Theater did carry on, but it went underground, and there are few records concerning the work of the time.

Presentational Acting

In 1660, Charles II was restored to the throne in England, ending the reign of the Puritans. Theater once again began to grow and flourish, and some respect for the actor returned. Women were introduced to the English stage, and companies were set up. Many companies had training or apprentice programs that took on young actors and taught them singing and dancing, but most actors learned from trial and error. Company apprentices would spend their first few years playing small roles. From this they would discover just what characters and types they were best suited for and would spend the rest of their careers playing those types.

The majority of acting for the next two hundred years was what is called presentational acting (see Figure 1.4), which is the mere presenting of the character from an external perspective. The goal for the actor is to look or appear as if the character is genuinely feeling or experiencing emotions by the proper adaptations of the body and voice. The actor would never experience any emotions or connect psychologically with the character. The work was purely external, and the style was oratorical. Actors always played the front of the stage and never turned their backs to the audience. This formal style persisted for years and was well received by audiences.

COSTUMES BY IVAN INGERMANN. LIGHTS BY RACHEL KONIECZNY. SET BY BEN PHILIPPS. DIRECTED BY KRISTIN KUNDERT-GIBBS.

Figure 1.4

Norman Ferguson and Jacqueline Carey as Oberon and Puck in a presentation model production of *A Midsummer Night's Dream* at the University of Georgia's Department of Theatre and Film Studies

A good example of the presentational ideology is the work of François Delsarte (1811–1871). Delsarte developed a system by which every part of the body could be used to communicate emotions, attitudes, characters, and ideas. Thus all characterization was based on a precise formula of stances, postures, and gestures.

Although the formal style of oration was the dominant mode of performance, certain actors began to change or adapt their personal acting styles for a more realistic approach. As early as 1750, actor David Garrick urged that characterizations should be based on direct observations of life and not a distanced formalistic approach. These ideas concerning realistic acting continued to grow and gain acceptance throughout the next two hundred years.

Stanislavski and the Moscow Art Theatre

The major turning point from presentational to representational or realistic acting came with the founding of the Moscow Art Theatre in 1897. The theater, under the direction of Constantin Stanislavski (shown in Figure 1.5), revolutionized acting. It threw out the old star system and opted for an ensemble style of acting. Stanislavski, an actor himself, set out to perfect an approach to acting. The results of his work led to the first fully realistic productions. His company was world renowned, and their work was studied by theater artists across the globe.

The heart of Stanislavski's work is based on the "method of physical actions." The actor must determine the "objective" or primary desire of the character, which leads to a through line of physical actions for the role. The actor then performs a series of actions to help him or her achieve this objective. Stanislavski discovered that acting becomes truthful by truly doing something to achieve an objective. The work of the actors in the Moscow Art Theatre was simple, honest, and emotionally realistic.

Figure 1.5

Constantin Stanislavski

DRAWING BY JASON ALLEN

Stanislavski established a training program for young actors. He stressed that actors needed to start by training their bodies and voices but then needed to focus their attentions to learning to analyze and study a text in order to determine the through line of actions for the character. He also urged actors to observe themselves and others to learn what truthful behavior was. He wrote about his techniques and ideas in three books about the work of an actor and one autobiography of his life in art.

The Group Theatre

Acting in America was revolutionized by the Group Theatre in the 1930s. Founded in New York by Harold Clurman, Lee Strasberg, and Cheryl Crawford, the Group Theatre sought to emulate the methods and ensemble approach of the Moscow Art Theatre. The group would cloister themselves away in upstate New York to train and rehearse a script for months before presenting their ensemble work in the city. Their productions were known for their theatrical realism, which moved audiences to their feet and set a new standard for truth in performance.

The acting was based in a psychological truth that was rooted in the inner motivations of the character. In the course of rehearsing a script, Strasberg led the actors through exercises that emphasized emotional memory as the key to truth in acting. Strasberg believed that this was the heart of Stanislavski's work in Russia, but unfortunately Strasberg's knowledge and understanding of Stanislavski was incomplete. Strasberg's bastardization of Stanislavski's work became known as the "Method." Countless famous actors have trained in the Method. One of the most famous performances attributed to method training is that of Marlon Brando playing Stanley Kowalski in *A Streetcar Named Desire*.

Many founding members of the Group Theatre went on to establish themselves as major theatrical artists. The director Elia Kazan started with the Group Theatre, as did playwrights Paul Green, Maxwell Anderson, Sidney Kingsley, and most notably Clifford Odets. Lee Strasberg, Stella Adler, and Sanford Meisner, arguably the three most influential acting teachers in the history of America, were founding members of the Group Theatre.

For an inspirational look at the Group Theatre, read *The Fervent Years* by founding member Harold Clurman (Da Capo Press, 1983).

Acting in America Today

Acting in America today is based on the realistic mode established by Stanislavski and introduced to America by the Group Theatre. Actors attempt to uncover the inner, psychological workings of a human being and present a truthful character to an audience (see Figure 1.6). All acting training today uses Stanislavski as a touchstone. A few theorists have rebelled against his work, but without Stanislavski there would be nothing to rebel against. Modern audiences have come to expect the truthful depictions of life on the stage that Stanislavski established as the height of the art.

Film and television have furthered the need for subtle, psychological honesty. With a camera only inches from an actor's face, there is no room for broad playing. An actor needs only to think the thoughts of the character for the camera to identify what she or he is feeling and thinking.

Figure 1.6

Psychological realism in a scene from *Balm in Gilead* **at the University of Georgia Department of Theatre and Film Studies**

SET BY JASON ALLEN. LIGHTS BY MICHAEL O'CONNELL. COSTUMES BY LINDSEY GOODSON. DIRECTION BY KRISTIN KUNDERT-GIBBS.

Most actors develop their own method of acting. Many of them (especially stage actors) have gone through formal training and take bits and pieces from different teachers and different techniques that they have studied. Film and television actors who aren't as likely to have formally studied the art often learn by trial and error as well as by watching other actors work. Ultimately every actor is an individual and will discover his or her own process for creating his or her art.

How an Actor Works

It is an actor's job to create a real, living breathing character, which is usually human but sometimes not. She does this by using her entire being: her breath, body, voice, mind, heart, and soul. When creating a character, the actor always starts with the script. She devours the script, looking for clues to who her character is. She looks for what is said about her, what is said to her, and what she says. She attends rehearsals, analyzes the script, learns her lines, does research, memorizes her blocking, all while working to create this new life. Ultimately every actor comes to her own process for doing this. Some of these processes are instinctual, some come from training, and some come from experience with the craft.

You may have heard that a great actor never needs to train or study acting because real talent is something that cannot be taught. This couldn't be further from the truth. Esoteric directors who have no understanding of the acting process, lazy actors who don't want to do their homework, or pretender movie stars who just got lucky by relying on their looks usually utter the comment.

What is talent anyway? This debate has raged since the time Thespis stepped from the chorus and uttered his first lines. Talent, in regard to the actor, has been said to include many things:

Sensitivity A great actor needs an enormous amount of sensitivity to just about everything. She needs to be sensitive to her environment, to her thoughts, to her feelings, and to those around her. She must allow herself to see, hear, touch, taste, and feel everything in her surroundings, and, more importantly, she needs to allow these sensations to affect her. Her sensory skills should be heightened and finely tuned.

Vulnerability It does an actor not one ounce of good to have heightened sensitivity if she doesn't allow all of the stimuli just mentioned to affect her. She needs to have an open heart and mind so that the sights, sounds, smells, tastes, and touches of the world move her. She must freely weep, rage, scream, howl, laugh, and love. She must be fearless in her willingness to make herself open to others and to her own emotions.

It is often said that actors are bleeding hearts and jump to the aid of every cause from saving the environment to stopping the death penalty. Well, of course they are and certainly they do. If they have talent, they will not only sympathize and empathize with every living and imagined creature, they will also eagerly walk in their shoes. This vulnerability to others is a necessary aspect of talent.

Imagination and willingness to suspend disbelief Perhaps your parents once told you not to let your imagination run away with you. Well a talented actor will freely skip the country with her imagination. Actors believe. Anything. Their imaginations are vivid and all consuming. They approach every moment with childlike innocence as if experiencing life for the first time. Actors live in their imaginations far more than in the "real world." They willingly, freely, and with abandon will embrace a whole imaginary set of circumstances and accept them as reality.

The need to share and exhibitionism Another aspect of talent revolves around the need to share. One can be sensitive and vulnerable but unless she possesses an undying need to share her discoveries about humankind, she will never be an actor—a writer or painter possibly, but never an actor. Additionally, talent takes a certain amount of exhibitionism. An actor must be free and fearless in sharing in front of a group of total strangers.

A responsive body and voice To share all of the sensations to which an actor has made herself vulnerable, her body and voice must respond freely. Her body must be free from tension and be able to mold and morph into new and unique characters. Her voice also must be free from tension and able to carry the nuances of emotion in pitch, rhythm, and tempo. You may have heard the phrase that an actor's instrument is her body, so she must be relaxed, strong, and flexible to play her instrument with the virtuosity of a maestro.

Determination and self-motivation Acting is perhaps the most difficult business in the world to enter. At any given point in time the majority of professional actors are unemployed. To survive as an actor, one must be incredibly self-motivated. An actor is a salesperson selling herself. No one else can do this for her. Even an agent can't get an actor the job. He can help the actor get the interview, but ultimately it is up to the actor, through strength of determination, to persevere in the field. I have often advised aspiring actors, "If there is any other profession or job that you can do, you should."

These are some of the many qualities that have been ascribed to talent within the acting profession. There are arguably others, but these six cover most of the bases. Many "talented" actors possess several of these qualities, and a few great actors are lucky enough to be endowed with them all.

If you study this list, you might come to the realization that most of these characteristics can be developed. Yes, acting can be taught. And it is. Universities across the country offer training programs designed to help aspiring actors learn their art. In any major city in the world, there are conservatories, schools, and private acting coaches that will instruct and develop the craft of the actor. The quality of training and instructors vary greatly from location to location and the exact techniques and styles that are espoused are wildly different, but the core of acting training is essentially the same anywhere you go. Actors train their inner resources, their outer techniques, and their business skills.

Inner Resources

The inner resources of the actor include sensitivity, vulnerability, and imagination. Additionally and very importantly, an actor trains to analyze and dissect a script. He learns how to use this knowledge to develop the psychology of a character (see Figure 1.7). There are many different means of developing your inner resources, and most modern acting teachers have focused on developing these inner resources.

As mentioned earlier, Constantin Stanislavski focused on developing the inner life of a character through physical action. Through studying the script, an actor learns what the character is doing and what the character wants to achieve. Many famous acting teachers have based their inner life training on the work of Stanislavski, including Stella Adler, Sonya Moore, and the famous Lee Strasberg of the Actor's Studio.

Figure 1.7

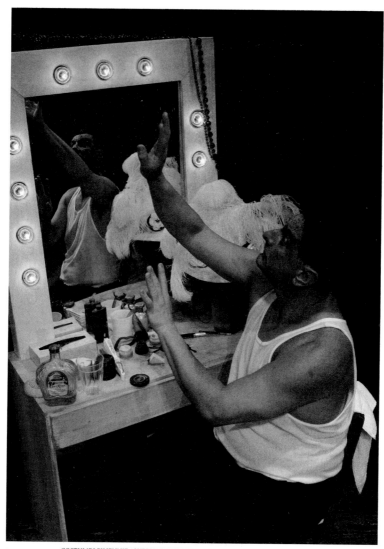

COSTUMES BY JENNIE ALVERNAZ. LIGHTS BY RICH DUNHAM. DIRECTION BY KRISTIN KUNDERT-GIBBS.

For more reading on Constantin Stanislavski, look to three books written by him: *An Actor Prepares, Building a Character,* and *Creating a Role* (all from Theatre Arts Books, 1989).

Childlike games and play are wonderful ways of developing or reawakening the imagi-nation; the leading proponent of this technique is Viola Spolin, who has a whole series of books on games for the theater. Additionally, improvisation is used to develop the imagi-nation and sensitivity to others and the environment. There are entire programs across the country devoted to improvisational training, including the famous Second City in Chicago.

Check out Viola Spolin's *Theater Game File* for handy index cards of theater games for the actor (Northwestern University Press, 1989).

Two of the greatest acting teachers of the 20th century, Uta Hagen and Sanford Meisner, focused their techniques on the training of these inner resources. Hagan emphasized training the imagination and sensitivity, while Meisner focused on developing impulse and vulnerability. All of their work was highly personal and intimate.

You can learn more about Uta Hagen and her work in her two books: *Respect for Acting* (Wiley, 1973) and *A Challenge for the Actor* (Charles Scribner's Sons, 1991). Sanford Meisner's book, *Sanford Meisner on Acting* (Vintage, 1987), will teach you his techniques for creating truth in the moment.

The training of the inner resources is twofold, affecting the head and the heart. It encompasses an intellectual understanding and analysis of character as well as the development and expansion of the imagination and senses.

Outer Techniques

There are two types of outer techniques: completely external techniques and external techniques that move to internal techniques. Completely external techniques are ones that focus on the external training and development of the actor's instrument—her body and voice—while external techniques that move to internal techniques are acting methodologies that focus on the external creation of character in order to awaken the inner life of the character.

Actors must train their body and voice. They need to have the flexibility, strength, and stamina of an athlete in order to physically create characters and sustain their energy during a performance. Their voices need to be free from tension to express the intricacies of emotion. They need to be able to run through a range of pitches and of course must learn the skills of vocal power and articulation in order to be heard and understood.

Actors train their bodies in many ways. Classes are designed especially for stage movement. They cover finding alignment, ridding oneself from tension, finding a neutral body, mask of character, expression of character, and even specialty components of period dance and combat. Actors also train by studying dance, gymnastics, and the martial arts. Additionally, most actors have some sort of personal physical regimen that they participate in to keep their bodies strong, fit, and responsive.

Actors also train their voices in specially designed classes for stage voice. Many actors study singing voice and voiceover techniques.

The outer/external to inner techniques comprise the majority of the content of this book. These techniques are acting theories, which are designed to externally create a character. They deal with molding, morphing, or changing the body physically. Ideally the external presentation of character awakens the inner life, desires, and emotions of the character. Change the body, and you change the way thought and emotions are expressed. Generally these types of techniques are learned in more advanced acting classes.

Business Skills

Any successful actor became that way by developing sound business skills. Since actors are salespeople selling themselves, they need to train in marketing and networking. They should develop sound interview and audition techniques to continue to land jobs. Actors can study these techniques through classes, but often these skills are learned on the job through trial and error.

How Acting Relates to the Animator

As an animator, you are basically doing the job of an actor. You are creating a living, breathing character that tells a story, shares an experience, and moves an audience. Your character becomes "animated" with the body, voice, and emotions that you breathe into it. So you need to understand the process of creating a real, living, breathing character on the screen from the actor's perspective as well as from the perspective of the CG artist.

In some ways, the animator's process is actually twofold. First you must create the character, and then you must transfer it to the computer. Perhaps you could argue that you are actually creating the character directly on the screen. But in either case your instrument is not the same as an actor who uses his own body, voice, and emotions to create the character. Your instrument is the hardware and software available to you. Nevertheless, your character still has a body, voice, and emotions as with the actor's character, so understanding and employing the techniques of an actor can only aid in your artistry.

We contend that it is virtually impossible to understand and internalize the work and process of an actor without participating in it. Reading about it will only increase your intellectual understanding. Doing it will allow you to viscerally experience the creation of a new life. In most theater programs across the United States, acting is a required element of a degree in theater. Even if an individual never intends to set foot on the stage but wants to design, write, or direct, he must fully participate in an acting class to understand the art of acting that is central to the creation of character. As you, the animator, are also creating characters, you too must participate in training as an actor.

Just as you began your work as an animator with elementary exercises to understand the hardware, software, and language of the discipline, actors begin their training and work with exercises designed to help them understand their instrument. The actors' exercises help them connect with their body, voice, and imagination. We will begin your exploration of the art of acting with basic exercises used by beginning actors.

Beginning Acting Exercises

As an animator hoping to grow in your ability to understand and communicate character, you will gain invaluable information and experience from training as an actor does. Although you are not attempting to become an actor, you will be best served by following the same training routine as the actor. The beginning exercises will help you develop a language and prepare you for the advanced work of character creation. The following exercises are often done in beginning acting classes. They might remind you of your games from childhood or even gym class, and that analysis would be correct. For the purposes of this book, the focus is on the physical self. The first exercises are designed to help you relax, warm up, and center yourself.

Actors are similar to musicians and athletes in their need to warm up. Since their body is their instrument, they need to relax, stretch, and start moving slowly to avoid injury. The warm-up also allows the actor to center herself and switch her focus to the work at hand, and free and limber her body to express character and emotion. Many actors study Eastern movement pedagogies such as yoga, tai chi, and qigong. All of these serve the purposes of warming up and centering very well. Although we will not discuss these topics in this text, feel free to use them as part of your warm-up if you have already studied the techniques.

It is helpful to start actor training with a childlike hunger of the imagination and freedom of inhibitions. We need to knock the editor that sits on our shoulder and screens and controls everything that we do into oblivion. This editor has grown from years of our parents and society telling us what is appropriate behavior and what we can and cannot do. While it may be useful to have an editor on your shoulder for polite society, it is detrimental for an artist to have anyone screen his impulses. So let's warm up and have some fun.

Solo Exercises for Relaxation

This is the preparation for the relaxation exercises. Read through all of the instructions first so that you can stay relaxed and do not need to refer back to the book during the course of the exercise. You may want to record yourself reading the instructions so you can listen and respond.

Start by lying on your back on the floor, as shown in Figure 1.8. If you have a hard floor, you might want to lie on a blanket or a towel. Stretch out very long and yawn, relaxing back into the floor as you exhale. You should end lying with your arms about 45 degrees from your sides and your palms facing the ceiling. Your legs should be extended and should not be crossed. If you have a troublesome lower back, you might want to bend your knees and place your feet on the floor.

Figure 1.8

Proper position for lying on the floor

Think about letting your back lengthen out long from the tip of your tailbone to the top of your head. Don't try to flatten the curve in your lower back or in your neck; they belong there. Just let the spine lengthen out. Then try to let your back spread out wide, letting the shoulder blades slip apart. (It sometimes helps to give yourself a bear hug to get your shoulder blades to spread.)

Relax your lower abdomen and let your breath drop deep into your belly. Inhale through your nose, then relax your jaw and let the breath fall out of the small opening in your mouth. Send your attention to your breath. Let it be relaxed and deep in your body. Allow the inhalation and the exhalation to become equal. Count the length of time it takes to inhale and the length of time it takes to exhale. An example would be to inhale for six counts and then exhale for six counts. Don't try to lengthen or change your breath just yet. Simply count the most natural pattern. Count your breath for several minutes.

Then send your attention away from your breath and the center of your body to the outside of your body by focusing on your sense of touch. While lying on the floor, with your stomach and jaw relaxed, send your attention to everything that is touching you. In your mind's eye, identify all of the things that you feel touching the outside of your body. It could be a ring, a watch, the hair on your forehead or the back of your neck, the waistband of your paints, the cuff of a sleeve, your socks, the floor under your body, or the air on your skin. Take about a minute to do this.

Then send your attention even farther away from your breathing center by focusing on what you hear. Listen for all of the sounds around you. In your mind's eye, identify what you are hearing. Listen for sounds within sounds or layers of sounds. Do this for about a minute.

Then send your attention back to your breathing center. Make sure that your lower belly rises and lowers as the breath drops in and out of you. It might help to flop a relaxed hand onto your lower belly (below the belly button) to feel it rise and fall. Make sure that your jaw is relaxed so that there is a small opening between your lips for the breath to fall out. Inhale through your nose and exhale through your mouth. Go back to counting your breath. Do this for several more minutes.

This exercise is a start to deeper relaxation. It can be used by itself when you are pressed for time, but if you have ample time, try it with one of the following exercises.

Mandala

Progress around the outside of your body using your mind to tell each area to relax. (If you don't have a partner to talk you through this, record the directions and play them back to yourself.)

1. Starting with the right side:
   a. Relax your right thumb.
   b. Relax your right index finger.
   c. Relax your right middle finger.
   d. Relax your right ring finger.
   e. Relax your right pinky finger.
   f. Relax the palm of your hand.
   g. Relax the back of your hand.
   h. Relax your right wrist.
   i. Relax your right forearm.
   j. Relax your right elbow.
   k. Relax your right upper arm.
   l. Relax your right shoulder.
   m. Relax your right armpit.
   n. Relax your right side from your armpit to your hip socket.
   o. Relax your right hip.
   p. Relax your right upper leg.
   q. Relax your right knee.
   r. Relax your right lower leg.
   s. Relax your right ankle.
   t. Relax the top of your right foot.
   u. Relax your right big toe.

    v. Relax your right second toe.

    w. Relax your right third toe.

    x. Relax your right fourth toe.

    y. Relax your right fifth toe.

    z. Relax the bottom of your right foot.

    aa. Relax your whole right side, from the tips of your fingers to the tips of your toes.

2. Repeat all of these steps for your left side.

3. Relax your belly.

4. Relax your chest.

5. Relax your throat and neck.

6. Relax your scalp and skull.

7. Relax your forehead.

8. Relax the space between your eyebrows.

9. Relax your right eye.

10. Relax your left eye.

11. Relax your right cheek.

12. Relax your left cheek.

13. Relax your upper lip.

14. Relax your lower lip.

15. Relax your jaw.

16. Send your attention back to your breath. Relax. Rest. Breathe.

Tense and Release

This is an alternative relaxation exercise to the mandala. Instead of using your imagination to relax the muscles, you will tense a muscle or muscle group and then relax the tension as you exhale. Some people find this method easier to find relaxation than a mere command from the mind.

1. Squeeze your feet into a ball tensing all of the muscles in your feet. Hold for a beat. Release on an exhale.

2. Isolate and tense only the muscles in your lower legs. Hold. Release.

3. Isolate and tense only the muscles in your upper legs. Hold. Release.

4. Isolate and tense only the muscles in pelvis and bottom. Hold. Release.

5. Isolate and tense only the muscles in your abdomen. Hold. Release.

6. Isolate and tense only the muscles in your chest and shoulders. Hold. Release.

7. Isolate and tense only the muscles in your neck, face, and scalp. Hold. Release.

8. Tense all of the muscles in your entire body, allowing yourself to curl into a ball. Hold. Release, uncurling.

9. Relax. Rest. Breathe.

Group Exercise for Relaxation

Start by pairing up. Allow one partner (let's call this person A) to lie on the floor and go through the first general relaxation process. After A has started to relax and find his natural breathing rhythm, Partner B will gently work around his body, stretching out all of his limbs. (These exercises are demonstrated in movie files available on the book's accompanying DVD.)

1. Start with the head. Partner B will gently take Partner A's head in her hands and lift it about an inch off the floor. Partner B will then start to gently turn the head left to right while gently pulling or extending the head from the neck, as shown in Figure 1.9. The neck is gently being lengthened here. It is important that the rock and pull of the head is gentle and slight. Partner A must relax his head and allow it to drop fully into Partner B's hands. Do this for about a minute and then gently place the head back on the floor. (See `RotatingHead.mov` on the DVD.)

2. Move to the right arm. Partner B will gently take Partner A's right arm and pull it from the shoulder while gently twisting or rotating it side to side, as shown in Figure 1.10. Again this is a slight pull and twist. Do this for about a minute (`RotatingShoulder.mov`).

Figure 1.9

An actor rotating the head

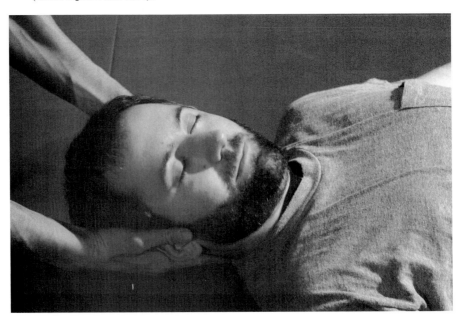

Figure 1.10

An actor stretching the shoulder

3. Partner B will then place Partner A's upper-right arm on the floor and work on the elbow joint. Partner B should hold Partner A's upper-right arm in place on the floor with one hand and then gently pull and rotate the elbow, as Figure 1.11 shows. Do this for about a minute (RotatingElbow.mov).

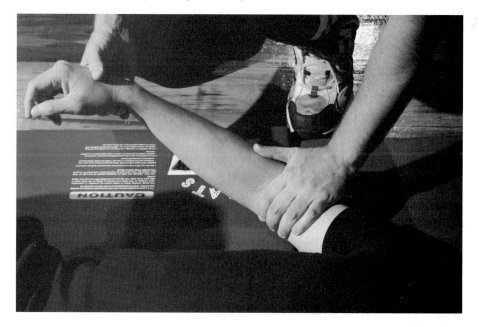

Figure 1.11

An actor stretching the elbow

4. Partner B will then place Partner A's lower-right arm on the ground and work on the right wrist. Partner B should hold Partner A's lower-right arm in place with one hand and gently pull on and rotate the wrist, as shown in Figure 1.12. Do this for about a minute (RotatingWristandFingers.mov).

5. Partner B will then work on all the fingers on the right hand of Partner A. Partner B will hold Partner A's wrist on the ground with one hand and with the other gently stretch and twist every joint on every finger on the right hand, as shown in Figure 1.13. Take several minutes to do this.

Figure 1.12

An actor rotating the wrist

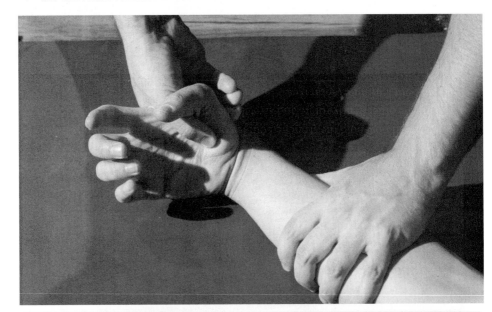

Figure 1.13

An actor stretching the fingers

6. Now move on to the right leg. Partner B will need to stand up and take Partner A's right leg in her hands. Partner B will gently pull, twist, and stretch the leg from the hip joint, as shown in Figure 1.14. Be careful not to twist the knee. Do this for about a minute and then gently place the leg back on the ground (RotatingHip.mov).

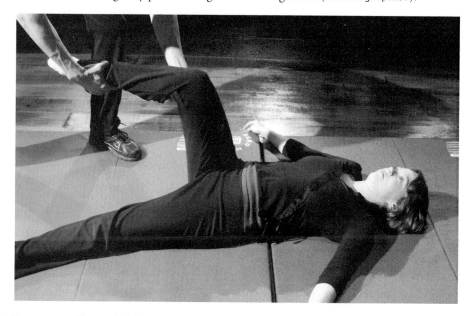

Figure 1.14

An actor rotating the hip

7. Partner B will now hold the stretched out leg of Partner A in place with one hand and with the other gently rotate and stretch the ankle, as shown in Figure 1.15. Do this for about a minute (RotatingAnkle.mov).

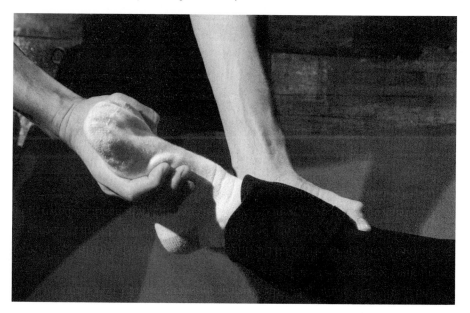

Figure 1.15

An actor rotating the ankle

8. Partner B will then work through rotating and stretching all of the joints on all of the toes of Partner A's right foot, as Figure 1.16 shows. Take several minutes to do this. If Partner A is extremely ticklish, you might need to skip this step (RotatingToes.mov).

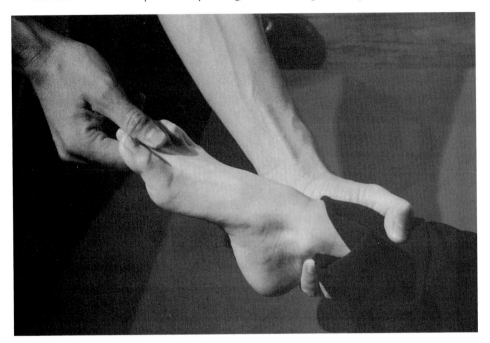

Figure 1.16

An actor stretching the toes

9. Repeat for the left side of the body.

10. End by returning to the head and gently rocking and stretching it one last time. Allow the fully stretched out and relaxed partner to rest for several minutes and then switch.

Exercises for Warming Up

These exercises can be done solo or with a group.

Stretch, Rotate, and Bounce

1. Start by standing with feet hip width apart, feet parallel to each other, and knees soft. Let your spine lengthen from the tip of your tailbone, which is pointing between your heels, to the top of your head. Imagine that your head is floating on top of your spine.

2. Allow your wrists to float toward the ceiling, taking your whole arm with them. Keep your hands relaxed as your wrists float up, as shown in Figure 1.17.

Figure 1.17
**Floating to
the ceiling**

3. When your wrists float your arms as high up as they can go, allow your fingers to start to float up to the ceiling, as you can see in Figure 1.18. Imagine there are strings on the ends of all of your fingers that are pulling your arms up to the ceiling.

4. Stretch through your sides. Gently raise your right hand higher, stretching your right side, and then raise your left hand higher, stretching your left side, as shown in Figure 1.19. Come back to center so that both sides are stretched.

Figure 1.18
**Fingers stretched
to the ceiling**

Figure 1.19
Stretching the sides

5. Let your wrists collapse so that your hands are hanging from the wrists, free from tension. Then let your elbows collapse so that your lower arms and hands are hanging free from tension. Then let your shoulders collapse so that your arms are hanging heavy and relaxed from your shoulder girdle. Then let your head and neck collapse forward so that your head is hanging heavy and relaxed from the top thoracic vertebra. Look at Figure 1.20 for examples.

Figure 1.20
Dropping down the spine

6. Let the weight of your head gently start to pull your spine forward so that you are releasing one vertebra at a time down the front of your body. At some point as you drop down your spine to the front of your body, the weight of your head will become so heavy that you collapse all the way down. You will now be dropped, over hanging upside down, as shown in Figure 1.21. You should release all the way from your tailbone. Make sure that your knees are not locked and are soft. Your head and arms should be heavy and dangling. Your hands might even be brushing the floor. Hang there for about 20 seconds, sort of bobbing up and down. Think about floating like a jellyfish.

Figure 1.21

Floating like a jellyfish

7. Slowly start to move to an upright position, stacking one vertebra on top of another. Go slowly, trying to imagine each vertebra stacking on the next. Your shoulders, arms, neck, and head should be loose and hanging until they take their place on the spine. Your head will be the last thing to come into place. Imagine it floating on top of your spine. Look to Figure 1.22 for guidance (Spinework.mov).

Figure 1.22

Stacking the vertebrae

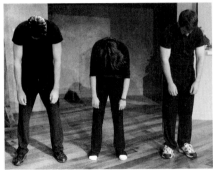

8. Imagine that you are a rag doll and everything in your body is loose and floppy. Then imagine that you have springs under your feet. Allow yourself to start to spring around the room, with your loose rag doll body flopping all over the place. Stop and shake all over like a dog shaking off water.

9. Stand on one foot and rotate the ankle of the other foot around in a circle. Change the direction of the rotation. Now rotate the knee around in both directions. Then rotate the hip around in both directions. This requires good balance and focus. It often helps to pick a spot on the floor far in front of you or on the wall in front of you to focus on. Then shake out the whole leg. Repeat on the other leg.

10. Rotate your wrists around in both directions. Then rotate your elbows in both directions. Then make great big arm circles in both directions. Shake your arms out.

11. Go back to the rag doll image and spring and bounce and flop all over the room once more.

Shake Out

This exercise has many purposes. It helps to relax and release tension while it builds energy in the body and focus for the mind. It also aids in a vocal warm-up.

1. Shake your right hand for eight beats, counting out loud: one-two-three-four-five-six-seven-eight.

2. Shake your left hand for eight beats, counting out loud.

3. Shake your right foot for eight beats, counting out loud.

4. Shake your left foot for eight beats, counting out loud.

5. Repeat with your right hand, left hand, right foot, and left foot, counting out loud for *seven* beats.

6. Repeat with your right hand, left hand, right foot, and left foot, counting out loud for *six* beats.

7. Repeat with your right hand, left hand, right foot, and left foot, counting out loud for *five* beats.

8. Repeat with your right hand, left hand, right foot, and left foot, counting out loud for *four* beats.

9. Repeat with your right hand, left hand, right foot, and left foot, counting out loud for *three* beats.

10. Repeat with your right hand, left hand, right foot, and left foot, counting out loud for *two* beats.

11. Repeat with your right hand, left hand, right foot, and left foot, counting out loud for *one* beat.

Exercises for the Imagination and Play

These exercises can be done solo or with a group.

Walks

If you are working with a group, you need to expand your awareness so that you don't run into other people. If you do happen to run into someone, just make contact and move on. Don't make a big deal out of it.

As you explore these different types of walks, see if any interesting patterns come to you that could be used in the development of a CG character.

EXPLORE SPACE WITH TEMPO, DIRECTIONS, AND LEVELS

Begin by walking around the room. Walk randomly. Don't fall into patterns or circles. Look to the horizon. Don't look to the ceiling or floor. Let your arms swing freely at your sides. Inhale through your nose and exhale through your mouth.

1. Continue walking around the room randomly, but now start to explore tempos and rhythms. See how slow, and then how fast, you can go. What happens when you vary slow and fast? Do any of these changes in tempo and rhythm suggest a type of person to you? Do any of these changes suggest a certain mood or emotion? If so, try to become that person or indulge in that feeling and continue to walk randomly around the room.

2. Go back to walking around the room randomly in a moderate tempo and start to explore your walking in terms of direction. Intentionally move from an imaginary point A to a point B. Explore direction to move between the two points. Try straight lines, curves, circles, zigzags, serpentine, and backward. Do any of these directionalities suggest a certain type of person or character to you or a particular mood or feeling? If so, continue to explore within the character or emotion.

3. Once again, go back to moving randomly around the room, but this time explore levels. How many different levels can you find within your space? Are there steps or

furniture? How many different levels can you create with your body? How close can you get to the ground? How high in the air? What about moving in every plane in between? How quickly can you change levels? Does moving at any certain level suggest a certain type of person or mood or feeling? If so, continue to move and explore within this type of person or emotion.

4. Put on some music and explore the space, tempo, directions, and levels as influenced by the music. Does the music lend itself to a certain direction or level? Is it possible to choose a different tempo or rhythm than what the music provides for you? Does the music suggest any mood or emotion? If so, continue to explore your space within that mood or emotion. Do this with many different types and styles of music and see how it affects your movement, body, and feelings. Figure 1.23 shows actors exploring levels.

Figure 1.23

Exploring levels

MEDIUMS AND ATMOSPHERES

After you have begun to explore your space and your body in space with the previous exercise, work on your imagination for this exercise.

1. Go back to randomly walking through the room. Now imagine that the floor of the room is coated with thick tar. Try to walk across the room while your feet are sticking to the floor. You must work to pull your feet free from the tar with each step.

2. Allow that tar to evaporate and imagine you are walking across a trampoline or one or those children's jumpers from a fair. Allow your weight to shift and throw you off balance with each step. Try to stay upright.

3. Let the trampoline become hot sand. Try to walk across the sand without burning your feet. Imagine that you are in the desert and the temperature is 110 degrees. Allow the heat under your feet and around your body to affect your movement.

4. Imagine that you are moving through a vat of Jell-O. It is surrounding you all the way up to your waist. Push and jiggle your way through the cool gelatin.

5. Imagine that you are underwater breathing with the aid of a SCUBA apparatus. You have been weighted so that you are walking across the bottom of the ocean. Feel the water surrounding you. You have weights around your waist but your arms and legs move freely and float in the water. Work your way around a sunken ship to view the fish.

6. Use your imagination to put your body on the moon. Try to move and explore the space as if you were completely free from gravity.

7. What if the room became the North Pole? You are freezing cold. The wind is whipping against your skin. You need to get to shelter but your feet are sinking in the snow, and the wind is pressing against your body. Continue to move, exploring these conditions.

8. Finally, place yourself on Jupiter. Here gravity is extreme because of the size of the planet. Don't get bogged down in the fact that there would be no oxygen; just try to move with the immense force of gravity pulling down on you. Every single movement will take great energy to pull you up from the ground.

CENTERS

For an actor, a center is the place in the body where energy comes from. It is usually found in the torso, hence the word *center*. This center leads or initiates movement. It is easy to see in some people where their center lies. A woman who is extremely pregnant often has her center in her pelvis and actually walks with pelvis thrust forward and leading the way. On the other extreme, a ballet dancer will often have a high center residing in her upper chest or even clavicle. She seems to lift and float as her movement is led from this place.

Training can affect the center. Athletes who train in wrestling, football, or the martial arts often have low centers as they are taught to drop their energy down to anchor themselves. Dancers, on the other hand, often have higher centers so they can jump, lift, and float with ease. For most people the center is somewhere between several inches below the belly button and the upper chest. Every once in a while you will find someone with their center in their forehead. It is usually someone with a very high intellect. You can actually see them pull their body through space by their brow.

Different centers suggest various types of characters and personalities, so trying out different centers in your walk can help you see and feel the differences. With all of the steps that follow, begin at an extreme and unrealistic exploration of the center. For example, with the pelvis center, really push your pelvis forward in an "inhuman" sort of way. Then slowly, as you move around the space, allow the center to become subtler and more naturalistic. Notice the difference between the extreme and the subtle.

If you are working with a group, at this point you can begin to interact with other members of the group. Different centers suggest different characters and might draw you toward or away from other people. At the end of each different center exploration, feel free to allow your energy and movement to be drawn toward another person.

Some of you may have difficulty exploring a certain center. If your own personal center is either very low or very high, you may not be able to change your center to the opposite extreme. Those of you whose center is more "central" will probably have an easier time switching your center around. Don't worry about it. Just do the best you can.

1. Once again start by walking around the space with your arms dropped and swinging naturally at your sides. Look to the horizon. Let your jaw relax so that it is dropped slightly and inhale through your nose and exhale through your mouth. Let your belly relax and allow the breath to drop deep inside. Now start to pay attention to where you believe your center lies. What part of your body is leading your movement? Where is your energy coming from? Does this suggest anything about you?

2. Shift your center down to several inches below your belly button. (If this is your natural center, skip to the next step.) You can do this by thinking about dropping your weight down into your body. Explore your space, moving from this center. How does this change in center affect your movement? Does it make you feel different? Does it suggest a certain type of character? If so, continue to explore the space within this character or feeling.

3. Shift your center even lower to your pelvis. (If this is your natural center, skip to the next step.) Allow energy to come from your pelvis and allow the pelvis to lead your movement. This usually suggests certain character traits. Explore the space with the pelvis leading. If a character or feeling emerges from this exploration, continue moving within the character. Figure 1.24 shows an actor leading from the pelvis (PelvisCenter.mov).

4. Shift your center up very high in your body to your clavicle. (If this is your natural center, skip to the next step.) You will feel light and lifted, perhaps as if your feet are barely touching the floor. Explore your space with this high center of energy leading the movement. Notice whether this movement brings up certain feelings or suggests a certain character. If so, explore the space within these emotions or character. Figure 1.25 shows an actor leading from the clavicle (`ClavicleCenter.mov`).

5. Drop your center down a bit toward your sternum and explore your space with the energy in this area leading the movement. (If this is your natural center, skip to the next step.) How does this movement make you feel? If it suggests any character or feelings, explore within these emotions or character.

Figure 1.24
Pelvis center

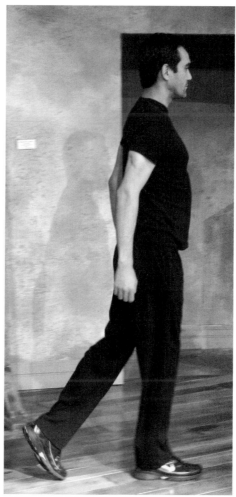

Figure 1.25
Clavicle center

6. Drop your center down one more time to around your belly button. (If this is your natural center, skip to the next step.) Explore the space, allowing the energy of this center to lead your movement. Does it suggest a certain character to you? Does this center bring up any feelings or sensations? If so, continue to explore within these emotions or character.

7. Finally, try exploring with some unique and rarely seen centers. First allow your center to reside in your forehead. Allow the energy of the forehead to lead your movement through space. This could change the tempo or pace at which you move as well as the quality of your movement. Does it suggest a character? If so, go for it, and explore within this character. Figure 1.26 shows an actor with her center in her forehead (ForeheadCenter.mov).

Figure 1.26

Forehead center

8. Try moving your center to a place that could be interesting for an animated character. Try leading with a knee, a toe, your right side, your rear end, or your left shoulder. While you wouldn't usually find these centers in daily human life, they have been seen in animated figures. Explore what it feels like to move within one or all of these centers. Observe what happens to the rest of your body when you change your center. Notice what type of character this might suggest. Figure 1.27 shows actors leading from many different centers.

Figure 1.27

Actors leading from many different centers

Alien Spirit

Assume a relaxed position on the floor, as described in the first exercise. Now imagine that you are an alien being that has never had a physical body. You have only existed in spirit form. But now, due to some strange space phenomenon, your spirit form has suddenly been placed in a human body. (Of course it must be yours.) As this alien spirit, and from a place of total innocence, begin to explore what this human body can do. Remember that you have never experienced gravity. You don't know how muscles work. You don't know how joints bend, flex, or rotate. You don't know how to stand, sit, crawl, or even lift a finger. You don't know how you hear or see. Slowly start to figure it out. Don't take anything for granted. Don't be afraid to make sound if something occurs that inspires sound. Give yourself 20 to 30 minutes for this exploration.

Then, if you have a class, discuss what you discovered, noticed, or learned from this experience. If you don't have a class, journaling helps you process your experience. This exercise can be emotional for some people, so don't be surprised if you experience some frustration, fear, anger, or joy. On the flip side, don't worry about it if no feelings come up for you. (If, however, in the future you find that you never feel anything for any exercise that you participate in, you may not be fully committing to and giving yourself up to the exercises.) The intricacies of the movement of the human body are quite extraordinary, and we often take our body for granted. This exercise can help you get back in touch with just how miraculous you are.

Exercises for Freeing the Body and Voice While Releasing Inhibitions

Learning to act is easier when done with a group than solo. Since acting involves communication, it makes sense that working with other people aids the process. Most acting classes have 10–20 students. Although these are ideal numbers, you can do these exercises with as few as four people. Working with others will help you listen and respond. Plus, it is just plain fun.

Sound and Movement

There are many reasons for doing sound and movement exercises. First, they help to free the body and voice by forcing a response quickly and without thought. Second, they force you to let go of your inhibitions because you are going to look silly. Everyone will look equally silly. In fact, if you don't look silly you aren't doing the exercise correctly. Third, and most importantly, it forces you to stop thinking and screening your impulses. You have to kick your editor off your shoulder and do something in the moment without thought. So let go with these exercises and just have fun.

PASS IT AROUND

This is a good sound and movement exercise to begin with for your group exercises. You will need to let go of your inhibitions and respond to your group.

1. Start by forming a circle. One member of the circle will then do a sound and movement. They should move their whole body into some position at the same time that they are making a vocal sound. The sound and movement should not be human. Don't try to assume a character or tell a story. Just throw your body and voice. The bigger and wilder, the better. Do not say words, just sounds. This is supposed to be preverbal, primal sound and movement. Try to move your spine as well as your limbs.

2. After the first member of the circle does his sound and movement, each successive member of the circle will repeat it as exactly as they can one at a time all around the circle, ending with the person who created the sound and movement repeating it one more time. This should move very quickly from one person to the next just like the wave at a basketball game.

3. Immediately after the sound and movement has completed the circle, the next person in line will do a new sound and movement and then it should whip around the circle like the wave. When it gets all the way around, the next person in the circle will start a new sound and movement, and so forth.

Keep in mind that speed is essential. You must go fast. Do not allow time to think. Just do it. Sheer speed can help to short-circuit your editor or screener that screams, "You are looking silly." Also, try to receive the sound and movement from the person ahead of you and try to pass it on to the next person in the circle. In this way you are communicating the sound and movement from one person to the next. Finally, even though you are going quickly, do not anticipate the sound and movement. Allow it to be passed to you before you receive it and pass it along to the next person.

SOUND AND MOVEMENT REPEAT

This exercise is essentially the same as the previous one with a slight variation. Instead of passing the sound around the circle, everyone in the circle will repeat the sound and movement in unison.

1. Start by forming a circle. One member of the circle will then perform a sound and movement as described earlier.

2. Immediately after this, the entire circle repeats that sound and movement in unison.

3. Very quickly, without leaving even one second for thinking, the next member of the circle will perform a new sound and movement and then the whole circle will repeat it in unison.

4. Do this all the way around the circle. Go fast. You should be out of breath.

Rhythm Jam

This exercise requires you to listen to other members of your group while you explore your own body and voice. It helps to grow an ensemble spirit within your group of actors.

1. Start by forming a circle.

2. Pick one member of the circle to lay down a beat. They should vocally establish a rhythm. It could be a sound like a beat box or a drum line.

3. Go around the circle and each member will add a vocal sound to this rhythm. Add only one sound at a time until each member of the circle is vocalizing. Just like the sound and movement, there should not be words, only sounds. The sound could be anything from animals to man-made sounds, to more rhythms, to things that are more musical. The only thing that is important is that all of the sounds keep within the rhythm established at the beginning.

4. When every member of the circle has added their sound, dance around the room continuing to make your sound. Dance and move around different people so you can hear different sounds next to each other.

5. Eventually reform the circle. See if, as a group, you can pick up the tempo of your rhythm jam and let it go faster. Then see if you can all slow down the rhythm jam. See if, as a group, you can slowly let it fade out and disappear.

CHAPTER 2

Foundations of Animation

Most character animation today is a stylized and exaggerated version of real life (or, more accurately, of the filmic representation of real life), where characters exceed or violate strictly realistic behavior. Yet these exaggerations are all grounded on our expectations from the real world. Therefore, it is of utmost importance that animators have a very deep sense of what makes people act and react in the myriad ways we do. A study in animation needs to have a technical component (how do we actually make a stop-motion puppet or computer-animated character move?), but just as importantly, it must have a psychological and performative component wherein human behavior is studied, especially as it relates to human performance or acting. Although numerous schools and books devote much study to the former, technical, component, there is a paucity of work relating to the human/performative component. This chapter introduces many historical and technical elements of animation; the rest of the book addresses the equally important element of performance and characterization.

This chapter discusses:

- **What is animation?**
- **A brief history of animation**
- **12 principles of animation**
- **Facial versus body animation**
- **Principles of rigging**

What Is Animation?

The term *animation* has its roots in the Latin word *animare*, meaning "to give breath to." Thus animation literally means to bring an inanimate object (or virtual object) to life. While there are numerous ways to animate something—from Dr. Frankenstein's re-animation of a corpse in his lab to making words fly across your computer monitor when a screen saver kicks in—here we are concerned specifically with character animation output to a visual medium. In the modern usage, character animation is the task of taking an inanimate element—a stop-motion puppet, pencil lines on paper, or pixels on a computer screen—and "breathing" life into it, making the "character" appear to act and react as we would expect a living being to do.

On a technical level, animation is the act of moving, drawing, and rendering *something* in one position; recording that image; and then moving, drawing, and rendering that thing again in a different place or pose and recording the new image. If enough pictures, drawings, and renderings are created that each vary slightly each from the other, when we combine these images in some medium and play them back over time, our minds will be tricked into thinking that the object is moving around as if it has some force or intentionality behind it. Normally the capture process is via either film or some digital format, and the playback medium is likewise either film or something digital. For stop-motion animation, for example, a character is placed in a given pose, and that pose is photographed. The character is then moved slightly and re-photographed. After several dozen to several hundred poses are photographed, each differing only slightly from the last, the photos are combined in a linear sequence, either on a film strip or in some digital playback format (like Apple's QuickTime container), and played back for an audience at several frames per second.

Our ability to perceive a number of individual photos, drawings, and renderings as a form of motion is related to a human feature (or, some would say, defect) called the persistence of vision. A number of theories exist concerning the physiology of persistence of vision, but the result is the same for all of them: we retain the image of something we've seen for a fraction of a second after it has disappeared from before our eyes. If within this fraction of a second another similar image is displayed for us, we will "see" the two individual images as a continuous whole (or action) rather than as two distinct images. Running a number of images together produces the effect of continuous motion, which was capitalized on in the late nineteenth century as film pioneers recorded individual frames on celluloid and then played these frames back via a bright projector for audiences amazed that they could see a "person" walking before them projected on a screen in a darkened room. Now, of course, projection of film, video, and digital content is so pervasive that we are unaware of the remarkable phenomenon occurring before our eyes on a daily basis.

You can easily witness persistence of vision for yourself. Stand in a completely darkened room and allow your eyes to adjust to the darkness. Then "flick" the light switch on and off again as quickly as you can while staring into the room (or have someone else flip the switch for you). As the room goes dark again, you will see an imprint of the room before you, even though there is no light in the room anymore. The effect fades very quickly, so you might need to try this a few times to fully grasp what you see.

While animated characters run the gamut from seven dwarves, to lions, to fish, to dragons, and even aliens, one common trait these characters share is some level of anthropomorphism. In other words, the characters are given an injection of humanness to allow us to relate to them on a gut level. Often, this anthropomorphism is selective: one animator (and modeler) might desire to emphasize the "cuteness" of a character, while another might wish to stress the horrific or the frightening for a different character (think Mickey Mouse versus the evil queen-as-hag in *Snow White*). Whatever the case, if we as audience are not engaged with the animated character on screen, then we don't imbue that character with personality and intention, and thus we are unlikely to remain emotionally involved and therefore become uninterested in the animation as a whole. Understanding the subtleties of human emotion and action, then, is at the root of understanding how to animate nearly any character you will come across, and thus it is critical to comprehend both how humans act and how we as observers interpret these actions, figuring out what a character wants or is feeling from the visual clues of their behavior.

Why Animate?

Animation is hard, plain and simple. It is far easier to get a friend to go outside and do a cartwheel for you while you videotape him than it is to create a model, rig the model, and go through the long, painstaking process of animating said model to re-create that cartwheel.

So why on earth do people go to the trouble to animate? The reasons are numerous, but the best of them share a common thread: to create something we can't easily see otherwise. Flying dogs and talking pigs are obvious examples of this (and yes, the pig in *Babe* and the dog in *Underdog* are animated, even if they're in a live-action movie). Though not character-based, animation of a blood clot moving through a virtual circulatory system is also a good example. Less obviously, but just as importantly, strongly graphic images— in the sense of simplified images with strong silhouettes, not extreme violence—can be achieved via animation more easily than in live action. Entire stylized worlds can be created that either approach something real, as in *The Incredibles*, or that eschew reality for a very abstracted or subjective environment, as in the scene in which Snow White runs from the hunter in the classic Disney movie.

Exaggeration, simplification, abstraction, and stylization are all good reasons to create an animation as opposed to filming something live. While these elements appear to divorce characters and worlds from the truly real, many argue that the refinement and freedom found in animation allows animators and directors to find the more truly, starkly real in animation than they can via live action. Just as a hand-drawn medical illustration of a heart is often more succinct and clear in presenting information about a heart than is a photograph of one sitting in a patient's chest, the ability to highlight some details while diminishing or eliminating others allows good animators to communicate more directly and possibly viscerally than filming actual actors on a set.

What you must do (and what we do with our animation students when they present an idea for an animation) is ask, "Can I do this any other way?" If you can, then by all means do it: animation is very time consuming and difficult, and if there is a faster, easier way to tell your story, you should do it that way. If, however, you clearly see how your story needs exaggerated, talking animals interacting with a simplified, stylized world, then animation is the way to go and can be a powerful medium with which to connect with your audience.

A Brief History of Animation

Animation—or at least the urge to animate—is much older than most people realize. Cave drawings from the dawn of humans show images of people and animals in dynamic, animated poses, and there are even a few that indicate motion via extra legs on drawings of hunters and their prey. While it took millennia to improve on this primitive suggestion of animation, the impulse to record "motion" from real life into a representational format appears to be as old as humankind.

The roots of modern animation as a format arise from the Victorian (and especially late Victorian) era and parallel the evolution of photography and moving pictures. One of the first forays into animation was the thaumatrope (often credited to John Paris), created around 1824. Meaning "magic created through turning," or, more concisely, "magic disc," the thaumatrope consisted of a two-sided card with a different image on each side hanging below two strings that could be wound up. When the wound strings unwound, the card would turn, and the two distinct images would appear to combine into one image. A famous example uses a drawing of a bird on one side and an empty cage on the other; when the thaumatrope is turned rapidly, the bird appears to be trapped within the cage. Paris used this inventive toy to demonstrate the theory of persistence of vision to his colleagues in London's Royal College of Physicians in 1824.

In the early 1830s, a more sophisticated device was simultaneously developed by Joseph Plateau and Simon von Stampfer. The phenakistoscope (or "deceiving viewer") as it came to be known, was often constructed of a disc with around a dozen similar images drawn around the disc, often drawn so that the last image would run into the first image, creating a looping animation when viewed (see Figure 2.1). In addition to the drawings, either the disc itself or a second disc in front of the disc with drawings had a thin slit cut between each drawing, and a cranking mechanism was attached to the disc(s) so a viewer could turn the machine as quickly or as slowly as desired. For the one-disc setup, the viewer would stand behind the disc and look through a slit at a mirror that reflected the images on the front of the disc. With the two-disc setup, the viewer would look through the slits in the first disc at the drawings on the second disc. By virtue of the narrowness of the slits, the viewer would primarily see a reflection of the drawing closest to a given slit. Upon spinning the disc around, each slit would in turn pass before the viewer's eyes, creating a quick "image" of each subsequent drawing, thus creating the illusion of continuous motion. The most important discovery of this tool was creation of a slit for the viewer to look through; without the slit (e.g., viewing the disc directly as it was spun), the viewer would see a blur of lines and colors rather than distinct images. Using the slit, however, "chopped" the passing blur of motion into distinct images, which were then reconstructed as motion by the viewer via the effect of persistence of vision. This "bright image, blackout, bright image" technique is at the heart of film recording and playback, allowing for the eventual creation of the movie camera and playback projector.

In 1849, William George Horner invented the zoetrope, or wheel of life. (Horner actually named his device the daedalum, but when it was imported to the United States, it was renamed the zoetrope, which is the name by which most people know the device today.) Rather than a disc, the zoetrope used a cylinder with around 16 slits cut into it inside of which a series of drawings on a strip of paper could be mounted, as shown in Figure 2.2. Upon spinning the device and looking through the rotating slits, the viewer saw the series of drawings appear to come to life. While still using the slit-and-image technique pioneered in the phenakistoscope, the zoetrope was self-contained (it didn't need a mirror to view the image), and placing the drawings around the inside of a cylinder allowed for many more drawings than on a disc, mak-ing the animations more substantial than before. Often, in fact, there were different "levels" of drawings, in different ink colors, on the same strip of paper, allowing one to view different animations, depending on which drawings were focused on. The zoetrope was highly successful as a household toy for the growing middle class in Europe and the

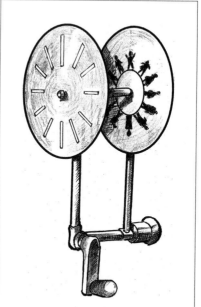

Figure 2.1

Drawing of a phenakistoscope by Jason Allen. Note the slits in the left-hand disc, through which the viewer looks as she spins the disc, creating the illusion of motion.

United States in the mid- to late-Victorian era. The device blazed the trail of separating medium from content, as numerous different drawing strips could be purchased once a family had purchased the zoetrope machine itself. The modern-day video console industry (with game content purchased for use with a specific console) is a descendent of the content-delivery system created by the zoetrope.

According to historical evidence, the Chinese invented a device very similar to the zoetrope at around 180 AD.

Figure 2.2

Drawing of a zoetrope by Jason Allen

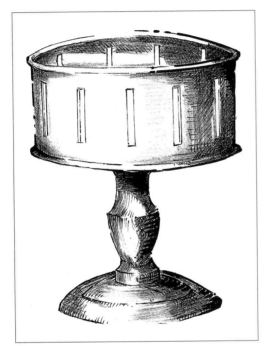

Oddly enough, the flip-book, which is today the purview of bored school children drawing stick figures in the corner of their notebook pages, was actually a patented device, and was invented relatively late in the Victorian era. In 1868, John Barnes Linnet patented the kineograph (moving writing or picture), his name for what we now call the flip-book. Rather than using slits to break up a sequence of images, the turning pages themselves act as dividers between each image, allowing the viewer to see each one (more or less) clearly. The important breakthrough of the flip-book as opposed to earlier devices like the phenakistoscope and zoetrope is its linear nature: rather than drawings moving in some circular manner, which forced them to loop around, thus limiting the number of drawings that could be animated and also the type of story that could be told via these drawings, use of the flip-book allowed for standard (linear) narrative format with a beginning, middle, and ending. Admittedly, due to the fact that flip-books can only contain a few dozen to a couple hundred drawings at most, the plot had to be fairly minimal, but the ability to create narrative was a major advance in conceptualizing animation. The mutoscope and filoscope, both developed in the 1890s, mechanized the flip-book, placing the drawings (or a series of photographs) into a housing and using a crank arm to flip the pages. These inventions had an enduring appeal, maintaining a place in the penny arcades of the late nineteenth through the mid-twentieth centuries. Some still exist in retro-style amusement parks, usually still for a penny apiece, which is a pretty good deal for today's entertainment dollar.

The last of the important pre-film animation devices created was the praxinoscope (or action viewer), invented in 1877 by Charles-Émile Reynaud. This device used a cylinder like the zoetrope, but mounted a series of mirrors onto a smaller cylinder inside the larger one, as shown in Figure 2.3. The viewer would look at one mirror, which reflected the image of one drawing on the outer cylinder, and spin the device; as that mirror quickly rotated out of view and was replaced by another mirror, the next mirror would reflect the next drawing in the sequence, creating the illusion of motion. The advance in this device is that the mirrors, rather than the slits of the zoetrope and phenakistoscope, act as the dividers between images, allowing for a more natural, less "flickery" image than either of the other two devices. Twelve years later, Reynaud improved on his own design with the Théatre-Optique, a version of the praxinoscope that feeds a long roll of paper with drawings into the device and projects the mirrored image onto a screen, allowing a large audience to watch at the same time. Unfortunately for Reynaud, this device's appeal was eclipsed in 1895 by the first film projectors, created by fellow countrymen Auguste and Louis Lumière. The film projector, which shone light through celluloid rather than reflecting opaque drawings (and photos) off a series of mirrors, was brighter, cheaper to produce, and more reliable than the Théatre-Optique, and thus gained favor during the earliest years of the modern cinema.

By the dawn of the twentieth century, the modern film projector and nascent cinema industry were gaining wide popularity with audiences. Oddly, however, what was shown in movie houses (such as they were at the time) were exclusively live-action events rather than hand-drawn animations. The likeliest reason for the disappearance of animation during this period was that movies were more of a curiosity at the time rather than a form of narrative entertainment, and it was far more impressive to see "real"

Figure 2.3

Drawing of a praxinoscope by Jason Allen

people and objects projected on a screen rather than drawings of people.

By the end of the first decade of the twentieth century, film had advanced to the point where actual stories were being told, and some even used relatively advanced special effects (see Melies's 1902 masterpiece, *A Trip to the Moon*, for example). Animation, however, was lacking until in 1911 Winsor McCay, a famous American (or possibly Canadian-born) newspaper cartoonist animated several characters from his popular "Little Nemo in Slumberland" comic strip. Using 4,000 drawings (and a silly frame story telling about the circumstances of his creating the animation), McCay in just one month brought his Little Nemo characters to life in a convincing way, and set the stage for modern animation. While a number of techniques were used in *Little Nemo*, from use of color inking, to a surreal form of squash and stretch, to particle effects, to changing forced perspective, to sight gags, there was no attempt to create plot, a factor that continued to plague animation for years to come.

Two other of McCay's numerous early animations deserve note for their pioneering advances. The first is *Gertie the Dinosaur* (1914), a 10,000-drawing animation that blended live action (McCay himself as Gertie's trainer) and animated drawings. McCay

Figure 2.4

Gertie the Dinosaur

would stand before a screen at a vaudeville house and "interact" with Gertie, shown in Figure 2.4, who was not a particularly obedient pet, drawing gasps and laughs as Gertie performed for them. This animation is considered the first true character animation: while the plot was very minimal, Gertie herself had a personality and motivations (hunger, thirst, and annoyance—and the need for dance!). The second is *The Sinking of the Lusitania* (shown in Figure 2.5), an impressive 12-minute animation containing 25,000 drawings and used as propaganda in the U.S. war effort against Germany. This animation was one of the first to use the new cel animation technique, patented by Earl Hurd in 1914, where different animation layers were painted on clear cells that were laid atop each other before being photographed. In this manner, foreground characters could be animated separately from a static (or repeating) background, easing the animator's job immensely. *Lusitania* is also groundbreaking in the level of realism it portrays, its art direction, its serious (rather than comic or silly) subject matter, and its narrative format.

Figure 2.5

The Sinking of the Lusitania

McCay and others in the 'teens and early twenties paved the way for animators like Max Fleischer and Walt Disney, who, with their studios, evolved animation to its modern-day form, invented several new technologies for animation (like the rotoscope and dope sheet), and solidified a grammar of animation that is still used today.

The Disney 12 Principles

Aside from the numerous technical and process (or pipeline) innovations studios of the 1920s came up with, they also established the philosophical tenets of character animation now known as the "Disney 12" principles of character animation. Although the technology behind animation has undergone a number of revolutions, the Disney 12 has endured as a touchstone for good animation for more than seven decades. The following sections list these principles, with brief descriptions of each one.

Ease in, Ease Out

Also referred to as slow in, slow out, this principle refers to the all-important need to approximate the physical law of conservation of momentum. While a virtual car (either drawn or otherwise animated) can accelerate from 0 to 60 miles per hour in 0 seconds flat, a supercar like this can never exist in reality, since it takes time and energy to accelerate or decelerate any object with weight. Generally, the heavier an object or character, the more energy and time it takes to accelerate the object. Thus, in general, slower or more ponderous changes in momentum (the up-down motion of walking, for example) convey greater weight than light, quick motion. Many new animators either forget or underestimate the need for ease in, ease out, making their characters appear too light or "floaty," and causing actions like throwing a ball to occur too quickly.

> One might argue that while it takes time to accelerate a car, if that car drove into a big concrete wall it would decelerate instantly. This, however, is not true. First of all, the car crumples under collision, so that its parts collapse onto one another, which takes time (a short time, yes, but it still takes time). Second, a number of parts of the car (tires, headlights, bits of the fenders) go flying off in an accident, transferring the energy of the car as a whole into a great deal of secondary motion (see the "Secondary Action" section later in the chapter). Thus even "instant" deceleration in the real world takes some amount of time.

Anticipation and Follow-through

Anticipation, which is linked to the principle of follow-through, has two functions: to mimic the real life need to prepare for an action, and to draw audience focus. When a person prepares to do an action, he or she first anticipates this action via a smaller counter-action that usually goes in the opposite direction. Consider throwing a ball: you don't just push the ball out of your hands; instead, you first "wind up," moving the ball and your body weight backward in order to store up the energy you need to actually do the throwing. The harder you plan to throw the ball, the more you will wind up, and therefore the larger will be the anticipation, leading to the common connection between the size of the anticipation and the size of the expected action itself. In addition to conveying realism, anticipation is a great way to draw the focus of the audience before an important action occurs. Nothing is more frustrating for someone watching an animation (or live-action movie, or even real event) than missing out on something important that happens. By using often exaggerated anticipation, however, you can ensure that your viewers are looking at the character you want them to be watching before something important happens. For "a guy hits a home run in the bottom of the ninth to win the game," spending a good deal of time on both the physical and emotional anticipation of both pitcher and batter is important to make sure everyone is watching at the crucial moment when the ball is pitched. Giving a lot of time to the anticipation of an action like this even helps viewers understand that what will occur is, in fact, important.

> One can, of course, play a discrepancy between the size of an anticipation and the actual action itself for comic effect. For example, a character might anticipate a "huge" sneeze, only to make a tiny noise—or perhaps they anticipate a small sneeze and their head pops off from the force of the actual sneeze.

Follow-through is the complement to anticipation: the action that follows after the main action has occurred. Using the ball throwing example, follow-through is the motion your arm and body make after you release the ball. (Try to stop yourself from moving after releasing a ball you throw hard and you realize just how much of a throw is follow-through.) While not generally as important as anticipation for drawing audience focus, follow-through is still critical to create believable action, as things don't simply stop after a primary action is accomplished.

Overlapping Action

Because character actions must be tied together into a whole, animators need overlapping action. Take, for example, a pitcher pitching to a batter, then catching the ball as the batter hits it back to him. Good (or believable) animation will avoid having the pitcher simply stop dead on releasing the ball, and then snapping up to catch the ball as it is hit back to him. Instead, the pitcher's arm and then leg will follow through, he will take up the weight of his off-balance body on his landing foot, his other foot will come off the ground and move under his body, his head will rise up to see what happened to the ball he just pitched, he will react to the ball being hit by the batter, and he will begin to adjust his position—all of this (and more) between the time he releases the ball and when he begins to catch it as the batter hits it back to him. While it is far simpler for an animator to animate everything stopping and starting at the same time, the pitching example shows how important it is for things to happen "on top of" each other, with different subactions stopping and starting at different points in time. The breakdown of when these actions start and stop relative to each other is tied up in the principle of timing, discussed in a later section.

Secondary Action

Secondary action is "all the little things" that animate (usually unconsciously or by force of physical interaction) when a main action takes place. For example, when a woman with long hair and a flowing skirt walks down the street, there are numerous secondary elements beyond the main action of the walk itself. Her skirt and long hair will flow back and forth, up and down as she walks. If she has a fairly tight top on, we will also see her breasts moving in rhythm to the walk, though this is a more restricted motion than that of her hair and skirt. Secondary actions like these three are based on physical forces—gravity and possibly wind in this case—and will occur out of phase with her walking stride; in other words, as she pushes her body upwards, her hair, skirt, and breasts will move downward under the force of their own momentum. The opposite happens as she descends to the lowest point of her stride. Physical forces will also force her skirt and body parts to continue moving for a time when she stops walking. The other type of secondary animation is unconscious action. Breathing is a prime example of this, as all living creatures breathe constantly, moving our bodies in some manner to take in and expel air. Other examples of unconscious behavior are blinking and nervous ticks or twitches. While primary animation is what a character is doing (consciously) at a given moment, secondary animation makes them appear truly alive, which is just as important.

Arcs

There are two ways to look at arcs: character arcs and motion arcs. Character arcs are a kind of personal drama occurring within the larger story your animation is telling. A character might be starving and desire some food in an animation. The character arc, then, is the desire for food, the character's tactics to try and get this food, and finally his success or failure in getting the food. This arc generates interest in a character and the story as a whole, and is very tied in to the objective-tactics-obstacles work actors do, which is discussed in the following chapter.

Figure 2.6
Skeletal motion is always an arcing motion.

The other type of arc relates to drawing (or rendering) and deals with the nature of human (and animal) motion. Because of the way we generate motion—muscles pulling on skeletons—all of our movements are in fact arcs, and not linear motions, as shown in Figure 2.6. If you wish to move your fingertip in a straight line, for example, you must rotate your shoulder, your elbow, your wrist, and perhaps your finger as well, to create the linear motion. This fact is often a revelation to beginning animators, but this factor is crucial to creating motion that looks realistic. Fortunately the rigging method for most 3D packages uses a simulation of muscles and bones, so it is easier to create arcing motion with these packages than it is drawing by hand.

Creating predictable, linear motion in a 3D package using a skeleton that only rotates is most often done today using IK, or inverse kinematics. This method is computationally complex and has some issues (most notably joint flipping under singularity conditions) but makes target-directed linear motion far easier today than it was before IK became common.

Exaggeration

Here is where animation breaks from reality in the most obvious way. Good animation differs from reality in some way (otherwise why animate, as we discussed earlier); exaggeration is one of the most commonly used (others are stylization and abstraction). Not only does this larger-than-life aura of animation help with humor, but it also serves to crystallize the essence of emotion and action in a very obvious form. In real life, a man seeing an attractive woman walking down the street might do a double take: he might look up from his reading, look back down at it, then look up again briefly to see the woman again. In an animation, this take can be exaggerated in numerous ways. Perhaps the wolf (a classic symbol for the sex-starved male) looks up from his newspaper to see the sexy female wolf passing by; he then looks back down again, only to realize how attractive she is; his eyebrows pop up; he does a large anticipatory counter turn of his head; his head snaps over to see the girl wolf, his snout stretching out and his eyes popping out of his head to follow her as she continues walking. Tex Avery was a master of over-the-top exaggeration. In his 1943 *Red Hot Riding Hood*, the big bad wolf's reaction when he sees "Red Hot" is even more exaggerated than what we've described here.

Squash and Stretch

Squash and stretch goes hand in hand with exaggeration in most animations. This principle is an exaggeration of the manner in which physical objects such as muscles and balls deform when under stress. In the real world, a tennis ball will compress when it hits the ground, storing up potential energy, which is converted back to kinetic energy as the ball returns to its original shape after overshooting this shape by stretching and thinning out too much. A muscle being used to lift an object will also deform, compressing in the medial direction while expanding in the lateral. A body can also seem to compress or stretch as multiple muscles are used to absorb the impact from jumping from a high wall, or to elongate the body to begin a jump. In cartoon reality, squashing and stretching takes these physical bases and runs with them. In a simple case, a ball might "anticipate" hitting the ground by stretching out to meet it (physically impossible, but hey, this is animation!). The ball will likely also squash in a much slower and more exaggerated manner than in real life when it hits the ground, and stretch much farther as it bounces off the ground. In more zany cases, entire bodies might act like springs, a head might remain in the air while the rest of a character's body stretches away as it falls off a cliff, or a character might suddenly behave like a rubber ball when another character collides with it.

One of the most important things to remember with squash and stretch is to preserve the apparent volume of the character. If a character shrinks in the vertical axis but maintains the same dimensions in the horizontal axes, we believe the character is shrinking or moving off into the distance rather than squashing under some impact. To preserve volume, when a character shrinks or stretches along one axis, she must do the opposite on the other axes. For example, a water balloon being pressed down squashes in one direction, but since the water has to go somewhere, it balloons out in the other directions. For whatever reason, we have no problem believing characters squashing flat as a pancake, only to bounce back into correct shape again, but if a character appears to lose or gain volume (without some reason, like a garden hose stuck in its mouth), we find this very disturbing. One can do some math to preserve more-or-less exact volume for the character, but with a little practice an animator can simply eyeball the squash and stretch to get close enough.

Winsor McCay's first animation, *Little Nemo*, includes characters stretching and compressing without preserving volume, making this portion of the animation both disturbing and amateurish.

Staging

As its name implies, the principle of staging involves placement of characters (and scene elements) relative to the camera in such a manner as to make the action clear and interesting for the viewer. In a way, the animator must think of the camera as another character—one that observes and reacts to the actions being played out before it. The camera is also a placeholder for the audience, since we will witness the action from whatever vantage the camera takes. One good way to work on staging skills is to silhouette the characters on a white background and see if the action is clear and interesting with only the silhouettes visible. As Figure 2.7 shows, the same exact action can be either clear or confusing in silhouette, depending on staging. Note that in the right-hand image it is difficult to tell what is happening, while in the left-hand image, it is clear the woman is kicking at something. Often staging for clarity is done from the side, so that silhouettes are easy to read and the action is clear. On the other hand, it is sometimes useful to stage from a first-person perspective to achieve intimacy or a higher level of threat. If the camera is in a first-person relationship to a character, the audience will react as if the character is talking to (or threatening) them; if a camera takes a more third-person view (often from the side), we will tend to feel like observers of the action rather than direct participants. Decisions about staging are crucial and should be considered carefully even before animation begins.

Figure 2.7

Two different stagings of a kick: left is from the side, right is from the front.

Storyboards are a great place to work through staging. By using sequences of these quick drawings, an entire team of artists can determine the best camera placement and staging for numerous shots that make up a given scene or even a whole animation.

Timing

Timing is the "other half" of animation (space being the first), and mastering this principle is considered proof that one has truly arrived as an animator. In timing, we have to determine how many frames (or how much time) occurs between each element of animation: Is the time to move an arm down to a table 40 frames (a gentle placing of the hand on the table) or 3 frames (slamming a fist down)? How much time does it take between a heel strike and the ball of the foot hitting the ground in a walk cycle? How much lag is there between a large character's feet hitting the ground and his belly stretching down from the impact? Timing is perhaps the most difficult of the Disney 12 to master. While most other principles allow the animator to examine a single frame to determine if something (pose, staging, squash and stretch, etc.) is correct, timing only exists in motion, making it a challenge to become adept at this all-important principle.

Timing is crucially important in giving weight to a character. Improper timing can make a character appear to float rather than walk, and make her look like she's lifting a feather instead of a feather bed. In addition, timing is crucial to the emotion or intention of a scene: a character that hasn't slept in days or has just heard some terrible news will walk at a completely different cadence than one who has just fallen in love or gotten a new job. Actors will often pause (or "take a beat") upon hearing something or making an important decision, and the timing of this pause helps the audience understand the mental process he is going through at the time. The same holds for animated characters, which must show us their state of mind and mental processes via this same method.

Straight-Ahead and Pose-to-Pose Animation

This principle is more one of process than result. The two main traditional "pipelines" (or methodologies) of animation use either the straight-ahead or the pose-to-pose technique. Straight-ahead animation is the more intuitive method in which an animator sits down and draws (or poses) frame 1, then proceeds to frame 2 and poses that frame, and so on. The advantages of this method are the intuitiveness of doing animation in this manner (it's easy to see where you just came from and determine where you're going), and also the naturalness of the resulting motion. The big disadvantages are the difficulty of synching up the motion of multiple characters or complex scenes, and the issue of having to go back and redo *everything* if the animation doesn't turn out right the first time (and when does it?). Pose-to-pose is a technique wherein an animator will draw (or pose) key moments in an animation without the intervening frames. The advantages to this method are that you can create poses before worrying about timing, that complex scenes are easier to create, and that reworking an individual drawing or pose is far easier than redrawing a whole section of an animation. The downside to pose-to-pose is that animation often comes out looking (or "feeling") wooden or mechanical due to the nature of its genesis. This lack of natural flow can make characters appear to be robots rather than living, breathing creatures.

The usual animation pipeline today is to combine elements of both of these techniques into a hybrid procedure. Pose-to-pose is used to frame out a block of animation, which are then timed out in a rough manner using a popping method where the character snaps from one pose to another. Once the poses and rough timing are approved, the animator will go back in and use a straight-ahead animation technique to move from pose to pose and to break up the poses so that different animation elements start and finish at different times.

Solid Drawing

Now often termed *solid modeling and rigging* rather than drawing to reflect the computer-generated nature of most animation, this principle states that characters should be clearly delineated from their backgrounds and from each other by their shape, and should additionally look "real" in whatever world they live. Solid drawing produces good silhouettes, which helps staging, and also creates characters that appear to have weight and will animate well, helping to bring the characters to life and give them weight and appeal.

Appeal

This is the most abstract of the 12 principles, stating that characters must be appealing or interesting to the viewing audience. This is not to state that all characters should be cute, cuddly, or good—in fact "bad guy" characters like Chef Skinner in *Ratatouille* or Lord Farquaad in *Shrek* are not cute or good, but they are very appealing to their audiences. What we need is a mental and especially an emotional connection to the characters on screen (just as we do with a live-action film), and appeal is the conduit to this connection.

Although the concept of an appealing character is straightforward enough, how to create one is a far more difficult matter. One thing that has worked over time is to use a talented actor as the voice of a character; the actor's voice will have good appeal in its own right, but can also drive the animation itself as animators work from the video footage of the actor playing the role. In addition, creating characters that are cute—or have the large head, big eyes, small mouth, and small body of an infant—works well, at least if you want a cute character. Writing a good character is also crucial: someone without big, identifiable desires and something standing in the way of them will fall flat on screen. It is difficult to get the recipe just right for an appealing character, but when you do, you can create an enduring cultural icon like Mickey Mouse, Bugs Bunny, or Pikachu.

Facial versus Body Animation

In CG animation, body and facial animation are often considered separate pieces of the animation pipeline (the path through which the idea of an animation is converted into fully rendered frames). Sometimes there are even different animators who work on facial and body animation for a given scene. Obviously body animation can be done without facial animation (as we will do in Chapter 4) and vice versa, but most often the body and face work together to create action and readable emotion. While there is a great deal of overlap, body animation is generally focused on action and silhouette (throwing a ball, walking, kicking someone, etc.) while facial animation focuses on intent and emotion (the desire to get that last cookie, sadness at not getting it, etc.).

Therefore, you might animate a character's face to show her fear of a ghost that jumps out at her, then her transition to anger as she realizes it was just her brother in a ghost costume, and next her intent to give her brother a whack over the head for scaring her. Her body, in the meantime, would be animated to jump back from the "ghost," then to straighten back up as she realized she was being teased, and finally to run threateningly at her brother, arms raised, as she tries to hit him. The combination of both facial and body animation work in concert to let the viewer know exactly what is going on and why.

We humans are exceptionally good at reading body language in other people (or human-like characters) and are even better at reading facial expressions. Since birth we have regarded others' faces and bodies to figure out what they are doing and to determine what's happening inside their heads. We are so expert, in fact, that we can often tell when someone lies, or when an actor on stage or screen is not delivering a believable performance. This level of expertise in even the most casual observer is both boon and bane to the animator: we can be incredibly subtle with our animation and trust audiences to read what's going on, but if we make any mistakes, they will be noticed for sure, either consciously or unconsciously. The level of perfection we must attain grows higher as the characters and settings become more realistic. While we can get away with fun approximations (and exaggerations) of human behavior when we animate simple hand-drawn rabbits and ducks, we must be far more careful when animating photo-real CG humans over live-action backgrounds. If not done just right, realistic animation can actually be unsettling, an effect known as the uncanny valley, an effect hypothesized by robotics expert Masahiro Mori in 1970, and since proven in films like 2001's *Final Fantasy: The Spirits Within* that come too close to reality without being perfect. The trouble, as set forth by Mori, is that as automata (robots or animated characters) get closer and closer to reality, the appeal of the creature will rise until a certain point where it is "too close" to real humans, but not close enough to pass as human; at this point their appeal actually goes down instead of up, as humans become very uncomfortable relating to the automata. The uncanny valley stands as warning to animators and directors alike that trying to exactly re-create humans and their actions is dangerous ground with serious consequences for failure. Animation is far better suited to exaggerating or crystallizing human (and animal) behavior, so unless you have a real need to reproduce photo-real animation, it is better to stay away from it.

The Facial Action Coding System

In the mid-1970s, Paul Ekman and Wallace V. Friesen, in researching facial expressions and emotions, noted that most emotions are related to facial expressions in a universal way, rather than a cultural one. Perhaps more importantly, at least for animators, is that Ekman and his fellow researchers "decoded" all human expressions into a few dozen muscle contractions they termed action units, or AUs. The complete set of AUs, which can be used to build up any expression on the human face, is called the Facial Action Coding System (FACS), and over the past several years has become a popular way for animation houses to rig characters' faces.

In essence, the AUs isolate sets of muscular contractions on the human face, which contains an impressive 52 (approximately) muscle groups. As each muscle group slides over the skull during contraction, it creates a distinct look on the face, which we have become extremely adept at "reading" or understanding. From birth we stare at other human faces, and by a mere few years of age can tell when someone is lying, or disinterested, or happy-but-trying-to-hide-it, or a thousand other things that can play across one's face. Our ability to recognize incredibly subtle differences in facial muscle contractions (and eye direction) is an amazing feat, but one that should scare the facial animator to death: we as animators have to take an inanimate object and reconstruct these subtle musculoskeletal interactions in such a way that an audience will believe they are seeing a real person with emotions and objectives behind the set of pixels rendered onscreen. Fortunately the FACS gives us everything we need to re-create these subtle motions; unfortunately it takes a skilled and experienced hand with them to get just the right effect. The best way to gain this experience is to observe faces doing specific things, which is where this book comes in. Over the next chapters we will have many occasions to re-create specific emotions based on pictorial reference.

The Maya rigs we have built for this book include a complete set of AU blend shapes for each character (except for a few involving head turns, which are easy enough to animate using the neck controls). These will allow us to precisely control facial "muscles" on the characters for lessons involving facial animation. While the faces are somewhat complex to manipulate due to the large number of blend shapes involved, we expect you will find that the level of control achievable with this setup is worth the learning curve. In addition, you will be working on a system similar to what large animation houses are currently using for their in-house facial animation systems, allowing you to achieve results similar to the best work being done today (assuming time and talent of course!). Figure 2.8 shows a complete set of AUs set together as a grid. The file `FACSActionUnits.jpg` on the accompanying DVD presents this image in substantially larger format so you can see the AUs more clearly.

Figure 2.8
_____

A complete set of facial action units (AUs)

We only touch the surface of this very deep research topic—as it pertains to animation specifically—on these pages. For further information concerning FACS, see www.face-and-emotion.com or search for Facial Action Coding System on the Web.

Rigging in a Nutshell

This book is not about rigging, which deserves an entire book of its own. However, it is difficult to be a good animator without at least a basic knowledge of rigging, so this section presents a basic outline of how modern rigging works, focusing on concepts and issues most relevant to animators.

For excellent references on body and facial rigging, see *Maya Techniques: Hyper-Real Creature Creation*, by Erick Miller, Paul Thuriot, and Jeff Unay (Sybex, 2006), and Jason Osipa's *Stop Staring: Facial Modeling and Animation Done Right, Second Edition* (Sybex, 2007).

Rigging in CG animation (as well as in stop-motion work) is the art and science of creating an internal skeleton/muscle system that allows parts of a given model to move in accordance with the model's logical pivot points (like knees and elbows) and the animator's desires. The arm of an octopus is going to move very differently than a human arm, for example, so a character technical director (character TD) must rig the octopus and human arms differently. At the same time, an animator might wish to "squash and stretch" a human arm for a given scene, so a rig used for that scene must accommodate scaling to create the squash and stretch effect. Two other very important elements of rigging are that a rig should be as intuitive and robust as possible, allowing an animator to quickly understand and feel comfortable animating a rig while simultaneously keeping said animator from breaking the rig by moving the wrong part or moving things too far or in the wrong direction. If a rig is difficult to understand or use, the animator will be hobbled and the rigger will be forced to spend a lot of time working with the animator to help them understand the ins and outs of a given rig, or to fix problems that are keeping the rig from doing what an animator wants. If the rig is not robust enough, animators will (nearly always!) break it while animating the character.

The job of an animator is quite challenging, then: He or she must create a method to move parts of a model that is in harmony with the model's ostensible musculoskeletal system—which can be difficult, especially in the case of fantasy creatures that have no real-life reference. They must also allow the model to move as the animator wishes in an intuitive manner that won't break when used (and abused). Animators like to push the envelope (to put it kindly): if given the chance they'll usually pull, bend, or twist any part they can get their hands on to create a given pose, often breaking the rig in the process. It is thus incumbent on the rigger to be sure animators can't get hold of anything that might break the rig, and that animators can't over-turn or excessively translate a given control.

A rig is most often broken down into body and facial components, which are usually created by different teams at large animation houses. While there are a number of each type of rig, the most common body rig in use today is a "cage" system whereby in-scene

elements (often curves) that either encompass or sit near their corresponding geometric element are used to control that element. Figure 2.9 shows the implementation of this setup that we have used for our supplied mod-
els. Not only is grabbing a circle around the wrist to manipulate the wrist fairly intuitive, but having the animator manipulate a control element (the circle) is far more robust than having them grab the skeleton itself, which should never be directly manipulated for fear of breaking something in the rig.

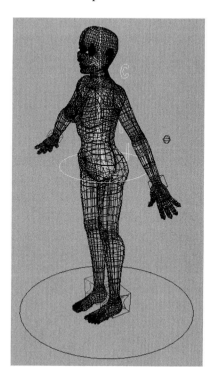

Figure 2.9

The female model and rig setup from this book's DVD

The most common facial rigs today use a set of blend shapes, which are modifications of the original, neutral head to create different facial motions like raising an eyebrow or opening the mouth. In combination, these different shapes create everything from phonemes (for lip synching) to emotions. The best of today's facial rigs use a control "board" set in the scene that allows the animator to move virtual controls for the eyes, mouth, and face, and have the actual face respond accordingly. These setups are fairly complex but allow excellent control over facial expressions.

> The models and rigs included on this book's DVD are for use with Maya 2008 or above. If you are using a different animation package, you can use your own models and rigs, or look on the Internet for sample model/rig combinations for your package. Often these setups are quite good and are available to the animation community for free.

Each of the two human models created and rigged for this book have a complex rig that allows them a substantial range of motion and a wide range of facial poses. They are general-purpose rigs, set up to allow for just about any natural human motion or emotion, and also include the advanced ability to do squash and stretch if the animator so desires. One issue with general-purpose rigs is that they can prove more complex to use, and are often incapable of creating some specialized pose or action for a really wacky scene or character. On the other hand, they are excellent tools to use for studying animation, which is what we are doing in this book. Taking time to get used to these rigs will be very beneficial as you work through the later stages of this book, so use the exercises in the next section to get used to the rigs while working on your animation skills.

James Orara, who works as a Creature Technical Director for Industrial Light and Magic (ILM), created the body rig setup used on the two models included in the book as part of his Master of Fine Arts (MFA) work at Clemson University. David Floyd and Lena Gieseke have created the female and male models, respectively, as part of their MFA work at the University of Georgia. David Floyd and John Kundert-Gibbs created the FACS-based facial rig for the models. All have kindly shared their expertise and time in modeling and rigging these characters for your use.

Animation Exercises

Animation theory is all well and good, but there is no substitute for a bit of practice to firmly ground the concepts, to get used to a given rig setup, and to hone your skills. The following exercises are fairly common, but completing them should get you up to speed for the more specialized work to come; plus they're fun to do and the later ones will help get you comfortable with the models and rigs we'll be using throughout the rest of the book. If you're already an accomplished animator, you might just wish to pick out one or two exercises rather than going through all of them.

Stop-Motion Animation

This is about as basic as it gets: animate a solid object like a coin or bottle cap by placing the object and taking a picture of it, moving it slightly and taking another picture. The focus here is to work with the two elements of animation—time and space—in their most essential form. For this set of exercises, you will need a digital camera (preferably one that you can set to full manual), a tripod, and a ruler. You will also need to use Maya's included FCheck program (or another program, like Apple's QuickTime Pro) to read in the sequence of images you will produce with your camera. Set the camera on the tripod facing down (or at a wall if you prefer), set it to manual exposure and focus if possible, and take pictures of the object as you move it.

The first exercise is to produce constant motion. Simply divide a length on the floor into 24 even, marked units; place the coin on one mark; take a picture; move it to the next mark; and take another picture, as shown in Figure 2.10. When you have taken all the pictures you need, dump the photos onto your computer and use a program like FCheck to read the file in as an image sequence (in FCheck, use File → Open Animation) and play it back at 24 frames per second. An example of this animation, `ConstantMotion.mov`, is on the DVD. This animation is fairly mechanical to create, but you can still see how the distance the object moves between frames creates different speeds, how there is a definite need for motion blur to smooth out the "stuttering" motion of the object as it moves (the result of taking "perfect" pictures where the object is not moving while the shutter is open), and the manner in which we as viewers meld the individual pictures together in our minds to create motion where there was none.

Figure 2.10

Moving a coin at a constant rate of speed

Next, we will create ease in and ease out for our animated object. Instead of 24 consistently spaced marks, you will need to mark several lines closer together near the beginning and end of the length the object will travel, along with a number of evenly spaced marks in the middle of the length when the object is traveling at full speed. As opposed to the mechanical animation before, here you will need to "eyeball" the marks at the beginning and end of the length, trying to get them spaced just right to convey that the object is starting and stopping. You will likely find that some experimentation with the spacing of lines at the beginning and end of the animation is necessary to get just the right acceleration and deceleration. Also note how differing acceleration rates make the object seem heavier and lighter on playback. EaseInOut.mov on the accompanying DVD shows an example of this type of motion.

The third animation exercise brings in a second dimension. Here we will animate an object falling and bouncing across the frame. In addition to adding in the "Y" dimension for this animation, the object must also change directions instantaneously as it strikes the "ground" and bounces back up again. Drawing arcs on a sheet of paper and then marking out where the object will travel is a good way to visualize where to place the object for animation. For this exercise, the focus is on the proper rate of fall for the object: if it falls too slowly, gravity seems too light (like it's on the moon or under water); if too fast, then things look too heavy. An example animation, Bounce.mov, is on the accompanying DVD.

Biped Walk

Creating a walk for a biped (human) character is one of the basic tasks any animator is asked to perform. While learned early on, however, walking is a series of complex motions, and age, gender, mood, and other personality-specific qualities can be read in a walk, so getting one just right is fairly challenging. Adding to the difficulty is the fact that we are adept at spotting anything that doesn't look "right" in a walk, making accuracy and specificity important when trying to create a convincing animation. We will outline the basics of how to create a walk here; you should add in elements like character, given circumstances, physical troubles, or anything else you can add to make the walk as specific as possible. We will use the pose-to-pose method to block out the major motion of the walk, and then go back and refine using straight-ahead animation.

> For walks and most other human-like animation work, video reference will prove invaluable. If you have even the most basic of video cameras, record yourself or someone else walking in the manner you wish to animate (in a hurry, sad, angry, etc.) and use this footage as a basis for your animation work.

 To begin, open either the male or female model on the accompanying DVD (or use your own model if you prefer). We will block out four poses for this walk: the passing position with the left foot up, the heel strike with the left foot forward, the passing position with the right foot up, and the heel strike with the right foot forward. For now, create the poses on sixes, or six frames apart. You can adjust the timing later on, but a 24-frame (or one-second) walk is a reasonable cadence from which to start.

> If you are using the included models (Genna and Marcel), which include built-in character/ subcharacter hierarchies, you can have Maya automatically select the characters as you go. First, place the autoCharacterSelection.mel file in your home scripts directory (~Autodesk/ maya/scripts on your home directory), then copy the line of code from ACSEnable.mel into the Script Editor input pane, and drag it up onto your shelf. When you start Maya, simply click the ACSEnable button, and from then on, Maya will automatically select whichever sub-character it needs based on what is selected in the scene. This makes selecting and keyframing characters far easier than having to remember to select and keyframe each sub character yourself.

1. Go to frame 1. Pose your character in a passing position with the left foot up, the arms hanging mostly at the sides, the shoulders fairly square, and the hips at their highest point, similar to Figure 2.11. The hip can tilt up slightly on the left-hand side to help lift the leg. Note that you should key every part of the animation on frame 1. To set keys on each of the characters on the rig (main, legs, torso, arms, head, etc.)— assuming you are using the autoCharacterSelection.mel script (see note, above)— just select any control item from one of the sub characters and press the "s" key. For now, leave all of your keyframes for every body part on the same frame. Later you will go back and divide up the different body parts to break up the animation.

> Male and female walks are not the same (as most people have observed many a time). For example, women tend to cross over their feet as they walk: on the left heel strike, the left and right foot will be directly in front of each other. Men, on the other hand, tend to keep their feet apart more as they walk—the more swaggering the walk, the more the feet stay apart. Women also tend to move their hips more when walking. "Rules" like these are not hard and fast; they are simply a place to start looking for variations in walk styles.

2. Go to frame 7 and pose your character so that their left heel is just striking the ground, as in Figure 2.12. Note that here the hips are at their lowest point in the walk, the right and left legs are spread out to their furthest distance, and the arms are opposite (so right arm forward, left back) and also at their furthest distance apart. The hips are twisted so the left hip is forward and the right back, and the shoulders are twisted opposite to the hips. The head should remain fairly close to square so that the character can see as they walk.

3. Go to frame 13 and create the right passing position. The right passing position is pretty much the same as the left passing position, except this time the right foot is up as it passes the left. See Figure 2.13.

4. Go to frame 19 and create the right heel strike pose. The right heel strike is opposite the left heel strike. See Figure 2.14.

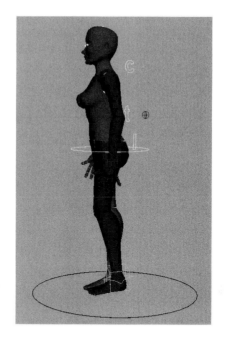

Figure 2.11

Passing position, left foot forward

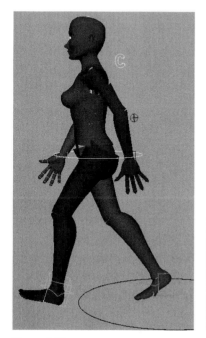

Figure 2.12

The left heel strike pose

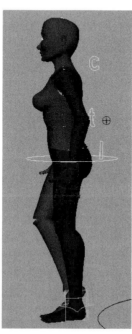

Figure 2.13

Passing position, right foot forward

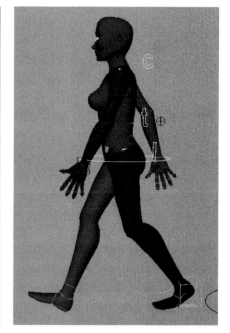

Figure 2.14

The right heel strike pose

Figure 2.15

Using stepped tangents in the Graph Editor

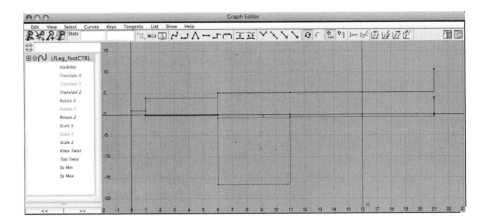

5. When finished blocking out the different poses, select the entire figure's control curves, go into the Graph Editor (in Maya, or the analogous curve editor in your package) and set the tangents to stepped, as shown in Figure 2.15. This will make the figure "pop" from pose to pose, which makes it easier to time the walk.

6. Adjust the placement of each pose by moving all the keys back and forth in the timeline and Playblasting the animation (Window → Playblast) to get a good sense of the actual timing. Don't rely on playing the animation in the timeline—there is a good chance it will animate at a different speed than "real time," which will give you an incorrect sense of timing between keyframes. Doing a quick render of the scene is always the best bet to get a quick look at timing for your animation.

7. Once you are happy with the timing, reset the tangents to spline (or clamped if you prefer), and start pulling apart different keyframes to create a more natural, overlapping motion. You might move the hips back about two frames from the foot keyframes (so 3, 9, 15, 21), the shoulders perhaps three frames back, and the arms four or so. If this variation makes the walk look too loose, or relaxed, tighten up the timing a bit by moving keys forward a couple of frames.

At this stage you have the basics. The rest is subtle refinement to get the walk to look natural and to invoke character and intention in the walk itself. Observation, practice, and several iterations of the animation will help you achieve the look you wish. Figure 2.16 shows a frame from a sample walk we have animated— girlWalk.mov—on the accompanying DVD.

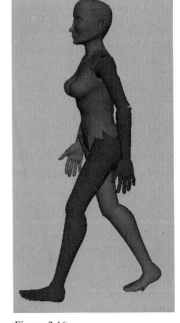

Figure 2.16

A frame from a fully animated walk

Facial Expressions

Your job here is to create a readable expression and then move it to another. For example, your character might be sad, and that sadness might transition to anger. The first task is to pick two emotions that you feel you can create in a readable way using the facial rig included (or your own rig). Picking two dissimilar emotions is best for this exercise; happiness and joy, for example, are too similar to create a good transition. You must then create a "script" or mental transition the character goes through to get from one emotion to the next, and animate this transition. To go from sadness to anger, for example, the character might be sad that his girlfriend is dumping him; he might then look up at her and see that she is not sad; he then considers why this would be the case; he then realizes that she is probably seeing his best friend and that's why she's dumping him; he then gets angry at her for doing such a dastardly deed. This sequence of thoughts is *very* different than just creating a "sad" look at one keyframe, then an "angry" look at another and letting the computer blend straight between the two, which will likely look strange and inhuman. The point, rather, is to get inside the head of your character and see what makes him or her tick. That knowledge will then generate any number of intermediate poses the character goes through to get from one state to another.

Start working out a script in your head with two distinctly different emotions as ending points. If you are able to draw the states, all the better; if not, you might want to search out photos of people with those emotions, or look in a mirror at yourself, or even photograph your own image in those states. Next, open either the male or female character on the DVD. Using the control "face" in the scene, as shown on the right in Figure 2.17, adjust your model's face until it reads the emotion you're looking for. You can show the facial pose to someone else and ask them if they can guess what emotion you're after to be sure you are communicating what you think you are.

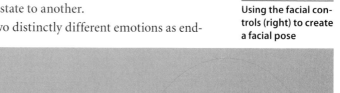

Figure 2.17

Using the facial controls (right) to create a facial pose

If you do facial animation, always carry a mirror with you. There is no better reference for facial animation than your very own face, which is always with you and can create whatever you need it to for reference. Visit any studio and you can pick out facial animators simply by looking for the mirrors on their desks.

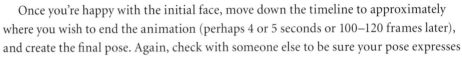

Once you're happy with the initial face, move down the timeline to approximately where you wish to end the animation (perhaps 4 or 5 seconds or 100–120 frames later), and create the final pose. Again, check with someone else to be sure your pose expresses the emotion you're after. Figure 2.18 shows one possible emotional state.

Now divide up the time between initial and final pose, and create the intermediate facial poses between them. When finished, you should have a sequence that moves from one emotion to another, with a clearly defined story being told to get from the first to the final states.

Figure 2.18

An angry face

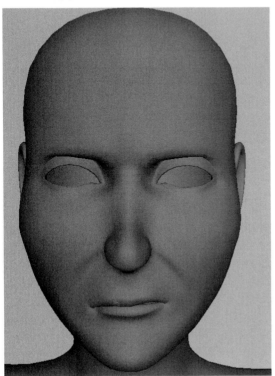

CHAPTER 3

Stanislavski's System

The work of Constantin Stanislavski is the foundation on which modern acting theory is based. It is imperative that all students of acting understand his methodology and are able to incorporate his technique in their work. For the animator, the ideas are also fundamental, as they will allow you to understand the exploration of character, the analysis of a text, and how to communicate with actors and directors.

This chapter discusses:

- A brief look at the life of Stanislavski

- An explanation of his system and its major components

- A means of analyzing a script

- Exercises to further understand the work

The Beginning of His Life in Art

Constantine Stanislavski (see Figure 3.1) was born Constantin Sergeyevich Alexeyev on January 17, 1863, in Moscow. His family was one of the richest in Russia and devoted to art and culture, so as a child he was exposed regularly to many different types of performing arts. Growing up he was especially interested in circus and puppetry arts. He and his siblings would regularly perform pageants and puppet shows for his family.

In, 1877 his father converted a building on his property to a theater for his family and friends, and Constantin began performing there. Later his father established a second theater at their home in Moscow, and this endeavor led the family to become leaders of culture in the city.

Figure 3.1
Constantin Stanislavski

DRAWING BY JASON ALLEN

After first working for the family business of manufacturing gold and silver braiding, in 1885 Constantine chose to begin the study of acting. He trained for a short period of time at the Moscow Theatre School and at the Maly Theatre but was disappointed in what he was being taught. Acting training consisted primarily of studying great actors and acting teachers and imitating their performances. By mimicking his teachers, he felt that he was learning tricks and conventions and not a true and consistent process to create a character on the stage.

He then saw the great Italian actor Tommaso Salvini perform Othello, and he began to rethink and establish what later became his system for acting. Constantin was so impressed with Salvini's performance on the stage that he changed his name to Stanislavski (he also did this in part to hide his theatrical work from his parents, who considered actors to be below their class) and began to pursue a full time career in the theater. He became known throughout Moscow as an innovative director.

After Stanislavski's debut performance at his family's theater, he began keeping a series of notebooks and journals, which later were published as *My Life in Art*.

The Moscow Art Theatre

In 1897, Stanislavski met Vladimir Nemirovich-Danchenko, an established Russian teacher and dramaturge, and after a famous 18-hour discussion of their ideas about theater the pair agreed to form the Moscow Art Theatre. The theater would be dedicated to a modern way of approaching both performance and production. Realism in production and psychological realism in performance were their goals.

After opening the theater with a production of a previously censored play, *Czar Fyodor* by Tolstoy, Moscow Art Theatre became famous for its productions of Anton Chekhov. Audiences were amazed by the psychologically complex characters that they observed on the stage. Minute details of character and life were acted with realistic truthfulness in these productions. As the reputation of the theater grew, the company toured Germany and Eastern Europe, and Stanislavski was heralded as a new artistic genius.

After much initial success, Stanislavski had a series of uneven productions and became depressed with the quality of his work. He took a leave from the theater to rest. When he returned, he put in place his system of acting. He began to train members of his company at the Moscow Art Theatre in a method of acting that revolutionized theater and all performance since that time.

The System

Stanislavski set out to understand inspiration. He wanted to be able to teach an actor how to achieve a state of inspiration so that while the actor was on the stage he would be living as the character. The actor would then do things as the character would do them, would think the thoughts of the character and experience the same feeling and emotions as the character. The actor would not participate in overacting or mannerisms but rather in simple action, and thus be living, as would a real human being in real life rather than acting. This, for Stanislavski, was psychological truth in performance (see Figure 3.2).

Figure 3.2

Actors performing simple actions as in everyday life in a production of *Balm in Gilead* at the University of Georgia Department of Theatre and Film Studies. Set by Jason Allen. Costumes by Lindsey Goodsen. Lights by Michael O'Connell. Direction by Kristin Kundert-Gibbs

Stanislavski called his system "The Elementary Grammar of Dramatic Art." He emphasized that his system was based on a scientific exploration of human experience and the re-creation of that experience on the stage. He sought to understand how people operate in day-to-day life and then discover a means for the actor as a character to do the same thing. He considered his system to be a scientific methodology.

At the same time that Stanislavski was creating his method, Ivan Pavlov was doing his research in conditioned responses. It is not clear whether Stanislavski ever encountered this research, but it is very interesting that his methodology follows a similar train of thought. Both ideas are based on neurophysiology.

Stanislavski identified three forces that determine the makeup of the psychological life of a human: the mind, will, and emotions. He set out to find a means of detailing and controlling these three forces. He ran into difficulty with the emotions because he believed that ultimately the emotions are out of the control of a human being because they are controlled by inner mechanisms, which he called the subconscious.

Stanislavski then set out to find a means of accessing the subconscious. He called this a "conscious means to the subconscious." He believed that internal experiences and their external physical expression were inseparable. If a person feels scared, she will jump or gasp. If she feels angry, she could attack. The internal emotional state is always expressed in external actions.

As Stanislavski began to understand human behavior, which he called action, he determined that the means to accessing the subconscious was through "a line of physical action." So an actor, who has no control over his subconscious, could, by essentially working backwards, access this inner life by determining the external actions that are tied to the inner life. By doing a series of actions, the actor would come to think and feel the same thoughts that would be experienced by the character.

This line of physical action goes beyond simple physical movement. Physical movement always has an inner need or desire. So in order to determine the physical actions, the actor must determine the needs of the character. The actor does this through an analysis of the script. This analysis comes from reading and rereading the script, breaking it down into smaller units and then piecing it all back into a whole. The key elements that Stanislavski determined were essential in determining the through-line of physical actions for a character were the given circumstances, objectives, obstacles, the "magic if," and tactics. Most of these things are hypothesized by the actor outside of rehearsal by doing homework on the text. The actor then tries out his or her discoveries in rehearsal and makes changes based on which ideas work and which don't.

Given Circumstances

As an actor begins to analyze the text, she must determine the given circumstances of the character. The given circumstances include the who, what, when, and where questions. They include the plot of the script, the time, the place, and any external factors that determine the environment of the setting. They also include any conceptual ideas that the director and designers are bringing to the production. The actor determines these given circumstances by repeatedly reading the script and asking herself questions about everything that she encounters (see Figure 3.3).

Consider the character of Dorothy in the movie *The Wizard of Oz*. What would some of her given circumstances be? She is a female teenager, living in rural Kansas with an aunt and uncle and not her parents. The year is 1939. She has a dog, which has bitten a mean neighbor who now hates that dog. She feels out of place on the farm and longs to find her place in the world. In a tornado she is swept away to Oz, a land where she has no friends, has a pair of magic slippers placed on her feet, and is being hunted by an evil witch. These are a few of the major given circumstances that shape the character of Dorothy.

Or consider the character of the Terminator in the movie *The Terminator*. What are some of his given circumstances? He is a cyborg assassin sent back in time from the year 2029 to 1984 in order to assassinate Sarah Connor before she gives birth to her son. He feels no pain and will stop at nothing to kill her. These given circumstances are what the actor needs to examine in order to develop the character and his through-line of actions, the through-line being a chain of logical, moment-to-moment objectives that build to the character's super objective.

Figure 3.3

Actors' take on given circumstances of the fairy characters Oberon and Puck in a production of *Midsummer Night's Dream* at the University of Georgia Department of Theatre and Film Studies. Set by Ben Philipp. Costumes by Ivan Ingermann. Lights by Rachel Konieczny. Direction by Kristin Kundert-Gibbs

The search for given circumstances sounds easy on the surface but actually is quite complex. It is not difficult to pick out the main plot points of a story and the time and place, but there are many more subtle details to examine when uncovering the given circumstances. Actors will read a script many times looking for clues to the character. They will examine not only everything that their character says and does but also everything that the other characters say about their character. They will look for clues in word choice and punctuation. Often these small subtle details will not become evident until the actor has spent a considerable amount of time studying the script.

Objectives

Everything we do in life is based on a desire or need. Some of our needs are purely physical and very easy to understand. We scratch our arm because it itches from a mosquito bite. We rub our back because we pulled a muscle working out and we are trying to get some relief. Some other desires aren't as obvious and perhaps are acting within our subconscious. We might eat because we are hungry, or it could also be because we are stressed, lonely, or sad. In all of these cases we are still trying to fulfill a desire: comforting ourselves. The things we do, the places we live, the friends we have are all chosen because of a specific desire or need.

Stanislavski called this need a super objective. He based his idea of objective on human behavior. Everything that humans do is done for a particular reason. It may be a subconscious reason that we don't fully understand, but it is still a reason. He says that every character, just like every person, has something they want or need, and this super objective will drive every moment of the play. So simply put, a super objective is the overall, or overwhelming, desire of the character.

In the case of *The Terminator*, the super objective is very obvious—so obvious, in fact, that it is stated in the character's name. His super objective is to terminate Sarah Connor. This desire is what drives the character throughout the entire movie. The pursuit of this super objective determines all the choices the character makes.

In the case of Dorothy in *The Wizard of Oz*, the super objective isn't quite so obvious. Most people would immediately say Dorothy's super objective is to get home. But remember, the super objective must take into account the entire script. It has to drive the piece as a whole and incorporate every individual moment. So how would the super objective of "to get home" work in the beginning of the movie when she is already at home? Her super objective needs to be something bigger that takes into account the beginning of the movie. Perhaps it is something like "to discover what home means," or to embrace home or even to find her place in the world. Any of these ideas would take into account both the beginning of the movie when she is in Kansas and later when she is in Oz. Ultimately at the end of the movie she wins her objective and is finally comfortable and grateful for her simple country home, her friends, and her family.

As an actor unearths the given circumstances of a script and starts to understand the needs and desires of the character, the actor must determine what she believes the super objective of the character is. She will then look to all the individual scenes within the script to determine smaller objectives for those scenes. Each scene will have its own objective, and each of these objectives needs to lead to and be a part of the super objective.

Thus in analyzing a script, an actor determines the given circumstances and from these determines the super objective. Once the super objective is decided upon, the actor will determine a smaller objective for each scene, all of which must add up to the super objective. If an actor comes upon a scene with an objective that they just can't fit into the super objective, something is wrong. Either the super objective is not yet correct or the individual scene objective is not correct. This is one reason why rehearsals exist: Actors need to try out their different objectives and determine if they work.

This breaking down of the script into scenes and objectives is the beginning of what actors call scoring a script, and it is the first step in developing Stanislavski's through-line of actions for the character. If you understand what the character needs and is trying to get, then you understand what they are trying to do. Thus you are developing actions to play to lead you to the psychological truth of the character.

When determining super objectives and scene objectives, there are a few things to keep in mind. First, an objective always needs to be positive. It is impossible to play a negative objective. How could you not do something? Say you were on a diet. Your objective could not be "to not eat cake." How would you not do this? Rather, turn this negative objective into something positive that you can do. Instead you could say the objective is to shun cake or to resist the temptation. This is positive and something that you can do.

Second, the objective *always must be expressed in the form of an action verb.* We cannot stress this enough. An objective is an action. The stronger, more immediate, and more visceral the objective, the better. This is highly personal. Words that move you to action are what are important. We recommend to actors that they start to think about everything in terms of action verbs. Carry around a thesaurus and find new and interesting action verbs each day. Wipe passive verbs or verbs that are states of being from your vocabulary. Don't think, "I am angry." Think, "I need to attack." Don't think, "I am sad." Think, "I need to mourn." Don't think, "I am happy." Think, "I need to rejoice." All objectives must be strong action verbs (see Figure 3.4). No exceptions.

Figure 3.4

Actors pursuing the action-verb objective of "to bond" in a production of *Death of a Salesman* at the Warehouse Theatre

Finally, an objective needs to be something that is immediately attainable. If it is not something that you can obtain within the scene, then you can't play it. Going back to the diet scenario, say, in the scene you are at work and someone has brought in a birthday cake for one of your co-workers. Your objective can't be to lose 20 pounds. Although that might be your overall goal, there is no way in the course of one day at work you are going to lose 20 pounds. Instead, the immediately achievable objective would be to resist the temptation for cake or to wrestle your hunger into submission. This specific objective could be immediately obtainable.

Obstacles

An obstacle is anything that stands in the way of the character achieving her objective. Without obstacles there is no drama. If there were no obstacles in the way of the Terminator's objective, then Sarah would be killed in the first scene and there would be no movie. If Dorothy had no obstacles, then she wouldn't have longed for "somewhere over the rainbow." Obstacles are the essence of drama.

Obstacles can be just about anything (Figure 3.5). They can be objects, people, time, knowledge, money, or understanding. They can be real and palpable, or they can be emotional parts of the subconscious. An obstacle to your resisting the temptation of cake could be the fact that you haven't eaten all day or that the celebration is for your boss and you don't want to appear rude by not sharing his cake. It is absolutely necessary for an actor to understand all of the obstacles that are standing in the way of obtaining the objective.

Figure 3.5

An actor encountering an obstacle of new information on the phone in a production of _Moon Over Buffalo_ at Crossroads Rep

The "Magic If"

Now here is the fun part. Stanislavski coined the term the "magic if." He says that once you have determined the given circumstances for the character and you understand the character's objectives and obstacles, ask yourself the magic if: If I were this character in this situation operating with these objectives and obstacles, how would I behave? What would I do? This magic if allows you, the actor, to use your imagination and put yourself in the place of the character to determine the character's behavior and choices (see Figure 3.6). It allows you to discover the vocal, physical, and emotional life of the character. It plays upon your imagination and creativity. It allows you to do things differently, to feel differently, and to act differently than your everyday self. The magic if is at the heart of character transformation.

Figure 3.6

Using the magic if to take on character and determine the actions and emotions of "if I had just killed my brother" in a production of *TopDog/Underdog* at the Warehouse Theatre

Tactics

So if you are working on a role and you have unearthed the given circumstances, fully understand the objectives and obstacles of the character, and have begun to apply the magic if, you will start to develop your "tactics." Tactics are things that characters do to overcome their obstacles and reach their objectives. Tactics are specific action verbs that are developed from the use of the magic if.

In a scene, the actor has a specific objective and obstacles in the way that are blocking her from achieving that objective. She must then determine different tactics that she can use to try to overcome the obstacles and reach her objective. Just like objectives, tactics must be strong, personal, positive action verbs. They cannot be passive states of being. Action is imperative, because acting is doing, not being (see Figure 3.7).

Say, for example, that you are a college student and you want to convince your father to allow you to take one of the family cars to school with you. You are back home on Thanksgiving break and want the car until Christmas. Your objective could be to win the car. You have a bad history of speeding tickets and never filling up the gas tank. These are your obstacles. So what kinds of tactics could you employ in order to overcome these obstacles and win your objective? You could start by buttering up your father. Sweet-talk him. Compliment him to put him in a good mood. Then you could request the car. When he says no, you could reason with him and explain why it is important for you to have the car. Then you could try to instill guilt and make him feel bad about how hard it is for you to have to walk everywhere. When this doesn't work, you could beg or plead for him to give you a break. When this doesn't work, you could demean him by telling him what an awful parent he is. When this doesn't work, you could try to make him feel bad by crying. So, simply put, your tactics would be to butter up, to request, to reason, to instill guilt, to beg, to demean, and finally to cry. Now, by developing your tactics, you have a series of actions to play within a scene.

This series of action-verb tactics is the final step in the development of your through-line of actions. You now have things to do, actions to play that will take you from one moment in the scene to the next moment in the scene, and every scene will eventually add up to the entire script. When you are dealing with discovering your different tactics, you always change to a new tactic when you realize that the one that is currently being employed isn't working. This is called a beat.

Figure 3.7

Actor pursuing the tactic "to intimi- date" in a produc- tion of *Macbeth* at the University of North Carolina- Asheville

Stanislavski used the example of eating a turkey to explain beats. (Actually he used the word "bit," but it was mistranslated into English to "beat" and that became the accepted word choice.) He said that you couldn't eat a whole turkey in one bite. You first must cut it up into the differ- ent pieces: wings, legs, thighs, and breast. But you still can't eat a whole wing or leg in one bite, so you must cut it up further into bite-sized pieces. This is just like a script. You can't ingest the entire script as a whole, so you must first divide it into scenes. This is still too big to fully under- stand and work with, so it must be further broken down into beats.

A beat change is determined by a change in your tactic—just like in the scene with your father and the car. When one method of winning the car isn't working, you move on to the next action- verb tactic. Every time you move to a new action-verb tactic, there is a new beat. A beat is the smallest unit of a script and is a way to fully analyze and understand a text.

Homework

Often a new actor doesn't quite understand what she is to do outside of rehearsal. She thinks that memorizing her lines and blocking (stage movement) is all that is required of her. In actuality there is an enormous amount of work for the actor to do outside of rehearsal. The actor must do everything that has been discussed so far on her own time. She must read and reread the script to discover the given circumstances. Then she must begin the work of scoring the script.

As we mentioned earlier, scoring the script is breaking it down and discovering what it is that you are going to do in every moment in time. You will start by identifying the super objective and obstacles standing in the way of this. Next you will note what the objective is for each scene and what the obstacles are that stand in the way. Then you will break down each scene into beats, identifying what tactic you are playing in each beat in order to reach the objective for the scene. You need to do this work in pencil in your script. Write notes and learn these things along with learning your lines and blocking.

The task of scoring a script or figuring out what you will do for each moment in time is part of the homework of the actor. You use rehearsal to try out all of the things that you have discovered in your homework. You try different objectives and tactics. If you find that something you have chosen doesn't work, then you will need to go back outside of rehearsal, re-analyze your script, and choose a new objective or tactic to try in the next rehearsal.

Although there are more details in Stanislavski's system, the ideas listed in this section are the heart of the work and will begin to help you understand the thought process and work of actors and directors on character.

> A complete guide to the teaching of Stanislavski can be found in *The Stanislavski System: The Professional Training of an Actor* by Sonia Moore (Penguin, 1984).

Exercises in Stanislavski's Method

These exercises are designed to cover the major areas of Stanislavski's training. Some of the exercises can be done solo and some require a group. It is always good to begin with the relaxation and warm-up exercises discussed in Chapter 1 before beginning any other training.

Although these exercises are designed for beginning actors, they are also valuable for you as an animator. They require that you heighten your awareness of human behavior and your environment, which is invaluable for animation. They heighten your sensory skills, concentration, and focus. They also lay the groundwork for further exercises in the book that may be applied more directly to animation.

JOURNALS

Journals have many different purposes. The everyday person uses journals to explore their feelings, values, and thoughts. Some people use journals simply to record their daily activities. Others use them to help work through emotional issues. Artists use journals to record inspirational ideas for their work.

Actors often keep journals. They record observations of people and environments. They write about images that move them to different emotional places. They record moments of epiphany from their lives or while working on a role. Many times they begin a new journal for every character they play to record the given circumstances, objectives, obstacles, character ideas, rehearsal discoveries, and anything that occurs in their life that would be useful to them for the character.

We encourage you to keep a journal while you work through this book. Write after every exercise about the experience. Use the journal to investigate your thoughts and emotional responses to the activities. Ask yourself questions. Dig deep into your feelings and why you feel the way you do. You will find that the better you understand your personal motivations and behavior, the better you will be able to identify the motivations and behavior of a character. This work will then be able to translate into your development of a character for CG animation.

You can write about anything in your journal. Beyond recording responses to the exercises, you can write about discoveries in your life. You can write about the application of the work to your life. You can write about anything that makes you think or question.

There are two things we believe are important when writing a journal. First, write immediately after something happens. The immediate response is the most visceral and emotional. Second, start each entry by writing positive things. So often new experiences are difficult for us and we want to discount them simply because they are unfamiliar. If you must first respond in a positive manner, you will not be able to immediately discount a learning opportunity. Try starting a journal as you work through the exercises in this chapter and continue using it throughout the book.

Exercises for Observation

Stanislavski believed that all behavior on the stage needed to be based on the behavior of real humans in real life. Consequently, he taught his actors to heighten their observational skills. Practice these solo exercises daily:

1. Many times our minds are racing so fast that we don't take in what is around us. To help you pay attention to your surroundings, try to identify the first thing you see when coming through a doorway, stepping out of a car, or rounding a corner. Actually speak what you see. So if you step out of the car and you see a tree, say "tree." If

you turn a corner in the hallway and you see the water cooler, say "water cooler." Try not to anticipate what you are going to see. Just open your eyes and discover what hits you. If you program this idea into your consciousness, this exercise can be done dozens of times every day.

2. Sit in an out-of-the-way place at a busy mall or shop. Watch people. Pick one person and observe him for a while. See how he walks, talks, and gestures. How does he interact with the world? Where do his eyes focus when moving? Do you get any distinct feelings or moods from watching this person? Watch all different kinds of people. It is a good idea to write down any observations, impressions, or discoveries from watching people in your journal. These details can come in handy in your work.

3. Watch someone who is performing more or less as himself, such as a teacher, lecturer, or minister. How does he gesture, walk, and talk? How does he use his voice and body to hold the attention of the audience? Do you get any moods or feelings from watching this person?

4. Make a journal of crazy walks. Sit in a busy place for a while and make notes of all the different walks that you see. Try to determine why different people walk in different ways. Is it their center? Their height? Their weight? The clothes they are wearing? When you go home, see if you can copy some of your favorite walks.

5. Try to do a physical imitation of a friend of yours. All you have to do is enter a room, walk to a chair, sit down, pick up a book, look through the book, set the book down, stand up, and walk out the door. Start watching your friend to see how she does all of these things. Try as best you can to copy her.

6. In general, watch children. Children interact with the world freely. They are doing and experiencing everything for the first time. They do it openly and with joy. They don't screen their impulses because they haven't had time for their editor to start telling then what is right and what is wrong. They will scream, cry, pick their nose, laugh, and scratch their bottoms at all the "wrong" times. Additionally they are learning how their physical bodies work and move as well as social interactions. You will learn huge amounts about the human being by watching children.

Exercises for Public Solitude

Stanislavski maintained that the actor needed to be able to completely lose herself in an activity on the stage in order to truly play an action for the action's sake and not for the sake of the audience. He called this public solitude. These solo exercises are designed to help you build your concentration and achieve public solitude:

1. Try to accomplish a mental task in a public place. For example, go to a sporting event or concert and attempt to balance your checkbook or study for a class. See if you

can isolate yourself completely and maintain your concentration on the task at hand while the roar of the crowd clamors around you.

2. Eat alone in a busy restaurant. Don't bring a book. See if you can place all of your concentration on the meal. Lose yourself in the tastes, smells, and textures of the food.

3. Try to read in a very busy public place. Lose yourself in a book while riding the subway or bus or while seated on a bench on a busy street corner. After ten minutes see if you can recount what you read.

4. Turn on your favorite television show and sit down by the TV with a jigsaw or crossword puzzle. Try to place all of your concentration on the task and not on the TV show.

Exercises for the Self

Just as Stanislavski wanted an actor to observe life around her, he also wanted an actor to observe and probe deep into understanding herself. Exercises on the self will help you to begin to do that:

1. Start observing yourself. See if you can identify at least three different characters that you play naturally in your real life. How do you behave different when interacting with your friends, your mother, your father, your siblings, your mentor, your boss, a lover, or an authority figure? All of these are different parts of yourself or different variations of character. Start observing how your different characters talk, laugh, stand, sit, and eat. Does their vocabulary change? Do they feel different from each other? Learning to notice the different aspects of yourself will increase your understanding of human behavior as well as increase your observational skills.

2. Dress for a night out. Imagine that you are going out on a very fancy date. Imagine all of the details surrounding the date. Who is it with and how do you feel about that person? Where are you going and how do you feel about that place? How was the date arranged? Be specific in figuring out all the details surrounding the event. The more given circumstances that you fully understand and believe, the better the exercise will work. Now, prepare for the night. Go through everything that you would do to get ready. Bathe, groom, and dress. Then walk around a bit in your best clothes and see what it feels like. Notice how everything that you did and every article that you put on made you feel different. The "costume" and the circumstances helped change the presentation of yourself. Now, here is the hard part. Do it again in exactly the same manner. See if you can repeat everything that you did in the exact same order. Try to re-create the exact same physical actions and allow your imagination to go to the same places that it went to in your first attempt. It is important to understand what it is you really do in life and to be able to repeat it over and over again as if for the first time.

3. Observe yourself waiting for someone or something. Notice what you do when you are waiting for a bus, or in the lobby of a doctor's office, or waiting for your lover to arrive at a restaurant, or for the mail carrier to bring the package with your first contract. What is it that you do? Do you pace? Read? Go through email? More than likely you are trying to distract yourself as you wait. Where is your mind going? What are you thinking about? Try to notice everything that you do physically and everything that your mind is doing. Are you trying to kill time, fill time, speed up time, or just stall? Does any of this action bring up emotions for you? Are you excited, bored, nervous, frustrated, or worried? After the event, go home and try to do it again exactly as you did it for real. Try to repeat everything that you did in order to do it as if doing it for the first time. If you were trying to kill time, then really try to kill time by physically switching your attention from the email, to the coffee machine, to looking out the window. If you are able to fully repeat your mental and physical actions, you should begin to feel the same feelings that you observed in yourself the first time that you did it. It is the action that brings up the emotion, just like Stanislavski says.

4. Have a friend of yours hide your key in your office or home. Then search for it. While you search, observe everything that you do. Where do you expect the key to be? Where do you look first? What do you do, say, and feel when you don't find it where you expect to find it? How do you feel after you have looked for several minutes and still haven't found it? What do you do, say, and feel when you finally have found the key? Again, here is the hard part. Repeat everything that you just did in the exact same manner. This time you know where the key will be but you must believe that the search is real. Make it even harder by believing that you need to leave for your big date from the previous exercise in one minute or you will be late. Don't try to show or pretend anything. Simply do everything that you previously did truly and fully. If you spoke out loud at any time, do it again. You will find that as you are fully doing the actions you will begin to feel the same way you did when you didn't know where the key was. If you don't, do it again, repeating all of the actions exactly until you do start to experience the feelings associated with a lost item.

For wonderful solo exercises to heighten your observational skills, understanding of self, and ability to perform an action as if it were the first time, look to Uta Hagen's book, *A Challenge for the Actor* (Charles Scribner's Sons, 1991).

Objective, Obstacles, and Tactics Exercises

These exercises are designed to help you explore and further understand the idea of playing an action. Once you start to truly pursue an objective, you are doing the work of an actor. The creation and exploration of given circumstances will further your understanding of the work an actor does in the process of developing a character within a script.

1. Take one of the following simple lines and try to say it with as many action verbs as possible. Make sure you are truly performing the action verb and not just playing an emotion or an emotional quality.

   • Possible lines:

      1. Can you take care of that for me?

      2. I love you.

      3. Have we met?

      4. Get out of here.

      5. How long has it been?

   • Now try the lines with these action verbs:

      1. To seduce

      2. To reprimand

      3. To dismiss

      4. To instill guilt

      5. To plead

      6. To demand

      7. To threaten

      8. To flirt

      9. To long

      10. To patronize

2. Take the previous exercise a step further by creating given circumstances for a situation in which to say one of the lines. Decide to whom you are talking and what is your relationship, where you are and what surrounds you, what time it is, what it is you want (objective), and what stands in your way (obstacle). Now say the line with one of the action-verb tactics listed in the previous exercise in order to help you achieve your objective.

3. Choose a simple, everyday activity. Develop a reason for doing the activity (objective) and clearly identify the given circumstances surrounding the activity. Then, with the given circumstances in mind, do the activity. Make sure you are truly performing the activity and not just *pretending* to do the activity. Don't pantomime anything. If the activity requires a prop, make sure you use the real object. For example, you could choose to read the newspaper want ads. The given circumstances could be

that you were just fired from your job through no fault of your own, have returned to your apartment, and are reading the want ads with the objective of finding another job. Make sure you clearly identify what the given circumstances are. The way you read the want ads looking for a job immediately after you have been fired is very different than the way you would read the want ads after you have been looking for a job for several months. Did you like the job you were fired from, or is it a relief to be rid of the terrible boss? Do you have some money saved, or are you living paycheck to paycheck? These different circumstances will inform how you do your activity in pursuit of your objective. Be careful not to illustrate or show the audience the circumstances. Simply do the activity with the circumstances and the objective clearly in your mind. Here is a list of possible activities:

- Polish your fingernails
- Read the newspaper
- Pack a suitcase
- Put together a jigsaw puzzle
- Write a letter
- Read your email
- Add contacts to your address book
- Straighten your room
- Sort your laundry
- Balance your checkbook
- Practice an instrument
- Style your hair
- Set your watch

4. Take the previous exercise a step further by developing a score of physical actions that you will perform in order to win your objective. Within the given circumstances that you have developed, write out every action that you do in order to achieve the objective. Make sure there is a beginning, middle, and end to the score. Be very detailed in writing out your actions so nothing is missed. Memorize and rehearse the score so you can perform what was at first an improvisation over and over again in exactly the same manner.

5. This improvisation requires two people and a chair. One partner sits in the chair. She has a simple objective of remaining in the chair. The other partner has a simple objective of getting into the chair (see Figure 3.8). The standing partner will enter the space and start an improvisation by setting up the relationship and location. He might say something like, "Excuse me, sir, but I always sit in this seat at the opera."

This will signal to the seated partner that they are in an opera house and that they do not know each other. Or he might say, "Son, I always sit at the head of the table at dinner." This would signal to the partner that they are father and son and that they are in the family dining room. The chair can be any chair in any location and the relationship can be anything, but it is crucial that the entering partner clearly establishes these things with her first line. Then the pair begins an improvisation based on pursuing their objectives. Try to do whatever it takes to win your objective. Don't hold back. Try as many tactics as possible. Don't stop until there is a clear winner to the improvisation. When you are finished, discuss all of the different tactics each partner used in trying to pursue their objective and the obstacles that were set up to stop the pursuit.

Figure 3.8

An actor pursues the objective of getting into the chair.

Figure 3.9

An actor pursues the objective of getting inside the door.

6. This exercise also requires two people and something that can simulate a door that will be placed between them. One side of the door is designated "inside" and the other side of the door is designated "outside." One partner stands inside the door and has the simple objective of keeping the other partner on the outside. The second partner will enter the scene setting up the location and relationship. His objective will be to get inside the door. He might say something like, "Mommy, please open the door, I have to pee" (see Figure 3.9). Thus he has set the relationship of mother and son and made the door a bathroom door. Or he may say something like, "Hello. This is Ed McMahon and you have won the Publisher's Clearing House Sweepstakes." He thus establishes that the door is a door to a home and Ed and the home-owner have not previously met. Again the door can be any door in any location and the relationship can be anything, but it is crucial that the partner entering the space establish these things in his first line. Then the pair begins an improvisation based on trying to win their objectives. Don't take no for an answer. Try at all costs to win your objective. After there is a clear winner, stop and discuss all of the tactics you used to win your objective and the obstacles that were placed in your way.

7. This exercise requires at least three people. Each member of the group finds a spot in the room to claim as their own. Then everyone tries to convince the other members of the group to come over to their spot. Thus every member of the group will have competing objectives. Each person will somehow try to convince the others that they simply must vacate their spot to come to a new one. Hold onto your objective and

fight for it at all costs. Think of as many different tactics as possible to get the other members of the group to join you in your spot. This game can go on for quite some time. After you have played until there is a clear winner, discuss which tactics were the most successful in winning people over.

Open Scenes

An open scene is one in which there are no given circumstances; consequently, the scene could take place anywhere, anytime, and between any two people. Sometimes this is referred to as a contentless scene as there are no contents. Working on simple, open scenes is an effective way to learn how to use tactics to overcome your obstacles and pursue an objective. The following open scene requires two people. The pair should talk out and develop the given circumstances. A useful guide to developing given circumstances comes from a list of nine questions that acting teacher Uta Hagen has developed. Here are her nine questions that must be answered whenever an actor is performing and should be applied to the open scene:

1. Who am I? (Develop an autobiography.)

2. What time is it? (Be specific and exact.)

3. Where am I? (Be specific.)

4. What surrounds me? (Be detailed.)

5. What are the given circumstances? (In the case of an open scene, you will make them up.)

6. What is my relationship? (Include your relationship to your scene partner, events, and location.)

7. What do I want? (This is your objective stated in a simple action-verb sentence.)

8. What is in my way? (These are your obstacles.)

9. What do I do to get what I want? (These are your tactics stated in action verbs.)

After you have answered the nine questions, determine which actor will play character A and which actor will play character B. Then memorize the lines and perform one of the following open scenes. Try them several times, utilizing different objectives. After you finish the scene, try to identify whether one of the partners won their objective. If so, determine which action-verb tactic solidified the win.

Open Scene: Been Waiting Long?

A: Hi.

B: Hi.

A: Been waiting long?

B: Ages.

Open Scene: Well?

> A: Well?
>
> B: Well what?
>
> A: You know what.
>
> B: Oh here and now?
>
> A: That's right.
>
> B: Tough luck.

Open Scene: Do I Know You?

> A: Do I know you?
>
> B: Does my face seem familiar?
>
> A: Don't play games.
>
> B: Is that a threat?
>
> A: It is what it is.
>
> B: OK.

CHAPTER 4

Commedia dell'Arte

As explained in Chapter 1, Commedia dell'Arte is a form of theater based on stock characters and improvised scenarios. Understanding these characters, their masks, their walks, and lazzi (comic "bits" or "takes" a character can perform over and over), is important for the CG animator because these characters form the basis for character types seen in today's animation and even in live-action films. As stock characters, commedia characters are "painted" with broad strokes: they take on obvious characteristics of a given type and are more caricature than truly human; in other words, they are not subtle. As such, they are obviously excellent candidates for the more over-the-top type of animation seen in everything from the classic Warner Bros. cartoons, to Scooby Doo, even to anime-influenced work popular today.

This chapter discusses:

- ■ **Learning the various Commedia characters**

- ■ **Looking at the Commedia masks**

- ■ **Understanding the characters' walks and lazzi**

- ■ **Transforming a mask to a character**

- ■ **Taking the Commedia work into CG animation**

Acting Commedia

Commedia originated in Italy somewhere in the mid-sixteenth century. It consisted of traveling actors performing improvised scenes or sketches based on stock characters in the middle of a marketplace. The actors made a living by passing the hat, so the players had to draw in a crowd and sustain their interest in order to do well. Consequently, performances were loud, fast, and funny. Prior to the performance, the actors would rehearse a scripted scenario or plot outline where all entrances and exits were set and a story developed. Then in performance they would improvise the individual scenes within the scenario. *Saturday Night Live*, *Kids in the Hall*, *Mad TV*, and other such sketch comedy shows are based on this tradition.

Every Commedia troupe had the same set of stock characters based on character types. Each of these characters had a specific mask, which crystallized the character traits. When actors donned these masks, their entire persona was transformed into that of the character represented by the mask. They stood a certain way; they walked a certain way; they interacted with others in a predictable manner. Most characters had an actual mask, but several of the types took on the mask of the character without the aid of a physical mask.

Every character also had lazzi that they performed. Lazzi were comic bits performed over and over again. Usually these bits were physical, but sometimes they were vocal ticks. The best lazzi were large physical gestures accompanied by voice. Audiences would relish and wait for the repetition of these bits. Today we anticipate and relish some of the quirks of character that we view over and over again on our late-night comedy shows. *The Three Stooges*, repeated characters on *Saturday Night Live* and *Mad TV*, and characters from classic cartoons like Warner Bros.' *Looney Tunes* and Walter Lantz's *Woody Woodpecker* provide wonderful examples of lazzi in use.

The Characters

The characters of Commedia can be divided into three categories: servants, (young) lovers, and (older) middle to upper class. Within these categories were many characters that were used repeatedly by almost every Commedia troupe. Additionally, there were characters that were unique to a certain Commedia troupe but still represented the common divisions of character and class. The following are some of the most popular and widely recognized Commedia characters.

The Old Men

There were several stock old men characters in Commedia. They represented the learned and merchant classes. These characters had more status and wealth than the others. They were often parents to the lovers and sometimes stood in the way of their children's amorous relations. They were usually rivals of one another. In animation, elements of Pantalone can be observed in characters like Scrooge McDuck, and we can see Il Dottore in the character of Dr. Frasier Crane in the *Cheers* and *Frasier* series.

Pantalone

Pantalone is a wealthy merchant who has risen to the top of the society within the Commedia world by virtue of his wealth. He is in charge. He controls his servants and his children. He is driven by greed and spends time and energy protecting his wealth. He is too cheap to provide a dowry for his daughter. His whole world revolves around buying and selling everything. Often plots reflect his underlings or children trying to put something over on this character, who is easily blinded by his greed.

As shown in Figure 4.1, the most prominent characteristic of Pantalone's mask is a long hooked nose. He has large eyebrows and often a bushy moustache to match the brows. He has a long beard, which narrows at the tip and points toward his nose. He is a very lecherous character and is often costumed with a phallic codpiece. Usually a large gold medallion, representing his wealth, hangs from his neck.

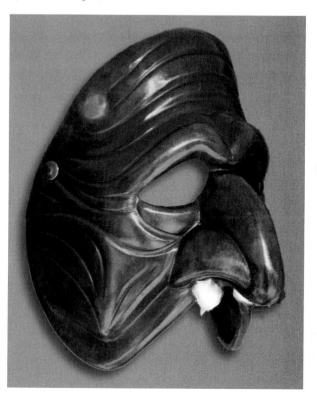

Figure 4.1

The mask of Pantalone, as constructed by Antonio Fava

The masks photographed in this section were constructed by Antonio Fava, one of the leading practitioners of Commedia dell'Arte in Italy today. We are indebted to him for allowing us to photograph these masks and also for the video of him performing character lazzi on the accompanying DVD.

As an old man, he is long and skinny, hunched over forward. This slouch restricts his movement but his hands, feet, and head are still very alive, often moving continuously. He always walks at the exact same tempo in very small steps. One of his lazzi is to fall over backward when he hears some negative news. Figure 4.2 shows both Pantalone and Il Dottore.

Figure 4.2

Jeff Morris and Truitt Broome as Pantalone (left) and Il Dottore (right)

Figure 4.3

The mask, Dottor PlusQuamPerfectus, as constructed by Antonio Fava

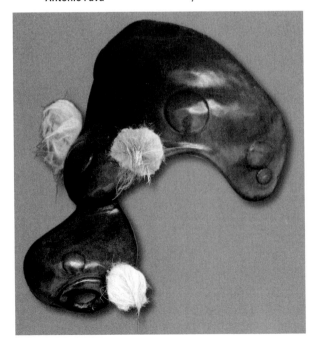

Il Dottore

Il Dottore is the long-winded academic. He actually knows very little about anything but could fool you with his talk. He is incredibly self-important and loves to hear himself speak continually. He is a quack and a pretender. He wants to appear as a man driven by intellect but in actuality he is motivated by his carnal appetites for women, food, and drink. Like Pantalone, he too is a letch and can be very stingy, but unlike Pantalone, he doesn't have any money to protect. He is usually a widower or bachelor. He often gives other characters a break from their high-energy antics with his self-indulgent proclamations.

Il Dottore's mask, shown in Figure 4.3, is one of the smaller ones, with only the nose and forehead covered. The nose is large and bulbous. A good deal of the actor's face is revealed with this mask.

Il Dottore is usually dressed in long, black academic robes. He is tall and larger than Pantalone. He stands with his weight back on his heels and his large belly protruding forward. His gestures are large and grandiose. He walks in small steps in figure-eight patterns. One of his lazzi is to lean forward while thinking and rear back to an upright position when he discovers an answer to his problem. Victor the gargoyle in Disney's *Hunchback of Notre Dame* is an example of Il Dottore in animation.

The Lovers

The lovers, or innamorati, are an important part of nearly all Commedia scenarios. The lovers have many different names, such as Silvio, Florindo, and Fabrizio for the men, and Angelica, Isabella, and Lavinia for the women. They are more in love with the idea of love than with each other. They are always star crossed and will try anything to get together. Unfortunately, they are unable to do this by themselves and require the assistance of other characters. The drama that ensues from their attempts to join together is often a central plot line of Commedia.

The lovers are young and quite lovely. Born of the upper class, they are usually children of the old men. They dress in the fashion of the day. Although they normally have no physical mask, they use heavy make-up for both sexes, creating a quasi-mask from the thick layers of stage paint. They are incredibly vain and not too bright. Today's cliché of the "dumb blonde" is in fact a Commedia innamorata.

The lovers, shown in Figure 4.4, are portrayed as light on their feet, perhaps because their heads are in the clouds as they focus on the idea of love or their own beauty. They stand in ballet positions and do not contact the earth fully. They are light and lifted, breathing only in their chests with a center on their hearts. Their walks are not grounded, and they tend to sway and lead from the head or chest. Their arms are often extended to display their physical beauty and dress or to hold out a token from their lover. One of their lazzi is to drop their breath down low in their bodies and sort of deflate their chests when life overwhelms them. Disney movies are loaded with variations of the innamorati.

Figure 4.4

Jake Cooper and Kelli Harrington as the innamorati Florindo and Angelica

The Servants

Although there are many different servants, or zanni, a Commedia scenario always contains at least two. One is clever and sly while the other is slow of body and wit. The zanni were the lowest class in society. They are servants to everyone, but often cause great confusion and chaos from their lowly positions. Zanni are driven by survival needs and basic instincts, living totally in the moment. They are constantly hungry and can fall asleep at the drop of a hat. They are ignorant, lazy, loyal, and very emotional. They will also use anything at their disposal—trickery, flattery, bullying, their sexuality—to get what they want. Zanni are the highest energy and most sympathetic of all the Commedia characters and the most often represented in animation. These characters are often involved more in the "B" plot (the zanier subplot) of a Commedia sketch, so they are frequently involved in the most comical moments of a given sketch, and audiences wait for their reappearance with bated breath. The character Skrat, in *Ice Age* and *Ice Age 2*, is a great example of a servant type (Arlecchino, to be exact) in contemporary animation: driven by hunger and instinct, and constantly thwarted by circumstance.

There are many different zanni walks that are employed by different characters and for different emotions. When running, a zanni might kick his feet out in front with his toes pointed and his arms swinging wildly in circles. When excited he could skip on his toes, shifting his center of gravity from side to side. These walks are still seen in animation today. Skrat uses a "quick burst, then stop" zanni for his movements; Bugs Bunny uses many variations of zanni walks; and as Road Runner speeds away from Wile E. Coyote, he incorporates the zanni running walk.

There are also basic stances used by the zanni. They can be seen standing in fourth ballet position with their back curved and chest sticking out on one side and their rear sticking out in the other direction. Their head always moves independently from the body with the mask leading the movement. They can also be seen doing a little jump with their toes pointed and the knees sticking out to the side, legs coming off the ground one at a time.

The modern English word "zany" comes from the zanni, as their energy, thoughts, and movement were indeed zany. Zanni were and still are the classic clowns and comedians. Although there are many different zanni, Arlecchino, Brighella, and Colombina are three of the most commonly occurring in a Commedia troupe.

Arlecchino

Arlecchino is usually a servant to Pantalone. He is very high energy, possessing great agility. He has enough wit to plot schemes, but not enough intelligence to unleash plots that will ever work out. He never simply performs a task. He must do it with great showmanship and extraneous movement. He is driven by hunger and lust. He lives completely in the moment and responds emotionally to everything.

Figure 4.5

Angela Savas as Arlecchino

Arlecchino's mask covers the upper part of his face down to his mouth. It has a lowered forehead and small round eyes. The longer his nose, the stupider he is.

Arlecchino employs all of the zanni walks and stances but he does them with high energy and agility. He is light on his feet and almost floating. He is often the carrier of everyone's loads, so he stands in a lowered position. But this is countered by an upward energy pull in the chest, resulting in a severely curved spine. He extends the elbows of his arms and tucks his thumbs in his belt. His movement is led by the mask. As seen in Figure 4.5, Arlecchino normally wears the jester's motley, made from scraps of cloth, representing his humble standing and inability to purchase new clothes. Donkey, in *Shrek*, is a four-legged Arlecchino character.

Brighella

Brighella is the highest or most important of the zanni. He is a workingman but not necessarily a servant. He is usually the keeper of a shop or an inn. He can, though, take on any job at any time and is willing to do so. He is quite devilish and ingenious, and he is an accomplished liar. He is bold and proud of his deceits. He is very quick witted and will do or sell anything for food, drink, or women. He lives for fights, secrets, and schemes. If there is a plot boiling, Brighella is in the middle of it.

The mask of Francatrippa, a character related to Brighella, is shown in Figure 4.6. This is a half mask with round eyes and small round cheeks and has a hooknose and large lips. The mask also has a thick, long moustache that extends off the sides of his mask. The mask can appear both jovial and devilish.

Figure 4.6

The mask of Franca-trippa (a character similar to Brighella), as constructed by Antonio Fava

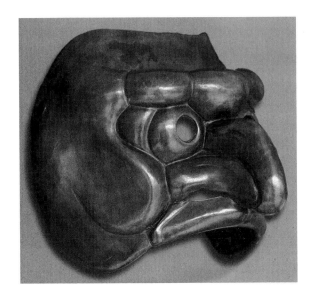

Brighella stands in first ballet position with his knees bent and his feet flat on the floor. His larger belly is protruded forward, and he has a curve in his spine similar to but not as great as Arlecchino's. His feet tend to hop and shift a lot as though he were standing on hot ground. Brighella also uses all of the zanni walks. He does, though, have one of his own in which he moves forward with his torso tipping side to side while his head stays upright. Figure 4.7 shows Brighella and Lisetta, who is a servant character similar to Colombina. In modern animation, Brighella often becomes a scheming woman like the evil octopus-like character, Ursula, in *The Little Mermaid* or the good "teapot" character, Mrs. Potts, in *Beauty and the Beast.*

Figure 4.7

Nick Abeline and Vivi Chavez as Brighella and Lisetta

Figure 4.8

Michael Stille as Pulcinella, Carole Kaboya as Colombina, and Angela Savas as Arlecchino

Colombina

Colombina, the female zanni, is a lady's maid to the innamorata. Unlike the other zanni she is self-educated and level headed. She is the most reasonable and rational character of the Commedia world. Although wise cracking and quick witted, she is extremely loyal and is never out for herself. She often places herself in the center of plots to try to solve the problems that have arisen. She is usually fairly young and attractive. She is in love with Arlecchino but realizes that he probably isn't the best choice for her. Babs Bunny, in the *Tiny Toon Adventures* and *Space Jam*, is a good example of Colombina in modern animation.

As seen in Figure 4.8, Colombina is unmasked, as is her mistress. She has wide eyes and like her mistress will wear heavy eye make-up.

Colombina also employs all of the zanni walks, but she has a special walk, flicking her foot at the end of each step. She stands with one knee bent and the other leg extended. This will show off her shapely legs and full breasts. She stands with her hands on her hips or in the air in front of her bosom as if holding a tray.

Other Characters

Many other masked characters appear in Commedia, but Il Capitano and Pulcinella are two of the most common.

Il Capitano

Il Capitano is a loner and a pretender. He probably never was a captain. He is a boastful braggart, telling mythic tales of his past battles and conquests. He is never from the town where the story takes place so he is able to maintain his lies until the end, when his cowardice is revealed. He is arrogant and lustful, showing off to all women in order to win them.

Figure 4.9

The mask, Il Capitan Matamoros, as constructed by Antonio Fava

He is especially fond of Colombina. As a military man, he is usually dressed in the uniform of the day and always carries a sword.

The mask of Il Capitano, shown in Figure 4.9, is a half mask. What distinguishes his mask is the long nose, which is incredibly phallic.

As seen in Figure 4.10, Capitano stands in a manner that displays him as a proud military man. His feet are far apart and his chest is puffed out. He has what is called a mountain walk, landing first on the heels of his boots and then rounding on to the ball of the foot. He has a bit of a bounce to what appears to be his large strides. He actually takes smaller steps but does them in a very large manner in order to gain time to display himself. His run is one of his lazzi. When he is frightened, which happens often since he is in fact a coward, he throws his head back and tries to run, but only succeeds at running in place. Warner Bros.' "cock of the walk" character, Foghorn Leghorn, is a wonderful example of a Capitano character.

Figure 4.10

Jan Lefrancois-Gijzen as Il Capitano

Pulcinella

Like Capitano, Pulcinella is also a loner. Usually he is depicted as an outsider. He can be a servant or an employer. He has no respect or love of anything human. He is mean spirited and does not give or accept love or kindness. He takes pleasure in the pain of others and even tries to set up confrontations and fights. Try as he might, he cannot keep a secret. He, like the zanni, takes pleasure in women, wine, and food.

The mask of Pulcinella, shown in Figure 4.11, is almost grotesque. He has a long bird-like nose with a sort of beak.

His forehead is deeply wrinkled with a large wart. The mask shows the inside of this repugnant character.

> The classic television series is chock full of commedia characters and plots. Sam is Arlecchino; Diane is an innamorata; Carla and Coach (replaced by Woody) are the zanni, Carla being mean spirited like Pulcinella, and Coach being the slower-witted one; Cliff is Capitano (he is even in uniform); Frazier is Dottore; Norm is Brighella.

Figure 4.11

The mask, Female Pulcinella, as constructed by Antonio Fava

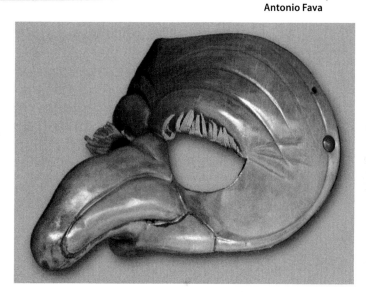

Pulcinella is a humpback, so his stance is bent forward with his weight on one leg to compensate for the hump. The hump also makes his walk slightly uneven with small jerky steps. During one historical period, he had two humps and was then presented as having a dual personality. He has big, expansive gestures that are not used often. He is an excellent mimic and will imitate people and animals to help set up his deceptions. Pulcinella is the character with the fewest redeeming qualities; thus his mask and stance are the most grotesque. *Shrek* uses the Commedia characters with a modern twist. For example, Shrek is a Pulcinella figure who grouses and complains throughout much of the movie, but turns into an innamorato who falls in love (against his will) with Fiona.

> For an excellent examination of the origins, style, and characters of Commedia, see *Commedia dell'Arte: An Actor's Handbook*, by John Rudlin (Routledge, 1994). This book contains more masks by and pictures of Antonio Fava.

Relating Commedia Characters to Animation

After reading through the earlier sections of this chapter, you likely already see a number of connections between stock Commedia characters and those that populate the animation world. This is no coincidence: Commedia is full of exaggerated, easy-to-"read"-at-a-glance characters that have simple desires that conflict with each other's and are used to create comedy in short scenario sketches. The classic use of cartoon animation as a short, enjoyable preamble shown before full-length movies in the 1920s through the early 1950s is an almost exact re-creation of the settings used to great comic effect by Commedia troupes over the centuries.

While animation, starting with *Snow White* in 1937, has grown well beyond these humble roots, the legacy of stock, exaggerated characters persists as a mainstay of most full-length animations and nearly all short-format ones, including those made for children's television channels like Nickelodeon and Disney Channel. For just a few of the multitude of examples, consider the following. First is Pepé Le Pew, the skunk "lover," who is always star crossed in his love for a cat, but who nonetheless holds on to hope and, as with Commedia lovers, gets his girl by the cartoon's end. He is extremely light on his feet, bouncing everywhere with hardly a touch on the ground to relaunch his amorous body back into the air again. Pepé seems more in love with love than with a particular cat, and while he is somewhat more lecherous than the classic Commedia lover, he is eternally positive and not overtly sexual beyond his desire to kiss and pet his beloved.

Lord Farquaad in *Shrek* is an excellent example of the Capitano character in a contemporary animation. He is a pompous, overbearing character who is, at heart, afraid of most things. While he is obeyed by his servants, he is not loved and thus is essentially a loner. Like Capitano, Farquaad likes to dress up in uniform or other regalia. To spite his extremely short stature, Farquaad stands very rigid and erect, his legs apart and feet splayed out, and his legs move a great deal when he walks. When he is frightened, Farquaad runs, though without much effect, due both to his short stature and inefficient running style.

Colette, in *Ratatouille,* is very much a Colombina-inspired character. In a servile role (as sous-chef in the restaurant), she is bright, self-motivated and educated, happy to stand up for herself, ready to help out, sometimes selflessly, very loyal, and more than a little enamored of Linguini, who plays the role of a rather klutzy Arlecchino. Colette commonly stands with one leg out and either crosses her arms over her chest or keeps her arms out in front of her large bosoms. Also, like Colombina, she is the most rational character in the movie, providing a balance for the excesses of the other characters.

Finally, consider Bugs Bunny as a reinvention of the Brighella character. Bugs is controlled by his baser instincts, loves a good intrigue, is devious, in charge, and normally gets his way. Bugs' origins as an homage to Groucho Marx make this relationship even more clear, as Groucho's character in his movies is very much a Brighella character. Note that Bugs normally stands flat on his (large) feet, that his belly protrudes, and that he has a very active torso and upright head when walking, all physical similarities with Brighella.

There are many other examples of animated characters arising from those in Commedia, but these should suffice to get you thinking about how much animation owes to this ancient comedic form. Of course, there are differences between classic Commedia and how it is used in animations. The most obvious difference is the ability animators have to exaggerate characteristics, walks, and lazzi, or, as they are commonly known in animation, "takes." Consider the lecherous wolf in *Red Hot Riding Hood* (1943), a classic

Tex Avery cartoon. When the lecherous wolf sees Little Red strip on stage, he does the equivalent of a lazzi, his whole body jumping out of his chair, and going rigid (yes, in a phallic manner), his eyes bugging out, and his body "boinging" back and forth horizontally until he finally comes to rest a foot or two above the table. While obviously influenced by real Commedia characters' lazzi, the wolf is able to do things no human can do. There are many more examples of exaggerated cartoon lazzi, including the bugged-out "multi-eye" take, the "jump out of your skin" take, and the head-whipping double-take. Walks also tend to be exaggerated in animation, with often large feet and smallish bodies generating crazy up-and-down and side-to-side motions. Moreover, hand-drawn animation has made use of inverse bending of joints (i.e., elbows and knees bending backward during parts of a motion) since very early on, generating great whip-snap motion to arms and legs that would be difficult (and dangerous!) to create for real.

In addition to exaggeration, animation often combines characteristics of two or more Commedia characters into one animated character. Bugs Bunny, for example, is very much a Brighella character, but has attributes that align him with Arlecchino as well: his energy level is high, he stands and especially walks with a severely arched back, and he is at times just silly, which is more Arlecchino than Brighella. Interestingly, Woody, in *Toy Story*, is also a combination of these two characters; while his persona seems very different than Bugs', their traits are fundamentally similar. Characters can also focus on just one aspect of a character. For example, Herbert, the old man who lusts after Chris in *Family Guy*, is the consummate old man lech, like Pantalone, but he is not concerned with money, as is Pantalone (not to mention the fact that he is interested in a young man rather than woman, which is not in the stock Commedia scenarios).

While improvisation, which is key to Commedia, is not really possible in animation itself, a great deal of improvisation can and does happen during voice recording sessions that lead to animation, and thus improv is in fact a part of the animation process. One need only watch video of Robin Williams creating the part of Genie in *Aladdin*, or Eddie Murphy and Mike Meyers going to town when recording for *Shrek* to see how much improvisation can do for an animation.

Now that we have had a chance to examine the roots of Commedia, its characters, and how it relates to animated characters we know and love, let's begin creating our own characters, first with your body and then with 3D models. As you work through these exercises, think about stock characters (both live and animated) that you have seen and imagine yourself in these roles—and of course creating your own!

Commedia Acting Exercises

Commedia is ultimately a group activity, so it is best to form a group to work on improvisation skills. However, you can begin the exploration of Commedia on your own by examining how to allow a mask of character to take over or become part of the whole physical body. You can also work on the individual walks and lazzi of the characters by yourself. Ultimately it would be wonderful to don some Commedia masks or even silly children's or party masks to help understand how the mask transforms the body.

Metaphor Masks

We will begin the exploration of mask and character by developing a character from a metaphor mask instead of a physical mask. This will help you understand how a simple idea can transform your entire being. Begin with a warm-up to prepare your body for work, then repeat several of the space walks from Chapter 1. This will help remind you of how to use your imagination to create the environment surrounding you.

Now pick a metaphor for one particular part of your body. Here are some examples to try. These are only a few of the countless possibilities for metaphors for pieces of the body. Try them all and come up with some more of your own:

- Your fist is a hammer or a tomato.
- Your mouth is an ocean or a piece of string.
- Your belly is a trampoline or a cannonball.
- Your eyes are burning coals or butterflies.
- Your skin is liquid metal or bubbles.
- Your legs are noodles or two-by-fours.
- Your head is a balloon or a ball of fire.
- Your fingers are skewers or diamonds.
- Your chest is the sun or a cave.
- Your pelvis is a rocking horse or a hula hoop.

We are going to use a metaphor as a mask that will transform your body, voice, and personality into a new and unique character, just as donning a Commedia mask transforms the actor wearing it. Begin to explore the movement of the given body part as your chosen metaphor. Use your imagination to allow the specific body part to become the metaphor. Move that part of the body through space. Try to do everyday tasks with the body/metaphor part. (It is useful to have a few simple props to interact with: chairs, books, phones, ropes, writing utensils, or anything you would find in a classroom will work. It is also nice to have some props that could be used as many different things such as blankets, ropes, or pieces of wood or plastic.) Notice not only how this metaphor makes the body part move, but also how it makes you feel. Then allow this metaphor to grow and overtake your entire body. Allow the movement of your entire body to follow the lead of the single body part in the exploration of movement through space and in performing simple, everyday tasks. Note whether the metaphor in your body brings up certain moods or feelings. Allow those feelings to further affect the movement of your body. Does the metaphor change your breath and stance? Does it change which part of your body leads the movement? If so, note these changes and allow them to further affect the movement.

Take time to write in your journal about what happens to your body as you explore these metaphors. How do your joints bend? Where is your center? What happens to your tempo and rhythm? What about fluidity versus staccato movement? Which muscles are tensed and which are relaxed? Noting these changes will help you remember physical details that you can later incorporate into animated characters, as you consider what physical masks (or characteristics) and metaphorical masks each character has.

Encounters

If you are working with a group of people, you can take the previous exercise a step further by developing a character from the metaphor and allowing this character to encounter another character.

Begin by reinvestigating a particular metaphor that worked well for you. Start moving through space, allowing this metaphor to take over your body. From the feeling and movement created, you have essentially become a character. You have taken a mask of character (the metaphor) and allowed this mask to transform your entire being into a new character.

As you move through the space, you will pass by other people. As you encounter someone, make eye contact and pause to take each other in. Follow any impulses you may feel from the eye contact with the other character. You may want to turn your eyes away. You may want to step closer. You may want to retreat or smile. Remember that all of these reactions are based on your new metaphor character encountering another metaphor character, not (necessarily) how you would react to that person yourself.

Next as you continue to move about the space and encounter other people, stop and introduce your character to another character. Say something like, "Hi, my name is Sally Wobblyknees." Use whatever name comes to you based on what you have created from the metaphor. Your voice should be affected: it should not be the same as your normal everyday voice. If you have allowed the metaphor to take over your whole body (as a mask makes an actor a new character), then your voice can't help but be affected. Let its new sound surprise you—whether it's higher or lower, louder or softer, slower or faster, or even from a different location with a different accent or dialect. You may also find that the voice changes even further in reaction to the character you encounter. Good. It should. Again, it is good to try different metaphor characters and see how they respond to other characters.

Now you are ready to set up a scenario with these metaphor characters, just as Commedia actors plan scenarios for their masked characters. Put a bench or several chairs together in the front of the room. Pick two members of your group to begin. Both people assume the metaphor character. The scene is a simple encounter between two strangers at a park. One character will begin on the bench, and the other one will enter the scene. At this point there is no specific objective for either character. Your goal is to discover how this character would react in the situation and how your character responds to other characters. Speak and move as your character would move. Continue this exercise with all different combinations of characters.

After you have explored how your character responds to others in this location, further the exercise by giving each character a simple objective. It would be easy to begin by using one of the exercises outlined in Chapter 3. Have one character on the bench with the objective to remain on the bench. The other character enters, and his objective is to take over the bench and remove the other character. Allow the metaphor mask of the character to determine just what tactics will be used by each character.

After this, you can try all kinds of other simple physical objectives. Have one character try to get a kiss, to become invisible to the other, to make a friend, or to scare the other character. There are countless possibilities here. It is particularly interesting to have a character try for an objective that is against the type of the character. For instance, if you have created a fairly intense, evil, or aggressive character from the metaphor of burning coals for eyes, have this character try to make a friend or find a lover. If you have a character that is unstable, silly, or vapid from the metaphor of a balloon for a head, have the character try to scare the other one away. By playing against the type, you will gain all kinds of new insights and layers for your metaphor character.

Again, take time to write in your journal after experiencing an encounter. These exercises can provide you with valuable information about a character's reactions and responses to other characters that can aid you later in your animations when one character interacts with others.

Real Masks

After you have come to an understanding of the development of a character from the use of a metaphor, you can explore the character further by using an actual mask. Any mask will do: Halloween masks, Mardi Gras masks, and children's character masks are perfectly suitable. If you don't have any masks, you can make one of your own easily by drawing something on a paper bag, cutting out eye and mouth holes, and placing it on your head. (This can be problematic, though, because it is often hard to totally give yourself up to the mask because you are simply trying to keep the bag on your head, so a trip to a dollar or party store is well worth the effort.) You will also need a mirror for this exercise. A full-length one is best, but a large face mirror will do if you don't have access to a full-body mirror. As you perform these exercises, consider how your animation character(s) are often physical masks due to the shape and exaggerations of their modeling. How does having a huge nose or a really long neck affect the way your character inhabits space and interacts with others around him? Think of the model as a mask that you, as the animator, take on, transforming the character into something unique based on its qualities.

To begin this exercise, sit on the floor holding your mask in your lap. Study it for a while. Observe the shape and contours, the colors and the expression. Allow these things to sort of seep into you. Also note if the mask brings up any feelings or moods. Don't rush: you should spend at least 5 minutes doing this.

Then, holding your mask, move to a position in front of the mirror. Turn your back to the mirror and place the mask on your head. Turn around and look at your new self in the mirror. Based on your response, you should immediately change your body and stance. The feeling and look of the mask on your face as well as the impressions you got from staring at the mask will determine the demeanor of your new character body. Some people will find that immediately, before they have even turned around to the mirror, they change their body. The emotion and feeling of a mask can be that strong. Start to explore the movement of the mask character in front of the mirror first. After you feel comfortable, move away from the mirror and continue to explore the movement of character through space. (Do not be surprised if you discover you cannot speak in a certain mask. Some masks are voiceless for some people.) As with the metaphor mask, try to perform simple activities with this new mask character.

If you are working with other people, after you have a good feel for this character you can go through all of the exercises listed in the "Encounters" section. Begin by simply making eye contact with another masked character and progress to the pursuit of physical objectives with another character on the bench. Be sure to try multiple masks. Different masks work better for different people. Some masks just don't speak to some people. And some people will find that they are strongly connected to one particular mask.

It is important to know a few things here about the fundamentals of working with masks. First, some terminology: when you don a mask it is called *shuing* the mask. The mask has a magical, transformative quality and should never be shued in front of the audience. You must turn your back away from people to shu and unshu the mask. Next, you should always be conscious of the presentation of a mask. The mask determines character; therefore, its gaze must be presented to the audience at all times. This means essentially that the actor must keep the mask facing front directly to the audience or it will lose the ability to communicate character. Finally, never, never touch a mask when it is on your face. If a mask is touched by hands that are flesh and blood, it reveals to the audience that the mask is not. The mask then loses its magic because it can no longer be perceived as the character. It is now just a mask.

Commedia Masks

If you are lucky enough to have a selection of Commedia masks to work with, you can begin your examination of the stock character types. Begin by laying out the masks in front of you so that you see which mask draws your attention. After you have selected a mask, go through all of the steps listed in the "Real Masks" and "Encounters" sections. There is one exception, though: only spend a moment in front of the mirror. It is important for the actor to draw the essence of the character from the look and feel of the mask and not from an external formal presentation. Spending too much time in front of a mirror can lead an actor to try to "perform the mask" instead of allowing the mask to dictate the character.

> If you become very enamored of Commedia and masks, there are a number of sources from which you can purchase masks, none better than the site of Antonio Fava, whose masks are featured in this chapter. While expensive (400 Euro and up), Fava's masks, available at www.commediabyfava.it, are works of art and are prized possessions for practitioners of Commedia dell'Arte. Just looking through his collection of masks can provide inspiration for character and physicality.

The Walks and Lazzi

To further your understanding of the Commedia characters' movement, it is good to explore their stances, walks, and lazzi. This will be particularly useful for the animator because these same postures and movements can be used for CG character development. If you have Commedia masks, practice the following with the appropriate mask on.

The Lovers

The lovers' walks are the same for both men and women. For the lovers, try to walk on air. Hardly contact the ground. You can even walk on your toes. Keep your chest pulled up high as if the chest is leading your movement and only breathe in your chest. Allow your head to be free and loose, almost floating like a balloon. Extend your arms out to the sides and slightly curved in front of your body as if holding a large round beach ball. Or float one hand in front of your heart and extend the other hand out to the side of your body as if showing off a long lacy cuff on your shirt. Now open your eyes wide and take a walk around the space. When you stop, place your feet in first ballet position and keep your eyes open wide, with your head floating on top of your body.

To practice a lazzi, begin walking around the room in a lover's walk and then imagine that you see your lover courting someone else. Very quickly inhale your chest huge and high as you see the betrayal and then quite suddenly exhale dropping your chest low and allowing your whole body to sort of deflate or collapse.

Pantalone

For the walk of Pantalone, try to curve your torso into a "C." Pull your pelvis forward, thrust your mid-back backward, and then pull your head, neck, and shoulders forward. This will cause you to bend over severely like an old man or woman. Pull your arms in close to your body, but allow your fingers and hands to move continually as if playing with gold coins. When you pull your pelvis forward, it will cause your knees to bend and your feet to turn slightly outward. Now start to walk around the space taking tiny, quick steps.

One of Pantalone's lazzi is to fall over backward when hearing bad news. Usually this news will involve a loss of money. So begin walking around the space as Pantalone, taking tiny quick steps. Now imagine you see Arlecchino spending your money on cake. Carefully, bend your knees into a low squat and roll backward as if beginning a backward roll. If you maintain the curved "C" position of your torso, you will roll back and forth on your back. Like a bug, Pantalone cannot get up without assistance from this position, so have someone give you a hand to get you back on your feet.

Il Dottore

For the walk of Il Dottore, imagine that you have a huge round belly that leads your movement. Now raise one arm curved over your head and curve the other arm around, but not touching, that large protruding belly. Slightly turn your feet out and begin to move through space by taking small steps in a figure-eight pattern. You will get nowhere fast.

One of Il Dottore's lazzi is to bend far forward while thinking and then rear suddenly back so that the belly sticks far forward and the weight is far back on his heels. While moving around the space in the figure-eight patterns, stop, lean forward, and think. Then, when a brilliant idea strikes you, suddenly rear straight back up. Be careful not to fall over backward.

Arlecchino

All of Arlecchino's walks are done with lots of energy. He is light and springy and very agile. The mask leads his movement as if the head is almost detached from the rest of the body. Begin by lifting and thrusting your chest far forward and your rear far back. This will result in a severely curved spine. Now bend your left knee and slightly shift your weight over to your left hip. Most of your weight will be on your left leg. Your right leg should be extended with your right heel resting on the floor and foot flexed so that your right toe is in the air. Your arms are extended out to either side of your body for balance, or you may tuck your thumbs into your belt. Standing in this position, think about allowing your mask and head to be independently moving about.

To walk as Arlecchino, start in the stance just described. You will now hop from one leg to the other by lightly lifting your right knee high in the air and placing your right heel gently on the floor and then lifting your left knee high in the air and placing your left heel gently on the floor. Make sure that you keep your chest protruding in front and your rear protruding in back while doing this.

Arlecchino's lazzi often involve the making and eating of food. There is one lazzi where he mimes making some unspecified dish in a bowl that is enormous and then devours the entire thing in one bite. Give this a try. Start by elaborately making your meal and then condense down into only the most necessary steps.

Brighella

Brighella stands in first position with his knees slightly bent. He has a belly like Il Dottore and a curved spine like Arlecchino, so he sticks his rear out in back and his belly and chest in front. He tends to fidget with his clothing on his belly and chest. He also hops between his two feet almost continually as if he is standing on hot ground.

Brighella has a special walk that shifts from side to side in the torso as he hops from one foot to the other. The peculiar thing about this walk is that his head actually remains upright as his torso shifts. Try this walk while moving around the room, focusing on moving the torso while keeping the head still.

Colombina

Colombina stands to show off her shapely figure. Start by slightly bending one knee and extending the other leg as if to show off a shapely ankle. Then suck in your stomach and raise your chest to show off your bosom. You arms are curved in front of your body, slightly under your breasts, with your palms facing upward as if holding a tray.

To walk like Colombina, shift your weight from one leg to the other with a slight hop from left to right as you slowly move forward in space. Then sort of flick your foot right before it lands on the ground. Now open your eyes wide and take a walk around the room, shifting your weight as you hop from one foot to the other and flicking your toes. Colombina often appears in the room just before or as her master calls her. Sometimes she can make her breasts or hips squeak as she moves. Both of these are lazzi for Colombina. See if you can make a vocal sound as you walk around the room each time your weight shifts from one side to the other.

Il Capitano

For Il Capitano, you need to stand very upright with your chest protruding—a proud captain's stance. Place your feet wide with your legs fairly rigid. Keep your chin lifted. Place your hands on the hilt of your sword. Think pride.

To walk, lift your leg high in the air and bring it down on the heel and then roll through the ball of your foot. Each leg is lifted very high as if to show off with great large strides, but actually allow each heel to land close to the other foot. Ultimately the strides are for show because the steps are very small.

Fear brings on one of Il Capitano's lazzi. When afraid, Il Capitano will attempt to run away but will get nowhere. To try this, walk around the room in the grand mountain walk. Then imagine that you have seen something to frighten you, which for Il Capitano could be as small as a mouse. Fling your head back and very quickly try to continue the large strides without going anywhere. Your arms will circle wildly to counterbalance your legs kicking forward.

Pulcinella

Pulcinella is a humpback, so bend forward and raise your right shoulder high in the air. Because of this change in posture, your left leg needs to bend, and most of the weight will be on this leg. Your right foot needs to turn out slightly. Put your hands in close to your chest and rub your fingers and thumbs together. Now take a walk around the room with small jerky steps. Marty Feldman as Igor in *Young Frankenstein* is an ideal example of this character's stance and walk.

Pulcinella will often do a lazzi of hopping around and peeping like a chicken (his name means "little chicken"). He does this to work all of the other characters into a frenzy and then when they are worn out, he, who still has lots of energy, can continue with his plot. Try bending over and resting one hand on the floor and then springing up off the ground, stretching your body out to its full length and then landing with your knees bent and one hand resting on the floor. Do this repeatedly, making a squeak each time you spring up.

Animation Exercises

Now that you have had a chance to practice creating character, posture, and movement in your own body, let's animate some characters to do similar things, but in a more exaggerated fashion, as is fitting for an animated world. Throughout these exercises, use your body and the discoveries you made in the acting exercises as a guide to what your character should be doing at a given moment: inhabiting the character yourself—at least as much as you are physically able to—is a great way to improve your animation technique. On the other hand, don't forget that this is the world of animation, so let your imagination take you in directions that aren't possible for human actors if that works for your specific needs. Replicating human acting is great, and a very valuable skill to acquire, but limiting your imagination to only that which is physically possible can be a detriment to your animating abilities. A careful balancing act is needed, and the balance changes for each project. For these exercises, don't forget to have a mirror and/or video camera to record your actions, as they will provide invaluable feedback.

> For many of the exercises in this chapter, we are privileged to have video capture of Antonio Fava (whose masks are shown earlier in the chapter), one of the great living practitioners of Commedia dell'Arte. Note in the videos how changed both his body and movement are by the different characters he takes on, and how precise and specific his posture and movement are. Studying Fava's work in these videos gives you access to someone who has spent nearly his entire life practicing this venerable art form.

Poses

To begin our study of using Commedia characters in animation, let's start by creating some character stances. Here we will focus on the readability of the silhouette and how the posture reveals each character. Masks cover the faces of most characters, so body posture is the preeminent way to "read" a Commedia character; thus we will focus in these exercises on body rather than face.

Let's begin by creating Arlecchino's pose. Open a new scene with your character in your 3D package. If you have Maya, feel free to use one of the two generic characters included on the accompanying DVD. (See the sidebar for more information about how to use these rigs.) Figure 4.12 shows Arlecchino (actually Arlecchina, as she is female) in one of his primary poses. This figure is included on the DVD (`ArlecchinoPose.tif`) so that you can add it as a posing reference in your scene, should you wish.

Figure 4.12

Angela Savas as Arlecchino

If you are using the included models (Genna and Marcel), which include built-in character/ subcharacter hierarchies, you can have Maya automatically select the characters as you go. First, place the `autoCharacterSelection.mel` file in your home scripts directory (`~Autodesk/ maya/scripts` on your home directory), then copy the line of code from `ACSEnable.mel` into the Script Editor input pane, and drag it up onto your shelf. When you start Maya, simply click the ACSEnable button, and from then on, Maya will automatically select whichever sub- character it needs based on what is selected in the scene. This makes selecting and keyfram- ing characters far easier than having to remember to do so yourself.

Import this image as a reference plane in Maya (or other package); in Maya, create a new camera, then under its attributes, choose Environment → Create Image Plane, and attach the image to this new plane. Because the model is large, you might need to set your camera's far clipping plane to 10,000 instead of the default 1,000 in Maya. Next, adjust the distance to the image plane so that you can see your model in front of it, and then adjust your model so it is approximately the same dimensions as the character in the photograph, as shown in Figure 4.13. Using this photo (or one of you posing in similar fashion) as reference, shape your character's body into the same pose. We started with the foot place- ment, then moved on to the hips and back, and finally the head and shoulders—then we went back and readjusted after the initial, "close" pose was achieved. We used squash and

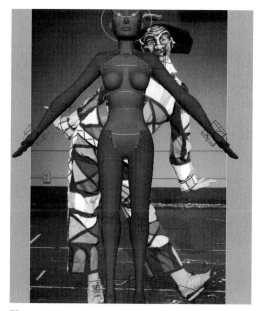

Figure 4.13

Adjusting the camera view so the model appears to have the same dimensions as the character in the photograph

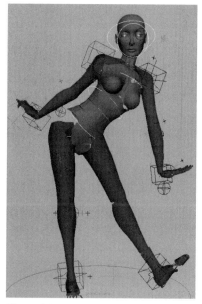

Figure 4.14

Arlecchino's pose in 3D

stretch to allow Arlecchino's left foot to stretch a bit extra to find the proper pose. If your character's dimensions are very different from the reference, feel free to adjust the pose to fit your character. Also feel free to exaggerate your character beyond the reference photo if it suits your desires. When you finish, you should have something similar to Figure 4.14, but with your own unique take on it.

For a different look, let's create a stock pose for Il Dottore. Using Figure 4.15 as a reference (you can find this image on the DVD under the name `DottorePose.jpg`), bend and pull your character into a similar shape, paying special attention to sticking the belly out, the placement of the feet, and the rotation of the hands. Also, don't forget to exaggerate the pose if you feel it works with your character. When you are finished, you should have something like Figure 4.16. Feel free to match other poses, and pose for your own photos so that you can feel the characters yourself as you manipulate your model to fit the poses.

Figure 4.15
Truitte Broome as Il Dottore

Figure 4.16
Il Dottore's pose in 3D

USING THE INCLUDED MAYA RIGS FOR BODY ANIMATION

If you work with Autodesk Maya, we have included two very robust, flexible rigs on the DVD for your use: Genna (or generic female) and Marcel (an homage to the late, great mime, Marcel Marceau). The rigs are designed to be generic enough to be used for the entire book (and for most animation tasks), while also providing enough control that very precise motion is achievable. Both rigs are the same, so we will cover their function together here. In this sidebar we will cover body animation. In a sidebar in Chapter 6, we will cover facial animation, since it is used first in that chapter.

All body animation is controlled via the NURBS curves that wrap around the figures when the Rig Layer (RigL) is visible, as shown in the following graphic. From bottom to top, the controls are as follows:

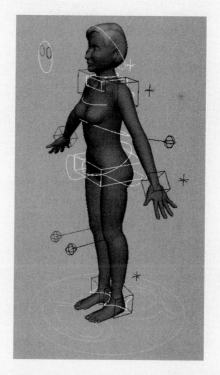

- `Rig Control:` The circle at the bottom with the "g" or "m" in it is used to move the entire model around the environment to place it in the scene. This control should not normally be keyframed. The rig control also has a setting, `showCOMCtrl`, which enables the center of mass (COM) control to be visible for the character (see COM Control later in this list).

- Left and Right Foot Controls (`Rt and LfLeg_footCTRL`): The boxes around each ankle, which allow for translation and rotation of each foot, also contain squash and stretch controls. Squash and stretch allows the rig to distort as if the body were made of rubber instead of bone. (See the last paragraph in this sidebar for more information on using squash and stretch.)

- Left and Right Foot Roll Controls (`Rt and LfLeg_rollCTRL`): The star-shaped curves inside the foot boxes, which, by moving the control about in the X and Z directions, provide ankle rotation and foot roll control for walking motions.

- Left and Right Leg Pole Vector Controls (`Rt and LfLeg_PVctrl`): The spheres in front of each knee, to which each knee is pointed. By dragging these controls around, you can change the orientation of each knee.

Continues

USING THE INCLUDED MAYA RIGS FOR BODY ANIMATION *(Continued)*

- COM Control (comPlacementCTRL): The blue circle around the hips (visible only when showCOMCtrl is enabled on the Rig Control), which is used to rotate the entire body around the center of mass. This is useful if the character needs to jump or spin in the air.

- Torso Control (torsoCTRL): The wavy curve around the hips, which is used to control the translation and rotation of the upper body as a whole.

- Hip Control (hipCTRL): The box around the hips (matched to the Shoulder Control, see later in this list), which is used to rotate and move the hips *independent of* the shoulders and head (whereas the Torso Control moves both). With squash and stretch on for the back, this effect can elongate or squash the torso area.

- Spine Control 1, 2, and 3 (spineFKctrl1, 2, and 3): The circles that surround the spine, which are used to rotate each portion of the spine, moving up the back.

- Shoulder Control (shldrCTRL): The box at the shoulders (centered on the neck), which is used to move and twist the upper back *independent of* the lower back and hips. With squash and stretch enabled, this control allows the upper torso to elongate and squash.

- Back Tweak Controls (backCluster1, 2, and 3Ctrl; only visible when Show Tweak is on in the Spine Config node, see later in this list): The series of boxes *inside* the geometry of the torso (visible when geometry is turned off) that allow for translation and rotation of specific spine segments. These controls provide very fine control over back poses, but are not generally needed for animation.

- Left and Right Clavicle Controls (Rt and LfClavCTRL): The boxes at each shoulder, which are translated to move the shoulders independent of the rest of the body.

- Left and Right Arm Pole Vector Controls (Rt and LfArmPV): The spheres behind each elbow, to which each elbow is pointed. By dragging these controls around, you can change the orientation of each elbow.

- Left and Right Arm Controls (Rt and LfArmCTRL): The boxes at each wrist, which allow for translation of the wrists.

- Left and Right Hand "A Joint" Controls (Rt and LfHand_Ajt): The semicircles within each wrist box, which provide rotation for the wrists and also provide open/close (flat to fist) and claw/tight (fingers spread wide to tight together) controls for each finger on the hand, as long as the hand is in SDK mode (see configuration controls, later in this sidebar).

- Neck Control (neckFK_Ajt): The circle around the neck, which allows the lower neck to be rotated while the head retains its orientation.

- Head Control (cervicalUpCtrl): The circle around the head, which allows you to rotate the character's head on all axes. Combined with the Neck Control, the two allow precise control over head rotation and orientation.

USING THE INCLUDED MAYA RIGS FOR BODY ANIMATION *(Continued)*

- Neck Tweak Controls (midNeckCtrl; only visible when Show Tweak is on in the Neck Config node, see later in this sidebar): The one box *inside* the geometry of the neck (visible when geometry is turned off) that allows for translation and rotation of the middle neck. This control provides very fine control over neck poses, but is not generally needed for animation.

- Look At Control (lookAt_CTRL): The circle with two inner circles in front of the character's eyes. By translating this control, you can have the character look wherever you wish. Also, by selecting just one inner circle at a time, you can cause each eye to look in a different direction for effect.

In addition to the NURBS curves controls, there are several "+" marks around the body that contain configuration controls. These controls are not moved around in space like the NURBS controls; rather, their attributes are adjusted to change the behavior of the rig. The attribute controls are as follows:

- Right and Left Leg Config (Rt and LfLegCONFIG): Behind each calf, just above the ankle. The roll control attributes delimit how far the foot will roll as each roll control curve (the star-shaped curve) is manipulated. The sticky attribute makes the knee stick to the pole vector control when 1, and not so when 0. The FKIK control causes each leg to be in inverse kinematics mode when the value is 0, and forward kinematics mode when it is 1. (See the following paragraph for more on FK/IK switching.)

- Spine Config (spineCONFIG): Behind the lumbar (lower) back area. The min and max scale attributes allow you to alter the squash and stretch attributes of the back. The Show Tweak attribute turns on (and off) the visibility of the Back Tweak controls (see earlier).

- Neck Config (neckCONFIG): Behind the neck. The min and max scale attributes allow you to alter the squash and stretch attributes of the neck. The show tweak attribute turns on (and off) the visibility of the one neck tweak control (see earlier).

- Right and Left Arm Config (Rt and LfArmCONFIG): Behind each shoulder blade. The ikSticky attribute makes each arm stay in place when set to 1, while the arm follows the body if the value is 0. The arm_PVSticky attribute makes the elbow stick to the pole vector control when 1, and not so when 0. The FKIK control causes each arm to be in inverse kinematics mode when the value is 0, and forward kinematics mode when it is 1. (See the following paragraph for more on FK/IK switching.)

- Right and Left Hand Config (Rt and LfHandCONFIG): Behind each wrist. The one attribute on each config node is the fksdk control. When 1, the control uses the set driven key control mode, where each finger is controlled by the attributes on the hand controls (allowing for finger open/close and claw/tight). When 0, you are presented with circles around each joint, allowing for direct forward kinematics rotation of each finger joint.

Continues

USING THE INCLUDED MAYA RIGS FOR BODY ANIMATION *(Continued)*

By adjusting the FK/IK switches above to FK, you can access a different control group, shown in the following graphic, that allows you to rotate each joint on a given appendage using forward rather than inverse kinematics. By rotating each circle in turn, you can rotate the underlying joint directly, rather than in an inverse kinematics method. For more on inverse and forward kinematics, please see a good reference book, like *Mastering Maya 8.5* by John Kundert-Gibbs, Mick Larkins, Dariush Derakhshani, and Eric Kunzendorf (Sybex, 2007).

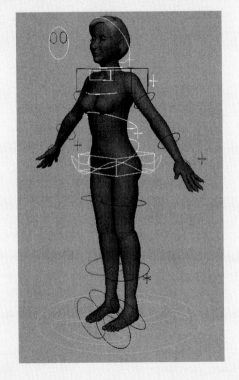

As is noted in the list of controls, many of the body controls allow for adjustment of squash and stretch on the character. This high-level rigging capability enables you to pull and push legs, arms, and spine beyond what is humanly possible, elongating and shortening the appendages as you go. The ssMin and ssMax attributes for each arm, leg, and torso give you control over how much that portion of the body will squash and stretch, respectively, before "sticking" to that length. The two controls are independent of each other (so you can have very long stretch but no squash, for example). During squash and stretch action, the rig has a built-in volumetric control where if an arm, for example, stretches, it also gets skinnier so that it looks like the volume of the arm remains the same; when the arm squashes, it also becomes fatter, again to preserve volume. A value of 1 means the rig behaves normally—as if there is no squash and stretch. A value greater than 1 for ssMin is equivalent to 1 (no squash), while a value less than 1 provides squash down to that percentage of the length of the appendage. An ssMax value less than 1 is equivalent to 1 (no stretch), while a value greater than 1 provides stretch up to that multiplier of the original length of the appendage. Good use of squash and stretch can create some wonderfully cartoony effects for the characters, so by all means experiment with this very cool aspect of the rig.

A special thanks to David Floyd for modeling Genna and creating the blend shapes for both characters; to Lena Gieseke for modeling Marcel; and to James Orara for building the amazing rigs that are used on both characters.

Animating a Commedia Walk

Now let's create a short animation sequence using video as a guide to animating the character. Several video clips are included on the accompanying DVD, so feel free to use as many clips as you'd like to practice animating a Commedia character. We will use a short clip of an innamorata or lover's walk, which has a nice chest lead and a slow but light motion to it—you might recognize Pepé Le Pew in this walk.

> The video clips of Antonio Fava were recorded during a motion capture session that is being used for other purposes. Unfortunately, the video capture is mostly of his upper body, not his legs, so you will have to imagine what his legs are doing below the camera.

First, import your model into a new scene. Then be sure your animation settings are for 30 fps, which is the native capture rate of this movie. (In Maya, this is under Window → Settings/Preferences → Preferences: Settings: Working Units: Time.)

Next, create an image plane behind your animation camera and place the movie clip on it. If you have Maya, create a new camera, separate from the Persp camera (so that you can move the Persp camera around), then in the Attribute Editor, add an image plane under the Environment tab. Once this is created, click the folder icon next to Image Name, and browse to the movie folder; you will have to select Best Guess from the Enable pop-up so you can select a QuickTime movie as an image plane. Scroll through the animation to be sure the movie is working (it should be 80 frames long).

Place your character in front of the first image of the video, to camera right. Be sure to adjust the camera and rotate the body somewhat so that it fits with the video source. Figure 4.17 shows our model in front of the first frame of video.

Now the task is to match this pose (and use your imagination for the legs and feet) for the first frame. Then move to the next keyframe you see— we chose frame 18, as it is the end of the anticipation move for the walk— and pose your character there. Move on to the next keyframe and pose, and so forth until you finish. We chose frames 1, 18, 28 (the collapse before the first forward motion), 48 (top of the first step), 62 (nearing the contact position for the left foot), 68 (the fully contacted, or "down" position for the left foot), and 80 (the last

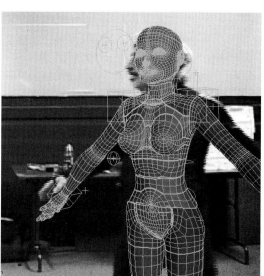

Figure 4.17

Placing Genna in position over the video file

frame of our animation). Once you have the major poses complete, go back and adjust the in-between frames to match the video there as well, using a hybrid pose-to-pose/straight-ahead method to animate your character.

As with the previous poses, feel free to tweak your poses and/or exaggerate them versus the video to make the animated character "pop" as much as you wish. Note that the beginning of the walk involves a major chest lead, where the character rises up and then "falls" forward (toward his or her lover) to begin the walk. Also note that the steps are not heavy on the strike portion because the lover is more drifting than walking heavily. The eye line is also generally up above the eye height, as if love is so wonderful it is just above the lover at all times. (Remember, the lover is in love with the idea of love much more than with an individual person.)

When you finish, you should have a nice 3-second start of a walk in the style of a Commedia innamorata character. Figure 4.18 shows a still from our version of the animation (LoversWalk.mov), which is on the DVD as LoverWalk.mb. We added more up-

Figure 4.18

The lover's walk, animated

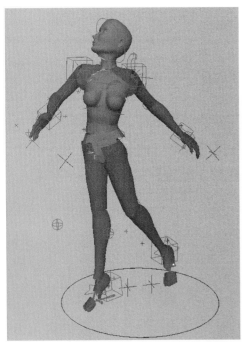

down motion at the start and made the walk slightly heavier than the video reference, mostly to get a better feel for the animation: following the video too closely led to a "floaty" feeling to the walk, which doesn't read well in animation, even if it is accurate in real life.

Using a few more of the included clips, continue to practice different Commedia walks and lazzi (or bits). Then be sure to record yourself performing as a Commedia character of your choosing, and animate to your recording. This is the best way to truly feel the way the character moves and translate your own body's motions into animation, which should be your goal whenever possible.

Now that you have a good sense of how to create a "stock" character both physically and in animation, let us turn to a more psychological/physical approach in the next chapter, where we will explore a psychological method, called bioenergetics, that has been used to great success by actors exploring character and motivation.

CHAPTER 5

Bioenergetics

Bioenergetics is a form of mind-body therapy, developed by American psychotherapist Alexander Lowen, that involves muscular tensions and character types that can be recognized by their external appearances. Lowen believed that each person has an energy core that wants to interact with the world, but due to different psychological traumas during childhood and adolescence, the energy is blocked internally, causing different behaviors that can be categorized into five character types. These characters and their external manifestations are prime fodder for animators, because they provide an external set of characteristics that reveal depths of internal psychological traits. For both actor and animator, an understanding of Lowen's character types aids in the creation of physical bodies that are embedded in emotional and psychological experience, adding realism—or hyper-realism—to the characters

This chapter discusses:

- A description of character and the development of muscular tensions

- An investigation into the five character types

- Exercises to find the characters in your own body

- Exercises to transfer these characters to animation

Energy

Alexander Lowen was a student of Wilhelm Reich in the 1940s; Reich believed that the mind and body were united as one and not two separate entities. After receiving his medical degree in Geneva, Lowen separated from Reich and founded the International Institute for Bioenergetic Analysis (IIBA). Lowen believed that the body built up chronic muscular tensions in reaction to perceived psychological trauma or in order to prevent feared forthcoming trauma. He analyzed these tensions and categorized them into specific character types. In his therapy, he worked with the body to release muscular tensions in order to free the mind. Currently there are over 1,500 members of the IIBA and 54 training institutes in countries around the world.

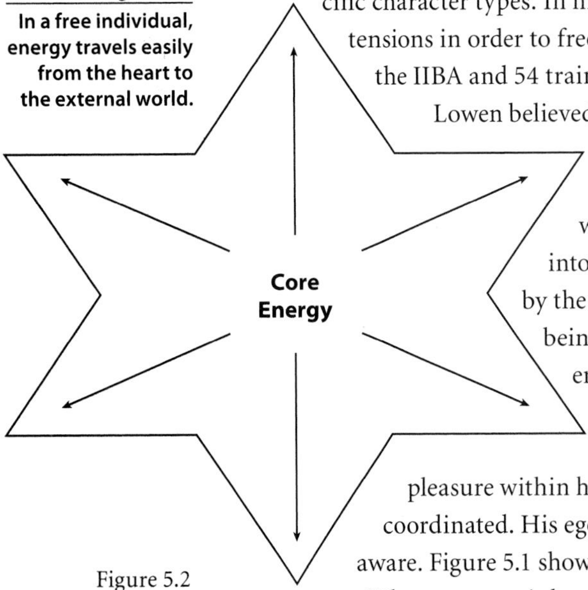

Lowen believed that everyone is born with a core of energy to love and to be loved. This energy has to travel through layers in one's mind and body to reach other human beings, where this energy can be either deposited or drawn back into the body. The first layer is the emotional layer, followed by the muscular layer, and lastly the ego layer. When a human being is functioning without psychological or physical barriers, this energy to love and be loved travels freely out from the center to others in the world and then back again to the heart. This ideal person is able to feel joy and pleasure within his emotional layer. He is muscularly free, graceful, and coordinated. His ego layer, which is the conscious layer of self-image, is fully aware. Figure 5.1 shows a schematic representation of this personality type.

When a person is bound, he feels pain, fear, rage, and despair in the emotional layer; he has chronic muscular tensions in his muscular layer; and his ego is full of denial, rationalizations, distrust, and blame. Figure 5.2 shows a schematic representation of this personality type.

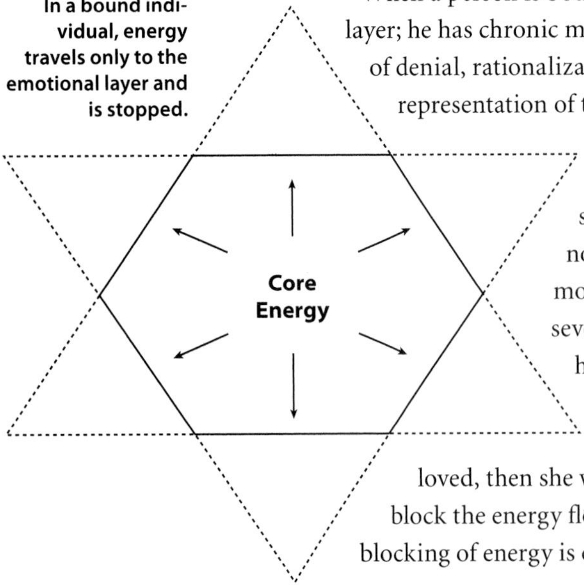

Unfortunately almost everyone is thwarted in the desire to love or to be loved, so all of us are bound in some way. As infants we send out our energy and we do not receive what we want. It could be as simple and common as not being fed or changed at our first wails or as severe as physical or emotional abuse. What's important here is the perception of the infant and not the intent of the mother or father. If the infant perceives some sort of disconnect in the flow of energy to love and to be loved, then she will feel rage, despair, pain, or fear and consequently block the energy flow so that it does not go beyond the emotional level. The blocking of energy is designed to prevent further painful feelings; the classic "If

Figure 5.1

In a free individual, energy travels easily from the heart to the external world.

Core Energy

Figure 5.2

In a bound individual, energy travels only to the emotional layer and is stopped.

Core Energy

I don't let others inside my defenses, I can't be hurt" scenario all of us feel to some extent or other.

To block the flow of energy, the infant will have to begin the process of building up chronic muscular tensions in order to hold her own energy in the emotional layer or to stop any painful outside energy from entering and affecting her feelings. Over time, as these chronic muscular tensions begin to set themselves in place, the ego will need to rationalize what is happening within the inner layers of the mind and body.

> Alexander Lowen's book, *Bioenergetics* (Penguin Press, 1994), is a marvelous reference resource for work in this area. If you are interested in reading further on this fascinating psychological theory, *Bioenergetics* is the book to read.

Character

Lowen believed that there are specific patterns to the means in which an individual strives to love and to be loved that can be observed in chronic muscular tensions within the body that limit impulse and also in the ego ideal of a person that affirms or rationalizes his means of behavior. Lowen organized these patterns into stereotypes of character and devised a physical means of representing these character types with the drawing of a star. As shown in Figure 5.3, the six points of the star represent the head, arms, legs, and genitals. In the center of the star is a core of energy, which is the energy to love and be loved, that is sent out into the world.

A solid line within the star represents a blockage of energy. A double solid line (the left hand in Figure 5.3) is a severe blockage and a dotted line (the right hand) is a weak blockage. Solid lines coming from the core of energy in the center are strong impulses being sent out while dotted lines coming from the center (the one toward the head in Figure 5.3) are weak ones.

The shape of the star is also important. Lowen believed that chronic muscular tension can actually alter the physical growth of an individual; consequently, different character types will have different body types. The body shape is represented by the outline of the star.

All of the character types are named with psychological abnormalities. Don't worry about this. Sometimes students get concerned that the names mean that everyone is somehow mentally ill, but this is not the case. Most individuals are a mixture of several different character types with one type dominating. It is rare to find a pure example of a character type in a human being. The names are simply for the sake of psychological categorization and are not to be taken as a stigma of the self.

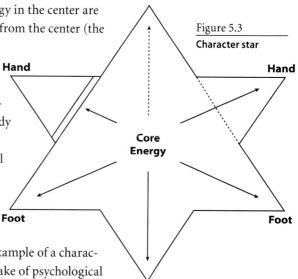

Figure 5.3
Character star

Head

Hand

Hand

Core
Energy

Foot

Foot

Genitals

As for animations, character types are often more obvious in animated work than in real life. Animated characters are more archetypal and/or caricatured than real humans, so it can be easier to observe the types in animation; sometimes the figure of a character alone can be enough to give away what bioenergetics type this character is. In addition, an animated character will often exhibit more starkly the characteristics of a given body type. This is not to say that modelers and animators are necessarily thinking of bioenergetics body types (though this could be very valuable in both the design and animation stages of the pipeline); more likely, because bioenergetics elucidates basic character types in life, designers, modelers, and animators are simply drawing unconsciously from what they see around them to create their work.

There are five character types: schizoid, oral, psychopath, masochist, and rigid. The psychopath type is further subdivided into the seducing and bullying subtypes. According to Lowen, everyone is made up of one or more of these types, described in the following sections.

The Schizoid

Historically, the schizoid character has suffered some sort of rejection by the mother from intentional or unintentional hostility. The infant perceived this as a threat to its existence. Consequently, the infant fears that reaching out, demanding, or any self-assertion would lead to its death. Thus the infant withdraws and feels no joy. The child will often have nonemotional behavior with outbursts of rage and sometimes night terrors.

Figure 5.4
Schizoid character

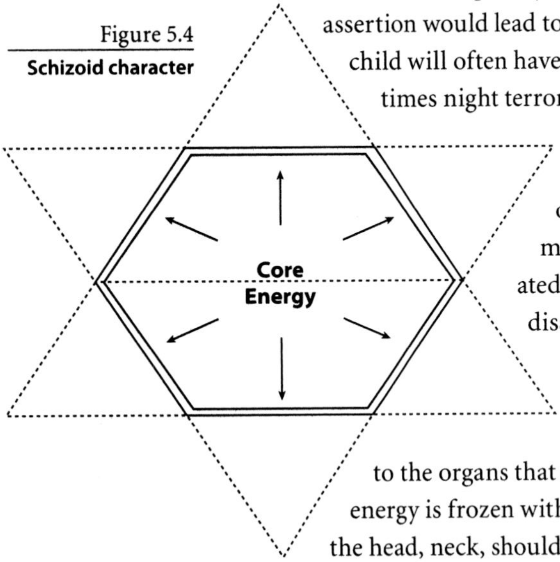

The schizoid's dominant feelings are of terror and fury. To deal with these negative emotions, the schizoid will often disassociate from either reality or from his body. This means that he could have an immense fantasy life if disassociated from reality or a highly developed abstract intelligence if disassociated from the body.

You will observe in the schizoid star, shown in Figure 5.4, that there is a strong flow of energy coming from the center, but there is a double line stopping the flow of energy to the organs that contact the world. This means that the inner charge of energy is frozen within the core and held there by strong muscular tensions in the head, neck, shoulders, pelvis, and hips. There is additionally a weak blockage in the center of the star, which represents a blockage of energy to the diaphragm, where there will also be a muscular tension. Since energy is held within the core, perception of impulse—the schizoid's ability to understand what he wants in a given situation—is very weak.

Physically, the schizoid character's body looks as if it is trying to avoid any contact between the self and the world. He tends to have a narrow and contracted body. His face is masklike. The eyes make no contact with the world. The feet are often contracted and inverted, meaning they walk on the outside of the feet in order to avoid contact with the earth. If there is any reason for the schizoid to be paranoid (fear of abuse or annihilation), he will often build muscles for protection.

The schizoid has an inadequate sense of self due to his lack of identification with the body. He is hypersensitive and has low resistance to pressure from the outside world. It is his will that motivates his behavior and not his feelings. His basic conflict is between the need to exist and the need to be loved. He believes that he can continue to exist only if he needs nothing, and consequently, he avoids intimate relationships. To rationalize these behaviors, the schizoid develops an ego ideal that sees himself as superior: rather than being lonely or underappreciated, he rationalizes that he is above and beyond all around him.

> Remember that the description of the schizoid, as with all the other types discussed below, is for a "pure" case. Rarely will you find a real person who matches the extremes of all of these characteristics. However, if you look around (perhaps at yourself even) you will begin to see more and more people who have attributes of this and other body types. Detecting body types of friends, family, and passers-by can be highly educational and entertaining—just be sure not to disturb your friends by discussing these matters too loudly.

Although the schizoid is a fascinating character, it is often a very unengaged and therefore unengaging one, as this type of character does not interact well with the world around him. Thus, in dramatic work, schizoid characters are most often the sidekicks of the hero if they are "good," or represent the schizoid who has "snapped" and now behaves cruelly, but with their own twisted morality if they are the bad guy in a given production.

An excellent case of the schizoid gone "off the deep end" is Heath Ledger's chilling embodiment of The Joker in 2008's *The Dark Knight*. Here is a character who literally cut himself a mask—out of his own face—for the outside world, and proceeds to wreak havoc on his world using his own twisted sense of morality to create chaos around him. Another character of this type is Hans Gruber (played by Alan Rickman), the villain in the original *Die Hard*. Rickman's character, while more realistic than Ledger's, is just as scarily out of contact with the real world, just as unempathetic, and just as prone to bouts of extreme violence coming, seemingly, from nowhere. The violence of these characters is particularly effective because it comes from their still, masklike demeanor, which embodies the schizoid character.

In the "good guy" category, the eponymous hero of *Monk*, played by Tony Shalhoub, is quirky, obsessive-compulsive, and "out of touch" precisely because he is a schizoid type. Interestingly enough, Shalhoub does another turn as a wonderfully funny schizoid in 1999's sleeper hit, *Galaxy Quest*, where he plays chief engineer Fred Kwan. In both of these roles, Shalhoub is dissociated somewhat from reality, following the logic of his own inner self rather than the way the world might wish him to behave. As opposed to the violence of the former characters, the schizoid type here provides comic relief due to his humorous lack of contact with the outside world.

The Oral

Historically, the oral character has suffered some deprivation of the mother due to her death, depression, or loss of some kind. While the oral type tends to be an early developer, her childhood is often filled with depressive episodes. If she has secondary disappointments or loss of a father or sibling, she can become bitter.

Oral characters, whose star is shown in Figure 5.5, have inner feelings of emptiness due to their loss, and consequently feel that the world owes them. They look to others to fill them up and provide their feelings; thus they tend to be clingy to others. They need to be held, petted, and taken care of. Their aggression is low and they find it very difficult to be alone. They have trouble breaking from their parents, who they need to take care of them. An interesting quality of oral characters is that since they draw energy from others, they have great mood swings based on the moods of the people around them.

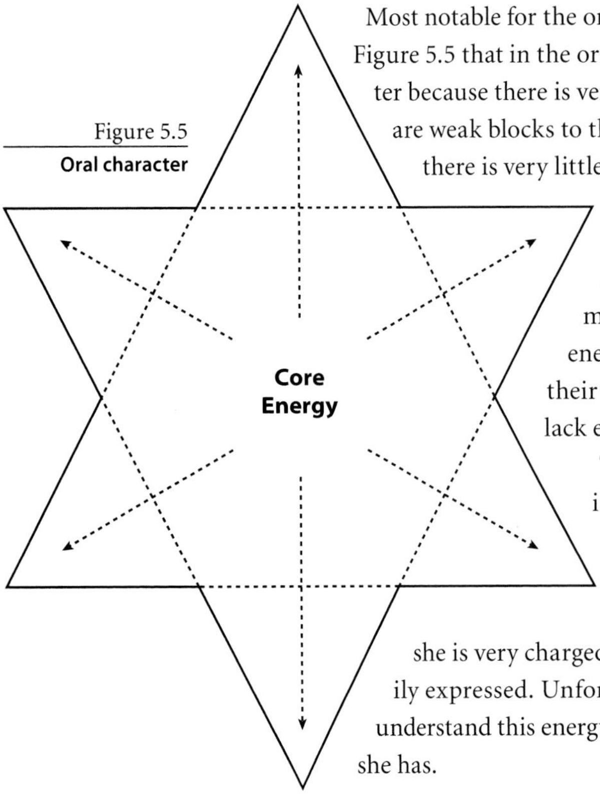

Most notable for the oral character is their undercharged state. Observe in Figure 5.5 that in the oral star there are only dotted lines coming from the center because there is very little energy flowing from this character type. There are weak blocks to the external organs, but that is all that is necessary as there is very little energy to block.

Also note that star itself is narrow and long. Physically the oral person tends to have a thin and long body type. They have loose, lean, underdeveloped muscles. They often slump because they don't have the energy to hold themselves up. They sometimes must lock their knees in order to keep from falling over. Even their eyes lack energy, and they have a tendency toward myopia.

The oral character has a fundamental conflict between independence and the need to be taken care of. She believes that she is independent and attempts to be so, but usually fails under pressure. To rationalize this, the oral character develops an ego ideal that she is very charged and very energetic with lots of feelings that are easily expressed. Unfortunately (according to this person) the world doesn't understand this energy, so others misunderstand all the energy the oral thinks she has.

Figure 5.5
Oral character

Core Energy

Because the oral type is very much of an energy hole, they are not generally the most interesting of characters for dramatic work, so they are somewhat rare as a pure type in either live-action or animated work. One good recent example of an oral character is Violet Parr, daughter of Mr. Incredible and Elastigirl in Pixar's 2004 *The Incredibles*. Violet's main character arc is, in fact, to go from being invisible to visible to others. Her body droops from lack of energy, which seems to extend even to her hair, which is straight and without body. She tends to whine a good deal, and she is unable (until the end of the movie) to generate the energy to create a force field to help out her family. Violet's lack of energy is highlighted by her brother Dash's extreme level of energy.

In live action, oral types are even more rare, usually only on stage as bit parts that can be funny in their lack of energy without draining the movie or television show for a long period of time. As an example, fans of *Cheers* might remember Norm Peterson's pining secretary, Doris, who generally wore a yellow raincoat, as a good example of a small role done as an oral character. Doris meekly follows Norm around, trying to get his attention/energy and affections, but she is too weak to make this happen. Interestingly enough, one place most of us are familiar seeing orals is a scary one: the iconic zombie character, with its weak energy, slow movement, reaching hands, and need for "BRAIN!" is a great example of the oral character type.

The Psychopath

In his youth, the psychopath's parents do not allow the child to have a separate identity from them. The parents often give to the child only for their own selfish reasons and not for the benefit of the child; thus if the child asks for something (a cookie or toy, for example) and this is not in the parent's interest at that moment, the parent(s) will attack or denigrate the child as the child's expression of need does not coincide with the parent's desires. Consequently, the psychopath character comes to feel that reaching out or asserting a need leaves him vulnerable to being ignored or slapped down for this need. The psychopath will then either rise above the need or will manipulate the parent into giving him what he wants.

Growing up, the psychopath quickly becomes an expert in control. They have a great need to control others, and consequently become dependent on those that they control. They have a need to be on top and be the best always. They have a fear of being controlled and are usually in an antagonistic relationship with the parent of the same sex. To control others, the psychopath must also control their own energy using strong blocks. Often they do this by the denial of feelings as well as physically. Figure 5.6 shows the character star for the psychopath.

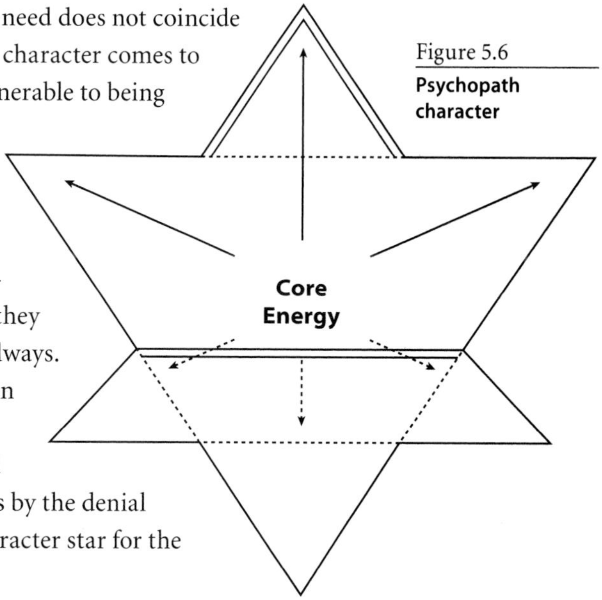

Figure 5.6
Psychopath character

Core Energy

There are two different types of psychopaths, the bully and the seducer, but both types share the same star. The muscular tensions, body type, and ego ideal are the same in both types. The difference between the two comes down to the means by which they control others. The bully pushes people around while the seducer manipulates. For both types, sexuality is always a factor in control.

The psychopath has a unique star. Note that there are strong lines of energy going to the top half of the star and that there are only weak lines of energy going to the bottom. This strong energy to the top makes the upper portion of the body large in comparison to the smaller, weaker lower part, which is very often revealed in the physical appearance of a person of this body type, which is the easiest to spot "on the street." Also observe that there are double-line blocks at the top of the head and at the diaphragm.

Physically, the psychopath has a big, blown-up, rigid upper body. The lower body is narrow and tight. The double block at the diaphragm splits the body into two parts, which makes it difficult for the psychopath to take deep, full breaths. It also means that they often have a flexible back. With lots of energy going to the head where it is blocked in, the psychopath has extreme tension around the eyes and in the back of the head and neck—often their eyes will appear to bulge outward from this tension. Their eyes are watchful and mistrustful and often close a lot. They need to control all of the energy they have radiating to the big upper body so they have a lot of muscular tension.

The basic conflict for the psychopath is the need to be close to others versus the need to control everything. They want desperately to be intimate with someone, but have difficulty in doing so, as it would require a loss of control. They also fail to separate their ego from the idea of power; consequently, they believe that whatever they control must be good. They justify these ideas with an ego ideal that they possess incredible, secret power.

The psychopath is a good character for dramatic work: they are generally very outgoing and want to control everything around them. Thus they can play well as either a hero or a villain; in either case, they put out a great deal of energy to the world around them. While in real life the bullying and seducing psychopath can be of either gender, in dramatic work (as one might expect) the bullying psychopath tends to be the male figure, while the seducing type is more likely to be the female. The Hulk is a good example of a bullying psychopath: his energy is barely contained rage, and his muscles tense and bulge due to his holding in that energy. The Hulk is a fairly barbaric psychopath, however; there are many who use more cerebral methods to control those around them. Syndrome, the bad guy in *The Incredibles*, for example, is clearly a bullying psychopath, but he uses his brains rather than his muscles to control—and try to take over—the world around him. The desire to take over the world is, in fact, a pretty obvious sign that a character is a psychopath. Bluto, Popeye's arch-nemesis, is also a bullying psychopath who is overinflated on top and wants to control those around him—or at least get Olive Oil away from Popeye. Interestingly enough, Popeye is also a bullying psychopath, this time a good-guy version. Placing two bullying psychopaths in close proximity is a good recipe for trouble, which is what usually happens in the plots of that cartoon.

A wonderful example of a seducing psychopath is the figure of Jessica Rabbit from the 1988 film *Who Framed Roger Rabbit*. Jessica is almost literally cut in half at the waist, representing the double block that psychopaths have at the abdomen in a physical way. She uses her sexuality in a very aggressive manner to wrap men around her finger, so to speak, and is used to the attention this gets her, as well as the control she gains over her world by displaying her sexuality. A seducing psychopath, while generally behaving more subtly than the bullying kind, can still be unsettling for those on whom she unleashes her sexuality.

The Masochist

Love and acceptance come to the masochist child from his parents with extreme pressure to earn it. Any resistance to the parents is crushed; therefore, the masochist experiences guilt for expressing any independence. Usually the masochist has a dominating and sacrificing mother and a passive, submissive father. The parents often place great emphasis on eating and defecation, so the masochist develops a fear of sticking out the oral and anal cavities and humiliation at letting anything out.

For masochists, their inside feelings are very different from what is expressed on the outside. On the outside, they remain passive and submissive while on the inside they have strong feelings of being trapped, negativity, hostility, self-defeat, spite, and even superiority. They tend to whine and complain but remain submissive. Their assertion and aggression is lowered, so as not to show any real resistance, but they engage in provocative behavior to egg others on. Passive-aggressive behavior comes from this character type.

When looking at the masochist star, shown in Figure 5.7, you will note that they have a very fully charged internal state, but that it is tightly held in the center of the body. They have great energy trying to escape, but the energy can't even get to the limbs because it is blocked completely in the center. This holding in creates a bend at the waist. There is an additional weak block to all of the organs of contact with the world, so there is very little energy in the limbs and reaching out to make contact with the world is limited. Also note that the head and genitals are smaller than the arms and legs. This is due to the holding in from above and below. The mouth and anus are pulled in and protected while the arms and legs may circle around the body to further protect the person, and to hold the energy in the center.

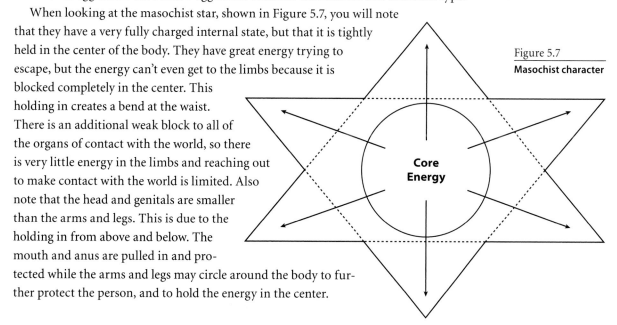

Figure 5.7

Masochist character

Core
Energy

Physically the masochist has a shorter, thicker body type, especially as they contract themselves vertically, making them appear shorter than they are. They tend to collapse or bend in at the waist or sternum. They tuck their pelvis and neck forward and in. This bend and tuck gives their torso a sort of C shape. Their arms are usually drawn close to the body, with one hand protecting the mouth area and the other protecting the abdomen or even the crotch. Sometimes they are even paler in complexion due to the tight pulling in that cuts off the blood supply. They give the impression of a turtle when it is pulling all of its limbs into its shell.

The basic conflict for the masochist is intimacy versus freedom of expression. They want to be close to another person but are incapable of expressing what is inside of them or reaching out to contact that person. Sometimes when the masochist actually does let go of the holding and lets out all of the internal feeling, the negative rage is so aggressive, hostile, violent, and spiteful that it will appear to come from nowhere and will often frighten others. A masochist pushed too far is the kind of "guy next door" that suddenly goes berserk on a violent spree that utterly confounds his friends and neighbors.

To rationalize this conflict between inner energy and outer behavior, the masochist adopts an ego ideal that he is superior to others. An interesting characteristic of the masochist is that he will often sabotage his work situations and relationships so that they fail. If something fails, he is not forced into intimacy, while at the same time, he can blame the failure on others, and therefore maintain his feelings of superiority.

There are quite a number of television and movie characters who are masochists, though often they are in the role of sidekicks or bad guys, as their personalities make them fairly prickly to others. A classic masochist is Cliff Clavin (played by John Ratzenberger) from the *Cheers* television series. Cliff is very nice on the outside, but one can easily see him gritting his teeth as he pushes the negativity that dominates his life down below the surface. In addition, he is slightly squat, as his body is compressed by the effort of keeping all his energy within his core. He tends to hunch over and use his hand to protect his face and lower belly (or uses the bar to protect him by leaning right up against it). Cliff even has a moustache, which helps hide and protect his mouth. Finally, exemplifying a masochist, Cliff is prone to negative outbursts as the blocked energy escapes violently, and tends to sabotage his own plans in a passive-aggressive manner, and then blame others when his schemes fail.

In the world of animation, one good recent example of a masochist character is Anton Ego in Pixar's 2007 film, *Ratatouille*. Ego is very thin, but his upper body is hunched and compressed, making him appear somewhat squat for his height. Ego consistently places his hands in front of his mouth and belly, protecting his vital areas and helping to hold his energy within himself. As the bad guy (or at least the threatening food critic who can ruin the restaurant's reputation), Ego has a very high opinion of himself, hates everything, but at the same time puts a thin veneer of politeness atop a negative worldview.

Interestingly enough, when Remy serves a delicious dish of ratatouille to Ego and he is invaded by pleasant memories, Ego's body relaxes, his hands drop away, and he straightens up in his chair, shedding most of the masochist body cues.

The Rigid

Historically the rigid character does not suffer any infantile trauma. Her troubles begin in her early erotic striving. The parent of the opposite sex disallows any physical expression of love so there are no hugs and kisses for comfort or joy. Since the child is then limited in her expressions and feelings of love, pride takes the place of intimate contact. For the rigid, love and pride become the same thing. The outcome for the rigid is often classic narcissistic behavior: too much love for and pride in the self, at the expense of relationships with other people.

The rigid character is afraid to let go of anything because of the pride that is giving her strength. She is materialistic, ambitious, aggressive, competitive, and stubborn. Many CEOs are rigid characters.

The rigid star, shown in Figure 5.8, is interesting because there are no blocks on the interior. The character has a lot of energy that travels freely to the exterior edge of the body where it is completely blocked with double lines. Physically, rigids are more integrated than any of the other types and have a good outside appearance. Their physical difficulty is that all of their energy is used defensively and so they become stiff. Just as their name suggests, their movement is not free and graceful as they are rigid/stiff with pride. Thus the rigid might look very good when standing still, but as soon as she moves, she reveals a lack of fluidity and agility. The Capitano Commedia character (see Chapter 4) is a great example of a rigid character type.

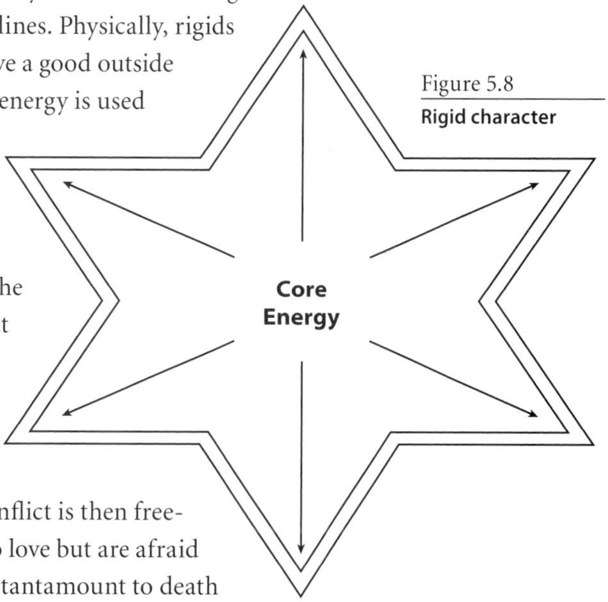

Figure 5.8
Rigid character

Core Energy

The rigid sees the lack of physical expression from the parent as rejection and betrayal. Therefore, the rigid makes sure that no one will ever get close to her, so she will not ever be betrayed again. The basic conflict is then freedom versus surrender to love: they want to surrender to love but are afraid that doing so would necessitate losing control, which is tantamount to death for this character. These ideas are rationalized with the ego ideal that they are a very loving person but no one appreciates or understands their love.

As might be expected, the rigid character type is often associated with the hero. This body type is both the most physically balanced and best integrated, so a rigid character looks good and, while moving stiffly, has a presence about her that makes others think she has a good handle on any given situation. At the same time, due to the heavy blocks at the outer edges of a rigid's body, she is cut off from the world, not truly integrated within it, which sets her off as a loner figure, which is, again, a hallmark of the (oft-misunderstood) hero. Examples of the rigid type abound, from movie presidents to military figures. Buzz Lightyear, from Pixar's *Toy Story* films (and television show spinoff), is an excellent example of a rigid type—as is, fittingly, the actor, Tim Allen, who plays Buzz. Buzz has a military/heroic demeanor to him, and an attitude to match. He is handsome, the other toys and even Andy, his "owner," finding him more attractive than the cowboy doll, Woody. At the same time, however, Buzz is a bit thick-headed and most certainly a loner. He accepts the adulation of others, but his character arc in the first movie is to find a place in society: to become integrated with others is his character challenge.

Perhaps even more iconic is the character of Superman, the ultimate hero—and the ultimate loner. Superman is generally drawn or played as a chest-out, feet-apart character who should have difficulty walking because he is so muscle bound. As it turns out, his lack of flexibility is not an awful detriment, because he is so powerful that he defeats most of his enemies without having to exert himself overly much. Clark Kent is a lonely man (and boy) who, it turns out, isn't even from Earth: he is the only survivor of Krypton's destruction, and as such is the ultimate loner. Moreover, while Superman is admired from afar, he is not loved intimately, instead pining after Lois Lane in a private purgatory that gives the character the pathos that keeps readers and viewers following his story.

Combination Types

While the five character types we have described are fascinating and starkly defined in their "pure" form, we more often see combinations of types in both real people and animated characters. A person combining two or more of the personality types will display elements of both types, the combination creating a unique personality based on the amounts of each of the elements they have from the pure types that are combined within them. Thus a combined psychopath and masochist, like the "Bowler Hat Man" in *Meet the Robinsons* (the grown-up Michael Yagoobian) combines the "C" shape of the masochist with the overblown top half and very tiny bottom half of a psychopath. In addition, Bowler Hat Man combines the scheming desire to control the future and wreck his friend Lewis' life (psychopath behavior) with the façade of pleasantness and the ultimate self-sabotage of his own plans that are the hallmarks of the masochist type.

As you observe people around you and characters in the movies, on television, and in animations, try to break down what types make up these people. If they are not pure types, observe what combination of types make them up; look at their physical postures and at their behaviors. Do they present a masklike visage and poor contact with the world while at the same time reaching out weakly for what energy they can get from the world—a combination of schizoid and oral? Are they big and energetic, projecting their energy outward but at the same time slightly curved inward, guarding some of that energy within their cores—a combination of rigid and masochist? How do they look, move, and behave? The better you can get at observing and breaking down how people and characters embody combinations of these types, the more effective you will be at re-creating them yourself for your animations. Whether you want to model or animate a pure type, or create a character who is a combination of bioenergetics types, your ability to observe the minutia of behaviors that indicate each type and combination thereof will help you immensely.

Bioenergetics Acting Exercises

The acting exercises for this chapter basically involve assuming the character types by taking on the different muscular tensions, energy, and psychic attitudes of each type. After the body is taken on, you then do simple activities and interact with the environment and others in this body type. For this work, it is often very useful to have monologues to speak within the character types. The different tensions that are adopted greatly affect the vocal mechanisms in the body, and therefore different bodies have very different voices. When looking for a monologue, it is important that you find one that moves you. If you don't like it, you will never be able to do anything with it. We recommend sticking with something contemporary so you don't have to deal with verse. Also, look for a monologue that has a strong, playable objective in it. Monologues that are just recounting stories from the past or memoires don't work well. In pieces like these, it is hard to find a good objective and easy to slip into playing mood or emotion. If you're working on an animation, you might find it useful to memorize a short monologue from one of the characters you're working on—especially one that could match a particular character type—to see how the words work with that character.

Monologues can be found in many places. If you are fairly well versed in plays, you can draw from texts that you know. You can find monologues on the Internet, but use these as a last resort: often they are new and not well written. As for writing them yourself, unless you are an accomplished writer, avoid that: this is an exercise in acting, not in writing. You can use monologues from movies or animation, but be careful that you are not trying to copy a given performance, or your exercise will end up becoming more about mimicry than acting. There are also many collections of monologues in book form, divided into all kinds of categories like monologues for women, male comedy, dramatic, classical, and contemporary. Most university libraries have copies. As long as you are not planning on using a monologue from a collection for an audition, look for one from a book. It is the easiest way to find a good piece for practice. Before speaking the monologue "in character" in the following exercises, try speaking it in a neutral voice a few times. This will give you a baseline from which to judge how speaking the monologue in character affects your voice and the flow of the monologue.

Before you begin any of the bioenergetics work, warm up fully using the exercises from Chapter 3. The bioenergetics bodies can cause a great deal of physical tension, and you want to be certain that you don't hurt yourself. Also, at the end of the session we suggest that you stretch and do a relaxation exercise so that you rid yourself of any remaining muscular tension.

As with the chapter on Commedia, it is useful to have simple props and objects around your space that you can interact with. Some of the objects should be recognizable and others should be somewhat abstract so that your imagination can make them become anything you want them to be. Have your journal ready so that you can write down your observations and discoveries.

Exercise for the Schizoid Character

Figure 5.9

Actor in schizoid body

After warming up thoroughly, spend some time looking at Figure 5.4, the schizoid star, to recall the shape and lines of energy and blockages. Next begin to walk around the space in your normal, everyday walk. Become aware of your body in space as you move around the room.

Now, think about the blocks in the schizoid character. There are blocks to the head, arms, legs, and genitals and a weak block at the diaphragm (the dashed line). To adopt these blocks, tense the muscles in your neck, shoulders, upper back and chest, armpits, abdomen, hips, and pelvis as you walk. You will find it more difficult to move as you put tension into all of these areas (you might also find it tiring to expend so much energy).

You should note that with all the blocks, there is now very little energy in your limbs. Your body will become narrower and contracted with the effort to hold the energy inside you, your arms dangling loosely at your sides, and your legs not very energized. Since the schizoid is holding a large amount of energy in the core, he will make little contact with the world. Figure 5.9 shows an actor adopting a schizoid body type.

Maintain the muscular tensions in your neck, shoulders, upper back and chest, armpits, abdomen, hips, and pelvis and try to make little contact with the external world. To do this, make your face masklike and unexpressive. Make your eyes inactive and don't let them contact anyone or anything. Also, don't walk fully on your feet because they shouldn't fully contact the earth. Instead, try walking on the outside edges of your feet, as shown in Figure 5.9. How does walking in this body make you feel? What moods or emotions does it bring up?

As you continue to move in this body, speak your monologue. If you have it memorized, great. If not, simply carry the text, or print it in a large font and place it where it is easy to see the lines. It is better to have the lines in front of you than to be trying to remember them. Note how these tensions affect your voice. Does the disconnect with the world show up in how you breathe and speak?

Now stop for a minute, breathe, stretch, and shake out the tensions. Because we are adopting the bodies in an extreme form, you may experience some physical and even emotional pain, so don't spend too long in the body, and be sure to release it fully. If you are having difficulty releasing the body, do a full stretch and then jump around.

Now go back to your body and start once again to move around the space. Keeping in mind the physical star and psychic attitudes of the schizoid, begin to interact with props and objects. Note how you touch, handle, and work with things. Are you actually interacting or just going through the motions? Do you fully touch and feel things? Are you in touch with your world, or looking at it from a disinterested distance?

If you have a group, you may now begin to interact with other members of the group. Continue moving around the space and working with objects, but add the condition that you must make some sort of contact with other people. Look at them or touch them. This will be difficult to do with the schizoid body, as it tries to avoid contact with the world, but force yourself to do so. Next speak with others. Notice how you sound and interact with other people.

Figure 5.10

Actor in oral body

Now relax and let it go. Stretch, shake, jump, and breathe. If you have a group, discuss what this experience was like. Write your observations in a journal, as this will help you when you translate your work to animation.

Exercises for the Oral Character

After warming up thoroughly, spend some time looking at the oral star shown in Figure 5.5 so that you can remember the distorted shape of the star and lines of energy and blockages. Next, begin to walk around the space in your normal, everyday walk. Become aware of your body in space.

While you are walking, think about the energy in the oral character. There is very little energy but it is extending equally to all parts of your body. The star is long and lean, so think about standing up very tall and walking almost on your tiptoes. But you have so little energy it is difficult to hold yourself upright, so you tend to slump slightly forward. Also your energy level is so low that you need to lock your knees to keep upright. Figure 5.10 shows an actor adopting the oral character type.

Try with your arms and head, and even the movement of your legs, to reach and pull in energy from the outside world: suck energy from the objects and people around you. Because you have a weak block to all of your extremities, you will barely be able to lift your arms before they drop again.

Continue to move about the space with your long, loose, underdeveloped muscles, reaching to grab energy from the outside. Note how this makes you feel or if the movement brings up any moods or emotions.

As you continue to move in this body, speak your monologue. Note how your lack of energy and need to draw in energy affects your voice. Is it a whisper? Is it whiny? Does your voice trail off at the end of sentences? Are you nearly unable to complete a sentence?

Stop for a minute, breathe, stretch, and shake out. Although the oral is not a particularly stressful body, it is still important to get rid of it and spend some time in a more neutral place before continuing.

Now go back to your oral body and start once again to move around the space. Keeping in mind the physical star and psychic attitudes of the oral, begin to interact with props and objects. Note how you touch, handle, and work with things. Do you want to draw things into you? To touch them and hold them? Do some objects give you more energy than others?

If you have a group, you can now begin to interact with other members of the group. Continue moving around the space and working with objects, but add in that you must make some sort of contact with other people. Look at them or touch them. You may find with the oral body that you touch and lean on people a lot. Then speak with your partners. Notice how you sound and interact with other people. How does interacting with others in this body make you feel?

Finally, relax and let the body go. Stretch, shake, jump, and breathe. Discuss your experiences and/or write about them in your journal.

Exercises for the Psychopath Character

After warming up thoroughly, spend some time looking at the psychopath star, shown in Figure 5.6, so that you can remember the shape and lines of energy and blockages. Note in particular how distorted the shape of this star is, and how much of the core energy goes to the top half of the body. Next begin to walk around the space in your normal, everyday walk. Become aware of your body in space.

First, think about the flow of energy in the psychopath body. Notice how there is strong energy flowing up the torso and out your arms and to the top of your head. Extend your arms straight out to the sides. Let your spine align and pull you up toward the ceiling. Puff out your chest and take a walk. There is little energy traveling below your diaphragm, so as you walk with this big puffed-out body, your lower body stance and steps should be smaller and close together. Note how in Figure 5.11 the upper body is expansive, while the lower body is small and contracted due to lack of energy there.

Now as you continue to move in this body, speak your monologue. It is difficult to speak in this body because it is hard to take a deep full breath. Your breath will remain in your chest rather than flowing throughout your lower belly. You will probably find that the pitch of your voice drops very low. Notice how the voice coming from this body feels and sounds.

Figure 5.11

**Actor in psycho-
path body**

Stop for a minute, breathe, stretch, and shake out. Because this body is particularly stressful, take a good amount of time to stretch and relax your muscles before beginning again.

Now go back to your psychopath body and start once again to move around the space. Keeping in mind the physical star and psychic attitudes of the psychopath, begin to interact with props and objects. Note how you touch, handle, and work with things. You may find that you are not particularly graceful or at ease with smaller, delicate objects, and that you feel as if you're overwhelming the space you're in.

Continue moving around the space and working with objects, and now add in the other people. Look at them or touch them. Psychopaths do not have difficulty invading another person's personal space, so you might find you will approach others uncomfortably closely. Next, speak with your partners. Notice how you sound and interact with other people. How does this body make you feel? Powerful? Sexual? In control of those around you?

Finally, relax and let the character go. Stretch, shake, jump, and breathe. Discuss and write down your experiences. Take plenty of time to void this body and the overblown persona that so easily accompanies it.

Exercises for the Masochist Character

Figure 5.12

Actor in masochist body

Once again, warm up thoroughly and spend some time looking at the masochist star, shown in Figure 5.7, to help you recall the shape and lines of energy and blockages. Next, begin to walk around the space in your normal, everyday walk. Become aware of your body in space.

Begin by thinking about the huge amount of energy the masochist type contains, and how it radiates out through the arms and legs. Now, allow that energy to get squished into a little tiny ball, represented by the circular block in Figure 5.7, that you hold in the center of your body. There should be a knot of tension in your solar plexus as you hold all the energy deep inside you.

Next, allow your whole torso and limbs to help hold this energy in. Collapse at the sternum and bend slightly forward at the waist. Pull your neck forward, down, and in as if you are a turtle pulling its head into its shell. Next, tilt your pelvis forward so that your lower back flattens out. Think about trying to pull your anus and mouth into your shell. Now wrap your arms across the front of your body to protect yourself. Place one hand up to protect your mouth and let the other hand drop a bit to protect your midsection. You should be sort of wrapped up and hiding, similar to the actor shown in Figure 5.12.

Begin moving around the room in this body. Think about being submissive and pleasant on the outside and negative, hostile, and spiteful on the inside. Allow the hiding, bending, and pulling in to help disguise the negative inside. How does this make you feel?

As you continue to move in this body, speak your monologue. What happens to your voice when you are smiling on the outside and bitter on the inside? What kind of choices do you make in acting the text?

Stop for a minute, breathe, stretch, and shake out. This body, like the psychopath, is particularly stressful because of the extreme blocks, so take your time to stretch and relax your muscles. Be sure to roll your head and neck around to release the tension built up in that area. When you feel ready, continue.

Go back to your masochist body and start once again to move around the space. Keeping in mind the physical star and psychic attitudes of the masochist, begin to interact with props and objects. Note how you touch, handle, and work with things. You should find that your gestures are very small and that you keep objects tucked close to your body just as if you are pulling them into your shell with you. How does reaching out for something feel for this character?

Next, start to interact with other people as discussed for the other characters. Do you have trouble looking at people? Is your smile forced? What happens when you shake a hand? Notice how interaction makes you feel.

Let your character type go. Shake, rattle, and roll the tensions away. Discuss your discoveries with the group and write about them in your journal.

Exercises for the Rigid Character

Before you spend some time with this star, shown in Figure 5.8, warm up thoroughly. Now, look at the rigid star to help you recall the shape and lines of energy and blockages. Next, begin to walk around the space in your normal, everyday walk. Become aware of your body in space.

The rigid character is the most well integrated in body and appearance. Notice that there is a lot of energy in this character and that it travels freely out through the entire body. Therefore, think about sending energy out through your whole body, radiating from your center and out of your limbs. This should make your arms extend straight out to the sides (similar to the psychopath) and your legs spread wide (which is unique to this type). Your spine should be long and aligned so that energy can travel up and out the top of your head and down through the tip of your tailbone. Your body should be extended like a starfish.

Next, you need to put the blocks for this character in place. All of this energy that is traveling freely through the body is stopped by a double block at the exterior edge of the body from flowing into the external world. To achieve this effect, think of slightly tensing all of the muscles in your whole body. Unlike the blocks of the other characters, these tensions do not need to be as severe because the entire body is engaged in holding the energy in. Try to concentrate on radiating energy out to the outer edge of the body where it gets stuck and is unable to extend to the world around you. As shown in Figure 5.13, this character is very big but painfully stiff looking—or rigid.

Figure 5.13
Actor in rigid body

Now, take a walk. It should not be as painful to move about as a rigid as it is for the psychopath or masochist, but it is somewhat awkward. The character is stiff and rigid with pride, so he moves angularly and tightly, not bending the knees well, thus creating a rolling type of motion. You might sense that you are a robot or military officer. How does walking in this body make you feel? Big, strong, in control, and blown up with pride?

As you continue to move in this body, speak your monologue. How does all of this energy affect your voice? Does it deepen in pitch? Does it strengthen in power and volume? How does the sound of this voice make you feel?

Stop for a minute, breathe, stretch, and shake out. Relax and deflate. After you feel like you have balanced and adjusted, re-create the rigid type and start moving around the room in this body. Keep in mind the physical star and psychic attitudes of the rigid and begin to interact with props and objects. Note how you touch, handle, and work with things. Are your movements angular and somewhat staccato? Do you have difficulty performing precise movements or handling delicate objects?

Continue to move around the space and start to interact with others. Look at them or touch them, and then speak with them. Notice how you sound and interact with other people. Do you feel proud, as if you should be showing off? Do you feel as if you might have control or power over others? Perhaps you feel like a puffed-up peacock.

Now relax and let this body go. Stretch, shake, jump, and breathe. Discuss what your experience was like with your group and write about it in your journal.

Bioenergetics Animation Exercises

Now that you have a good sense of each character from having "inhabited" them using the acting exercises, let's put this knowledge to use in posing and moving characters to create these types in a virtual world. We will first create basic poses for a couple of the character types, and then use video footage to move our models around as that type of character. You can, of course, use your own model, or take one of the generic models from the DVD. See Chapter 4 for more on how to use the included model/rig setups.

Posing the Oral Character

Let's start with a low-energy type, the oral. As shown in Figure 5.10, the oral character is weak and needs energy, reaching out to suck it in from her surroundings. She stands on the balls of her feet, locking her knees and thrusting her head forward to pull as much energy as she can from the world around her. While we will not concentrate on faces in this chapter, you can, if you wish, create the slackened look of the oral character to complete the pose. Create a camera from which to pose your character, and import oralPose.jpg from the DVD to use as a guideline for the pose if you wish. Then match up the feet, hips, and head of the model as closely as you can to the actor in the image, as shown in Figure 5.14. You will need to move the image plane back to around 1,000, or move your model forward in order to see the model in front of the image plane. Figure 5.15 shows our model posed as the oral character.

To pose our model, we ended up using a little stretch on the legs to lengthen them out more than a real person could in order to exaggerate the effect of stretching upward. While the picture is from a front angle, we decided it looks best to push the oral character forward on her toes as much as possible so that, with her arms out front, she is almost tipping forward in her need to pull in energy from around her. We also tipped her pelvis back just a bit and her mid and upper back forward, to reinforce the idea of reaching, and moved her shoulders forward while at the same time keeping them low, helping generate the feeling that she lacks the energy to rise up on her own. Our version of the project, `oralPose.mb`, is on the accompanying DVD.

If you are using the included models (Genna and Marcel), which feature built-in character/ subcharacter hierarchies, you can have Maya automatically select the characters as you go. First, place the `autoCharacterSelection.mel` file in your home scripts directory (`~Autodesk/ maya/scripts` on your home directory), then copy the line of code from `ACSEnable.mel` into the Script Editor input pane and drag it up onto your shelf. When you start up Maya, simply click the ACSEnable button, and from then on, Maya will automatically select whichever subcharacter it needs based on what is selected in the scene. This makes selecting and keyframing characters far easier than having to remember to do so yourself.

See Chapter 4 for more information on importing images and using the book's included rigs in Autodesk Maya.

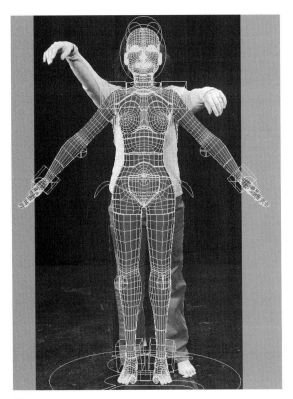

Figure 5.14

Importing the image for the oral type behind the generic model

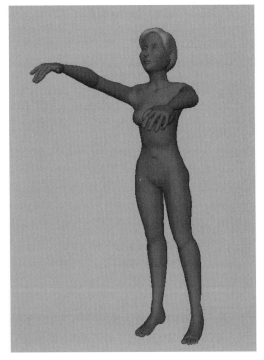

Figure 5.15

The model posed as an oral character type

Posing the Masochist Character

Whereas the oral type is lengthened and open, masochists are a good contrast, shrunken and closed off from the world around them. As Figure 5.12 shows, the masochist has great

energy internally but cuts it off from a world he fears might destroy him if he extends out into it. Therefore, posing the masochist is an exercise in wrapping the core of the body (the lower abdomen) with as many protective layers as possible. When you first match up your model to the actor's picture (masochistPose.jpg on the accompanying DVD), you will likely notice just how much taller the model is than the actor, as shown in Figure 5.16. This is due to the amount the actor has compressed himself, both vertically and horizontally, in order to protect himself and hold his energy inside.

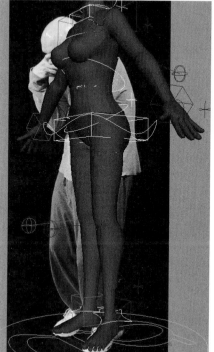

Figure 5.16

Placing the model in front of the masochist image

As you pose the character, keep thinking about compressing and compressing and compressing it into as much of a ball as is possible given the human shape. You can even exaggerate the actor's pose by tucking the pelvis in further and making the upper back into more of a C-shape than is already there. The squash-ability of the spine is particularly effective in exaggerating the compression of the character's torso area. We also stretched the arms just a little around the body, so they could protect even more of the abdomen and face. Raising and bringing in the shoulders also helps with the protective posture. The results are shown in Figure 5.17. Our version of the project, masochistPose.mb, is on the accompanying DVD.

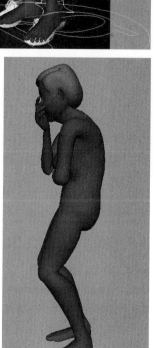

Figure 5.17

The model posed as a masochist character type

Experiment with posing for the other character types, using either the included images or photos of yourself or friends. Feel free to pose character types without references as well, but we recommend using a photo the first time you pose a new character type to help you get the nuances of each character.

Animating the Rigid Character

In addition to the posed characters, the DVD includes short clips of actors performing as each of the character types so that you can use the video files as reference in your work. Each clip starts with the actor in a neutral stance. They then start performing a character type in a pure, exaggerated fashion (at a higher intensity than you should see in real life); the actor then reduces the type back to a more realistic level, and even interacts with some props, performing tasks such as climbing a ladder, moving a book, or grabbing a lectern. By observing how each type moves and interacts with their environment, and especially by animating to this footage, you will get a better sense of how each of these types acts and interacts, giving you a solid basis from which to work as you animate other characters for your work.

Figure 5.18

The model placed in front of an actor performing the rigid character type

As an example, we will animate the rigid type in its most exaggerated form, where the actor looks a great deal like a starfish trying to walk on two of its legs. Figure 5.18 shows our model placed in front of the video footage (rigidExtremeShortSample.mov on the accompanying DVD), ready to pose and animate. Be sure to set your animation preferences to 30 fps (NTSC standard), create a new camera to look through, create an image plane, check the Image Sequence box in the image plane settings, and set your timeline to 144 frames; that way, the video footage just fits within the set number of frames. Now place your model in front of the character, zoom the camera, and move the model around until your model matches the size of the actor in the video sequence.

From this point, move to the first frame and pose the model to fit (or exaggerate) the actor's stance. Keep in mind that the rigid type has great energy, but it ends with double blocks at all the extremities; as you pose the model, try to imagine all that energy trapped within the skin of the character, imagine how that would feel, and try to make the character exude that radiating but blocked energy, using the video footage as reference. What subtle changes are there due to this energy and blockage? You might even notice on closer examination that the actor is just getting into character in the first several frames, and thus there is not as much of that highly blocked energy in these frames. Train your eye not only to see this, but to determine exactly why this is happening; then see if you can correct that lack of blockage in the early frames of the animation—you might want to run through all of the poses first, and then go back to fix the beginning after you have a better feel for the character's animation. The subtle nuances of character, as well as training your eye to see them, are crucial to getting these characters just right, especially if and when you have to animate a more subtle character where the movements are not as obvious as they are in this case.

The animation is a simple walk cycle, so we chose to key the down and passing positions, which come at approximately the following frames: 5, 20, 37, 50, 66, 80, 98, 111, 125, and 141. What is quite interesting about the footage is that the foot strikes (20, 50, 80, 111, and 141) occur almost exactly every 30 frames, which is very much in line with the rigid character type, who will not only pose rigidly but should move about in a rigid, metronomic manner. Also note that the body tends to stay very much over the feet as the

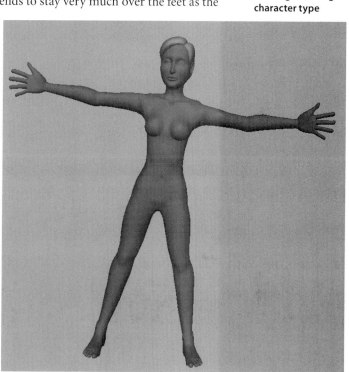

Figure 5.19

Walking as the rigid character type

actor walks, which keeps him balanced but awkward looking, since his hips don't anticipate the motion of the body. The hands in this walk also move along with their corresponding legs, rather than opposite, which is backward from a "normal" walk cycle.

After you have created the key poses, go back and fix any problem spots for the in-between frames. Because this is a rigid type, you will find that you don't need to add as many in-between corrections as normal, though the ones you do need are important, so it takes some work getting things just right. One subtlety that reveals itself as you go back over the video footage is the bobbing of the extended arms as the actor walks, due to the difficulty of holding arms straight out and walking. When you finish, you will have a character walk that looks a great deal like a starfish is walking around on two of its legs. Figure 5.19 shows a frame from the animation included on the DVD (`rigidExtremeWalk.mov`). You can also find the Maya file of this walk (`rigidAnimation.mb`) on the DVD.

Using Bioenergetics Types to Discover Animated Characters' Motivations and Physicality

Although this book is not about modeling, and thus we have used our generic characters for work here, it is obvious how much bioenergetics characteristics can affect the design and modeling stage of an animated character. If you enjoy modeling, you might wish to model (or even sketch) some characters based on these types, just to see what you come up with. If, on the other hand, you have previously built models, you should look at them and think of what type or combination of types would make up a character with the given physical attributes. Read the script and see how this character acts. Do their actions match what you would think of for the character type(s) you chose? If so, you are well on your way to using bioenergetics to reveal this character through posture, motion, and behavior. Don't forget that you are working to reveal emotion, character, and "soul" through physical presentation, so review what each bioenergetics character type reveals about the inner character and work backward from that, considering what the character's physical appearance and type reveal about their inner workings.

Next, take these observations and combine them with the acting exercises earlier in this chapter for that type (or types), adopting the character type *and* the physicality of the character. Once you think you have found the character, video yourself doing some actions similar to what the character does in your project, going for your objectives but with the character's blocks and problems working against you (or for you, if that turns out to be the case). You should find that your character becomes very real, with clear drives and emotions, by the time you finish this work. Take the video footage and work off that to begin animating the character to fit your project's needs. This character work can end up being fairly intense physically, so be sure to warm up first and cool down afterward.

Remember, animation is often much more starkly rendered than "real life" characters, so don't be afraid to really push one or more of these character types as you work with it. You can always dial back the performance later, but you might very well find you want to take it even further than you'd thought and that the character is more appealing (or frightening) due to the intensity of the bioenergetics character(s) you present in them.

CHAPTER 6

Using the Work of Michael Chekhov in Animation

This chapter was written by the authors and George Contini, Associate Professor in the Theatre & Film Studies Department at the University of Georgia.

In order for animated characters to appropriately convey a sense of realistic movement, they must portray a believable psychological depth. This chapter will explore the acting theories of Michael Chekhov, whose well-regarded technique is a psycho-physical exploration of character development and is utilized by actors to create distinct, full, and highly charged characters. At the time he was developing his techniques, Chekhov's work was deemed so controversial that his books were banned in Russia, yet now many actors look to this technique to grant their characters easily readable depth and truth. Chekhov's series of interrelated techniques thrive on a sense of the theatrical and a heightened sense of reality. For this reason, it is extremely helpful to character animators in creating detailed and one-of-a-kind characters. Chekhov's process, which uses atmospheres, qualities, actions, imaginary body, and psychological gesture, provides a simple and direct way for anyone to undertake the creation of a new character. This chapter discusses:

- A short Chekhov biography

- Physical awareness and the Four Brothers

- Incorporation for animators

- Working with atmospheres, qualities, and sensations

- Working with will/objective/psychological gesture

- Working with centers/imaginary body/grotesques

- Working with polarities

- Acting and animation exercises

Michael Chekhov

If you are a student of film, you might know Michael Chekhov, shown in Figure 6.1, as Ingrid Bergman's lovable psychoanalyst in Hitchcock's 1945 film *Spellbound* (a role for which he received an Oscar nomination for Best Supporting Actor). If you are a student of theater, you might be more familiar with his uncle, Anton Chekhov, the writer of such world classics as *The Seagull* and *The Cherry Orchard*. However, it is Michael's profound work as an acting teacher that is his true legacy. At one point, Chekhov's teaching technique was considered so controversial that he was banished from his homeland of Russia, and his writings were burned and banned. It is only in recent years that his illuminating theories have resurfaced and quickly become a hallmark of creating honest and theatrically engaging characters.

Born in Moscow in 1891, Michael was the son of Aleksander Chekhov, an amateur cartoonist, so he was exposed at a very early age to the concept of getting to the heart of a character in a few broad strokes. Michael went on to study under Constantin Stanislavski (see Chapter 3), who regarded him as one of his best students. At the Moscow Art

Figure 6.1

Drawing of Michael Chekhov by Cameron Bogue

Theatre, Chekhov made a name for himself in performing idiosyncratic, audacious, and memorable characters. Chekhov eventually felt too limited by Stanislavski's use of "affective memory" in performance and expanded his work on the connection between the actor's psychology and his physical state—the psychophysical connection. The two men's differences as performance theorists can be simply stated: Stanislavski worked using internal stimuli leading to external action, whereas Chekhov worked using external stimuli leading to internal emotional release. Although this is an overly simplified view of the multilayered philosophies of these two great teachers, it is helpful in showing animators how important Chekhov felt the external was for communicating the internal world of the character. In addition, Chekhov felt the actor had a personal stake in the creation of the character and was working to a point of inspiration where his or her creation would exercise its independence under the actor's guidance, almost as if the character were a semi-independent puppet under the control of the actor.

In quest of his goal of controlled independence of character, Chekhov used metaphoric image to drive his creations. His strong image work is most evident in his concepts of the imaginary body and the psychological gesture, both serving as backbones of his process. He was strongly influenced by Rudolf Steiner's work in eurhythmy, where sound and color are transformed into movement: sound becomes gesture and one form creates another. Chekhov also owes much to Vsevolod Meyerhold's work with biomechanics and the kinesthetics of performance. Chekhov took these ideas and layered them over an actor's performance, linking the expression of the body to archetypal psychological truth. In the same manner in which Steiner strove to discover the essence of a sound or color through the body, Chekhov used images and archetypes to develop essence of character.

After being banished from Russia in the 1920s, Chekhov roamed the world searching for an artistic home, crossing paths with artists spanning all disciplines, including Max Reinhardt in theater, Rudolf Laban in dance, and Wassily Kandinsky in painting. All of these artists, in their own ways, were in dialogue with the ideas of image, archetype, and symbol, and their abstraction into physical form. Eventually Chekhov connected with Deidre Hurst, who was creating a utopian community of artists and intellectuals at Dartington Hall in Devon, in the United Kingdom. During his time in Dartington Hall (1936–1939), Chekhov was able to further explore his groundbreaking ideas in a laboratory setting. At the beginning of World War II, Chekhov emigrated to the United States, and after spending the early 1940s working in New York, Chekhov moved to Los Angeles, where he made a career as a character actor in film. He also gave lessons and taught master classes for actors, including Yul Brynner, Marilyn Monroe, Clint Eastwood, Robert Stack, and Jack Palance. His book, *To the Actor*, was published in 1951, but was heavily edited. A revised and corrected edition was finally published in 2000, and it has since become a leading theoretical text for actors and directors. It's important to note that Chekhov's book was really the first "how-to manual" for actors. As opposed to Stanislavski's three books, which merely gave dense and detailed descriptions of what occurred in his classes, Chekhov provided practical exercises that encouraged actors to work on their own and immediately experience the joy of the creative act. His exercises lead the actor on a journey assimilating all arts and media so as to heighten their artistic sense and intuition. Chekhov died in 1955, having achieved what he hoped all his students would achieve: to be a singular artist in his own right.

Chekhov's voice is that of an experienced actor speaking to actors and directors using the terminology they can understand and immediately incorporate into their performance. Never satisfied with his first choice, he pushes the actor/animator to explore all sides of the psychological and physical complexities of their character. This journey requires an observant eye, a compassionate sense of humanity, and a practical under-standing of the realm of the physical. In the end, characters formed through Chekhov's process will resonate with audiences long after the performance is over.

The Chekhov Technique

The perennial question for animators is how to give an inanimate object or drawing the illusion of a body that possesses an incorporated soul and life force, and as Chekhov spe-cifically works "out to in," linking the semiotics of the physical to psychological truth, his technique is well suited to animation as well as acting. Leonardo da Vinci is quoted as having said, "The soul desires to live in the body… because without it, it can't act or feel." This quote clearly reminds the animator/actor that, whether dealing with real or gener-ated characters, they must strive to create the image of a character having free will that motivates their actions and choices.

Figure 6.2

Da Vinci's Vitruvian Man

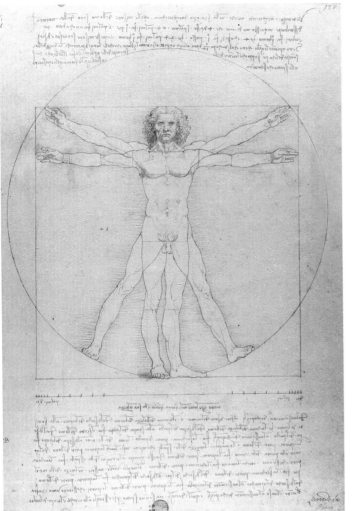

© LUC VIATOUR/GFDL-CC

It's interesting to note the various ways in which da Vinci's own work mirrors Chekhov's theories of character creation. Da Vinci explored what it meant to inhabit a body in this world, as exemplified by his famous "Vitruvian Man," shown in Figure 6.2, and his work was both scien-tific and metaphysical. In his ontological journey to understand what it means to be human, da Vinci combined all sciences, just as Michael Chekhov combined the arts and psychology to explore the metaphysical realm. Da Vinci's myriad areas of study have direct corollaries in Chekhov's work, which involves incorporation, composition, atmo-spheres, qualities of movement, sensations, psychological gesture, and imaginary body. Both Chekhov and da Vinci affirm what all actors and character animators are working toward: the discovery of the many facets of human behavior through artistic explora-tion of character.

Clearly, when working with live actors you have their brains and emotions to process this theoretical work into practice. But as an animator, you are the brains and emotions of the character you are creating. You are their life force and will. So, the question is, how do you bring your internal emotional and psychological world to the external world of your character? Interestingly, the answer with Chekhov is to clarify the external image and the internal will follow. Image is all. Understanding the semiotics of performance is crucial to the success of creating a truthful character that seems to act with believable intentionality behind it. Early film theorists like Sergei Eisenstein proved that an audience places emotion onto character depending on the context of the image. Eisenstein's use of image montage explicitly aided the audience's understanding of a character's psycho-physical state. Chekhov's work is also all about image and composition, which makes his techniques very well suited to the animator. Using Chekhov's developmental process, characters are sharply defined in space, while at the same time grounded in naturalistic psychology.

Physical Awareness and the Four Brothers

There are four tenets, often referred to as the Four Brothers, that provide a great base from which to operate when using any of the Chekhov techniques:

Feeling of ease Don't let there be any unnecessary tension in the body. Only use muscles needed to perform a task but always keep the entire body engaged in the action. The performance should not look like work.

Feeling of form Keep asking yourself, "What is the image I am making?" Is this image conveying what I mean to convey? Is what is physically occurring how I saw it in my head? Is the performance readable by the audience?

Feeling of beauty Quite simply, every movement you make is a little work of art. Enjoy that and allow that joy to lead you. For animators, who spend far more time on a given gesture than most actors would, this feeling of joy can get lost in the minutia of details of a motion; remember the joy and beauty of the poses and motion as you perform them.

Feeling of the whole You should always have an awareness of the group picture and your place in the larger artistic composition, whether you are a solo artist or working in a large studio to produce your work.

For actors, these are four manners of physical awareness that should operate constantly in any performance. For animators, these are excellent reminders of your artistic autonomy as you create the world of your characters. Keep these tenets in mind as you perform the exercises in this book, and indeed as you animate in general.

Incorporation

There cannot be a creation if there is no incorporation. Incorporation is the basic transformation that occurs when an artist seeks to take what is in his or her head and make it a physical, or corporeal, reality. The mantra of many a Chekhov teacher as they guide a student through creating a character is "See it. Be it." By this, the teacher is suggesting that the actor must first get the image clearly in their head, down to every minute detail, then, using their imagination, they place the image in the space before them and step into the image (like putting on a costume), allowing this new body to lead them. The actor has quite literally "taken on the body"—incorporated themselves into the character they imagined.

Transferring an insubstantial idea into physical reality is the heart of every creative act. Like actors, as animators you need to constantly expand your awareness of the details of human action and intention and increase the range of techniques and observations from which you can draw when it comes to realizing your vision. When you get to the point of the mechanics of creation, take the time to see your character and their actions fully; then create what you see. In other words, see it; then be it.

Atmospheres

Chekhov always began his work with atmospheres because he felt that from this foundation all other work sprang. Atmosphere is a constant in the physical world. No one can act in a void, even animated characters. So the first question you must ask yourself is, "What is the atmosphere the character has been placed in?" Another way to ask this might be, "What is the tone of the scene?" We deal with atmospheres every day and don't realize how every choice we make is based on our relationship to them. Is it hot? Is it depressing? Is it oppressive? Is it airy? Is it tense? Each of these different atmospheres will create a different physical response. In some ways related to Stanislavski's given circumstances (see Chapter 3), Chekhov's atmospheres are the environmental circumstances upon which character and action are layered. As animators you must be aware of the physical and emotional reactions that occur when bodies interact with atmospheres.

It is also important to note that a great deal of delicious dramatic conflict can be mined from the moment when two atmospheres collide. According to Chekhov, two atmospheres cannot be in the same place at once. One must always win. That competition is the heart of the interaction: who will win? Think of moments in your life when two atmospheres collided. The moment at a funeral when a honking carload of drunken teenagers drives by, disrupting the service. The moment when you run into an old friend years later in a different city, and you either connect, reforming the atmosphere you shared back in high school, or the current atmosphere wins out, and you feel estrangement from someone you used to be close to. The moment when you don't want to leave some place because the atmosphere is so strong: the warmth around a fireplace, the soft tranquility of a snowy evening. When reading over an animation script, consider where atmospheres might collide, and mark those places for later reference as you animate those scenes.

Qualities and Sensations

Chekhov defines the word "qualities" in two ways. The first is what he has designated archetypal qualities of movement, each related to one of the elements: molding (earth), flowing (water), flying (air), and radiating (fire). The second refers to the qualities an actor assigns to the execution of a particular movement: "I kissed her slowly, quickly, languidly, etc." Chekhov's use of "sensations" refers to the body's sense of relationship to the earth. There are three sensations: floating, falling, and balance. As an animator, you are already using qualities and sensations: every time you determine the manner in which your character moves, you are assigning a quality to it. The important factor for Chekhov is that by assigning the correct quality to a movement, he believes one unlocks the necessary emotional response for the actor/character, thereby realizing psychological depth via external poses, or signs (semiotics), and motions. It follows from Chekhov's observations that if an animator assigns the correct quality to a movement a character is performing, the audience will ascertain the desired emotional state that fits the context of the scene. Your practice with qualities and sensations will ensure that your characters truthfully inhabit the space around them and seem to be reacting with the appropriate emotional and psychological response to the atmosphere and actions around them.

In describing Chekhov's Four Qualities of Movement, it is best to remember that they are connected with the four elements. A body that moves with a molding quality leaves a firm imprint in the space around it: associated with earth, it is as if the air was clay and the body of the character molds into it. (Older people tend to be molders.) A body that moves with a flowing quality, associated with water, moves fluidly from position to position. A body moving with a flying quality is suspended and supported by the air but still moves strongly forward. (Think of a bird in flight.) Finally, with a radiating quality, associated with fire, the power of each movement extends beyond the physical and radiates outward into the environment.

Sensations (sometimes referred to as the Three Sisters) remind us of our connection with the earth and sky. Floating gives the sensation of weightlessness, like a balloon floating on the breeze. In animation, a floating character could be anything from a cloud creature to a duck that has swallowed a helium balloon and then floats around the room (before inevitably popping!). Falling is a strong sensation of weight being pulled downward; the moment at the top of a tall roller coaster when you begin to descend mimics this. Animated characters often fall in parts (e.g., a character's legs stretching downward as her face looks at the camera pathetically); thus as animators, we can draw out the moment of falling, increasing the anticipation for comic or dramatic effect. Balance informs us of how the character's body (live or animated) relates to its immediate surroundings. Is it balanced? Unbalanced? Does its center of gravity seem to be pulled toward a particular part of the body, or is it centered? As with floating and falling, balance can be exaggerated for wonderfully dramatic or comic effect in animation, for example, a character perhaps stretching far forward and off balance in anticipation of a kiss, only to be smacked across the face and fall down once his desire no longer holds him up.

Quality + Action = Emotion

If there is one part of the Chekhovian process that applies most to animators, it is the following equation: Quality + Action = Emotion, where Quality here is a physical quality (quickly, powerfully, etc.) rather than an emotional one (sad, happy, etc.).

For a live actor this formula represents the most practical application for exploring the psycho-physical connection. Rather than attempting to play an emotion (which can often come across as forced), it is better to perform an action required by the character with a specific quality (for which adverbs work very well) and the necessary emotion for the moment will follow. For example, consider two alternatives to create anger in a character: first, you can simply say, "I want an angry character here, who punches a wall." This, however, will likely generate a forced animation in which it is obvious the character is trying to present the emotional quality "anger," rather than psychological truth. Instead, using Chekhov's formula, you could say "I will have the character punch (action) forcefully (physical quality)." The combination of these terms creates anger: punch + forcefully = anger.

The animator is in an excellent position to take advantage of this formula, as it is image that holds the key for the animator to create a believable emotional moment for the character. Thinking as the character, you must execute the animation with a clear action and a strong quality that leads the viewer to place an emotional context around the action.

Will/Objective and the Psychological Gesture

Any animator wishing to create a believable character must understand what the character's objective is in the situation in which they are placed. As outlined in Chapter 3, Stanislavski created the grammar of acting that is still used today. The basis of his technique is that knowing a character's objective and motivation is the key to all that character's action.

In this regard, it is also important to identify the character's superobjective. What does the character want, not just in this moment, but also in life? What is its driving force that colors everything it does? Think of your own actions today. Your superobjective (or primary goal in life) might be to win the Oscar for Best Animation, which directly feeds into your present objective to read this book, and which fed into your action to go to the store and buy the book. According to this theory, no character action can be fully initiated unless you understand your character's superobjective or, as Chekhov often refers to it, "the will."

As previously mentioned, Chekhov continued exploring the work that Stanislavski began in reconciling the character's inner and outer lives. Chekhov's study of the psycho-physical relationship led him to consider that the actor must first abstractly explore the character's objective/will through physical image and then work toward internalizing that image, after which the image would subconsciously drive the actor's performance.

The concept of the psychological gesture (PG) gives the animator a practical and image-based manner in which to display a character's psychological motivations. Chekhov identified 11 basic archetypal gestures under which most human actions would fall. It is helpful to compare these to Rudolf Laban's qualities of movement (see Chapter 8). The archetypal gestures are open, close, push, pull, throw, embrace, lift, smash, penetrate, tear, and wring. In working with the psychological gesture, you begin by physicalizing the character's will through an external full body gesture that is fully formed and often looks pain-ful or grotesque. Then, you "veil," or soften, the gesture to some degree (depending on the style or genre of the piece as a whole), working toward incorporating it internally, the external becoming much more subtle or realistic. The memory of the gesture will then, according to Chekhov, activate the character's actions during performance. The psychological gesture becomes, in essence, a crys-tallization of the character's will. The obviousness of the gesture depends on the style of the piece being done; the more zany or stylized the piece, the less veiling occurs to hide the original gesture.

Figure 6.3

The miser's psychological gesture: wring

To a large extent, animation has made use of this technique already without recognizing the underlying formalism of what is being done. Characters are often realized possessing a physical outward trait that reflects their inner life.

An excellent example for both animators and actors is seen in the following figures depict-ing actors undertaking the role of a Scrooge-like miser. An actor undertaking that role might determine that the miser's psychological gesture is wring, because he wrings every last dime out of those around him. The actor would develop a full-body image that suggests wring, as shown in Figure 6.3.

If the actor is doing a broad farcical comedy, a style that calls for highly theatricalized physicality, he might adapt the character body in Figure 6.4 for his miser. Note the exaggerated hunched shoulders, closed body posture, and obvious hand wringing.

If the actor were playing in a more realistic drama, he would mute the physicalization to something more naturalistic, like that shown in Figure 6.5. Perhaps the PG becomes subdued enough that it only remains in the wringing of hands.

Figure 6.4

A farcical miser using the wring gesture

Figure 6.5

A realistic miser using the wring gesture

If the actor was in a movie, a medium where the camera sees all and magnifies it, he might choose to only use the PG as an internal impulse, with barely noticeable outward manifestation, as shown in Figure 6.6.

Inspiration for a character's psychological gesture can come from anything or anywhere. The gesture is about an external image signaling a character's internal world, so it could be taken from a gesture the character performs while doing their job (the mechanical pulling of a handle on an adding machine is mirrored in the bobbing of their head) or the habits of an animal (the tearing of a lion's claw is reflected in the character's savage grasp), or it can be based on a prop they use (the invasive penetration that occurs when a character spies through a telescope might be reinforced by the character having ever-popping eyes). There are no true rules for psychological gesture; its use is very flexible.

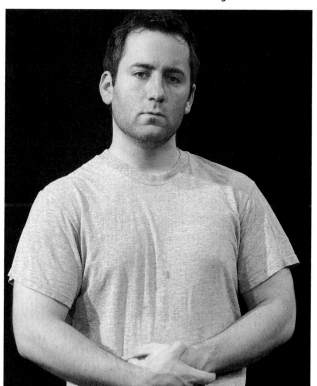

Figure 6.6

A cinematic miser using the wring gesture

Many cartoons already use PG in the broadest manner. Think of the classic Tex Avery wolf, whose eyes bulge out of his head when he sees a curvaceous woman. The wolf's eyes "penetrate" in a suggestive yet inoffensively sexual manner. A great example of PG using objects to define character is seen in Disney's *Beauty and the Beast,* in which the house staff at the Beast's castle have all been magically transformed into objects that suggest their personalities. Mrs. Potts, the cook, takes the form of a teapot. Her son Chip is a small cup with a chip in its rim. Cogsworth, the meticulous valet, is seen as an over-wound clock, his mustache becoming the hands on the clock. These are terrific images that reflect both their characters' positions in the story and a key to their internal life. (They are also great examples of the grotesque, to be discussed in the next section.)

Sometimes a group of characters might all possess the same psychological gesture. The Orcs in *Lord of the Rings*, for example, are all of one mind and body, created to destroy. Thus, "smash" seems most appropriate to describe their collective PG. Indeed, an animator could even regard any composition created with these characters as somehow displaying this communal PG. A long shot showing an army of Orcs could reflect one large destructive psychological gesture, while inserted close-up shots show the individual PGs of each Orc.

In short, using the PG is an effective and easy way to transform a character in your head or on the page into a breathing person. Again, harking back to Chekhov's cartoonist father, the psychological gesture is great for creating character in big broad strokes. Figures 6.7, 6.8, 6.9, 6.10, 6.11, and 6.12 show actors creating each of the archetypal psychological gestures; we will work on creating animated characters using some of these gestures later in the chapter.

Figure 6.7

The push (left) and pull (right) psychological gestures

Figure 6.8

The open (left) and close (right) psychological gestures

Figure 6.9

The lift (left) and smash (right) psychological gestures

Figure 6.10

The tear (left) and penetrate (right) psychological gestures

Figure 6.11

The wring (left) and embrace (right) psychological gestures

Figure 6.12

The throw psychological gesture

Centers, Imaginary Body, and Grotesques

Once you have essentially built a character from the ground up using atmospheres, qualities, sensations, actions, and psychological gesture, you are ready to put an "imaginary body" over the top of the underlying psychology. The Chekhovian approach to creating the imaginary body involves the identification of the character's center and the use of a concept Chekhov terms the grotesque. The center is that part of the body from which all impulses to move originate. Chekhov identifies three centers, which correlate directly with the areas that drive humans: their thoughts, their emotions, and their will. The head is the thinking center. For a character driven by thinking, the impulse to act comes from the character's thoughts, or head. The chest is the feeling center. For a character driven by feelings, the impulse to act comes from the character's emotions, or chest. The groin is the will center. For a character driven by will, the impulse to act comes from basic human needs (sex, hunger, survival, etc.), which is centered in the groin. Consider those types of people who you would call thoughtful, emotional, and willful. Where do their actions seem to stem from? Consider the brainy professor who seems to be led by her nose. Consider the mooning lover whose heaving chest seems to guide his movement. Consider the cowboy in a high noon shootout who stands firmly, legs spread, slightly hunched, hands at groin level. What about other character types you have seen in theater, film, and animation? Can you spot where their motion comes from, and is their physical center related to the center of their being?

Although Chekhov hoped that actors could reach a psycho-physical unity for themselves, where all three centers are working together (a sort of "neutral" state), it is important to note that interesting characters usually do not have such an accord. They carry their center in unusual and idiosyncratic places. What happens if your character carries their center in their shoulder? Eyes? Buttocks? How does shifting the place where the impulse to move comes from affect the physicalization of the character? How does this alteration affect their perceived psychological motivations?

The imaginary body, which is based heavily on imagery, is another crucial aspect of the Chekhov technique. The character's body must be fully seen in the actor's (or animator's) mind before being able to be incorporated into the actor's body. Often, in order to fully incorporate the body, it is necessary for the actor to maximize the manner in which the body, takes on the image. Some might call this "overacting" or "very broad" acting, and for stylized animation, this over-the-top action might be the place to stop, rather than the place to start. Chekhov refers to the full-on physical incarnation of an imaginary body as the *grotesque*, a necessary part of the process of finding a particular character. To fully feel the image in his or her mind, the actor must take it to its extreme, then, little by little, "veil" the grotesque until it becomes more natural and second nature, fitting within the world of the play or movie they are acting in. As might be expected, animators already use the grotesque. Disney's Seven Dwarves are an excellent example of thinly veiled grotesques, where each of the dwarves' physical characteristics directly correspond to their names and personalities.

A wonderful way to get to the heart of the grotesque is to use abstract images that, ostensibly, have no obvious relationship to the character's psychology, but instead serve to offer strong visuals. A typical way to explore this is after visualizing the character in the mind's eye, the actor is then asked to describe the imaginary body in abstract terms. For example, the actor might say, "Her head is like a stalk of celery, her eyes are red marbles, her torso is a washing machine, her legs are springs." The actor then takes on these physical characteristics as fully as she is physically able to, stretching her face long, widening her eyes, churning her torso, and bouncing up and down on her legs. In performing these actions, sound most likely will begin to come from this body, and a voice will be found for the character.

As animators, you are used to using such anthropomorphism with inanimate objects. You know that if you had to make a "brave little toaster" walk, it would involve the realities of what a toaster is shaped like, and it would move accordingly, but with human characteristics layered atop the physical limitations of a walking toaster. In taking on a grotesque, the actor is applying the abstraction of imagery to their whole body as they discover traits of their character. The early Max Fleischer cartoons like Koko the Clown, Fritz the Dog, and Betty Boop are great lessons in this style of character creation.

In Figure 6.13, you see one actor's physical incorporation of a grotesque for the character of Uncle McBuck in Augusto Boal's play, *The Misadventures of Uncle McBuck*. The far left shows an over-the-top version of the character. The middle version shows how this grotesque becomes more veiled as the character is realized. Finally, the far-right version shows how the grotesque can become very veiled, leaving only slight suggestions of the original abstract grotesque in a realistic embodiment of the character.

Figure 6.13

A fully realized grotesque for Uncle McBuck (left); turning the grotesque into a more veiled state (middle); a highly veiled grotesque for a realistic character (right)

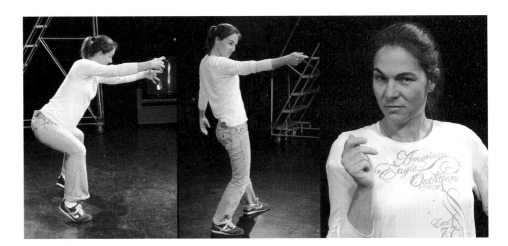

Polarities

Characters change. That is their nature. They are human—or in animation they are at the least anthropomorphic. They move forward in life and learn from mistakes—or perhaps fail in their attempts to learn. To create a fully realized character, you must take into consideration the character's arc, or journey, in a given piece, and the transformation involved. Acts of violent physical transformation occur frequently in animation. Toads become princes, princesses become crones, and people die and become ghosts. Animation is built on getting a character from point A to point B, sometimes in an obvious way, other times in more subtle ones.

Chekhov realized that human beings aren't static. A character may begin a play with the psychological gesture of push, but circumstances in the dramatic action might lead the character to undergo a psychological change so that by the time the curtain falls their PG becomes pull. At heart, most drama, whether on stage or on screen, is about such change, and the audience comes to the theater to see these transformations. It is also true that characters can often be "two faced," or have a hidden side, so they can be both open and closed, depending on the situation. (Nowhere is this polarity more obvious than in the *Batman* character Two-Face, who, quite literally, has two opposing faces.) This is being human. There is no black without white. We are naturally at any given moment a combination of forces. Chekhov allows the actor to explore this tension through his concept of polarities.

Through a physical exploration of a given character's two extremes and the transformation that must occur to get from one to the other, we can learn a lot about the manner in which that character and its body inhabits and manipulates space. For animators, it is crucial to clearly define an animated character's movement and motivation while getting from one state to another. In keeping with the Four Brothers' feeling of the whole, it should be remembered that each movement from point A to point B has a little of the whole movement in it. For example, there is always a remnant of push in pull, and vice versa, so a character journeying from A to B already has a little of B in him at the beginning, and has something of A remaining even at the end. Polarities are inherent in psychological gesture work, and most are polar opposites: open versus close, pull versus push, embrace versus throw, lift versus smash, penetrate versus tear. Your job as an animator is to flesh out each PG at any given moment, even (and especially) when the gestures are in competition with one another. This ability to work with and within polarities reinforces the character's essential qualities as well as his character arc, or journey throughout the piece.

Exercises Using the Michael Chekhov Technique

There is a great deal to digest when considering Michael Chekhov's acting techniques, and there is no better way to get a feel for his physical work than to try it out for yourself. This section puts the theory we have outlined into practice. As always, the more fully you participate in the exercises, the more you will get out of them, and the better you will understand the concepts both mentally and physically.

To start with, let's do a basic incorporation exercise. After warming up (see Chapter 1), find a relaxed position and imagine yourself performing any action (something simple, like picking up a glass, is better to start with). Close your eyes and see it clearly. Note every detail in the execution of this action. How does your weight shift? Which muscles tense? How are all parts of your body engaged? Then open your eyes and actually perform the action as you saw it in your head. Is it exactly as you saw it? If not, close your eyes and recapture the image and note what you missed. Continue visualizing and then performing this action until you feel you have successfully captured in your body what you saw in your mind's eye. Note down in your journal what steps it took to perfect your psycho-physical match.

Atmospheres

To begin exploring atmospheres, let's do an atmosphere scavenger hunt. Grab your acting journal, and take a half-hour stroll through your neighborhood, or some trafficked and interesting area of your city. Discover the varied atmospheres you come upon. What defines the atmosphere? How do people act within it? How does it affect you? What is your emotional or physical response to it? How do you enter or leave it? How is that liminal moment of transition between atmospheres defined? How can you tell the atmosphere has changed? Note down your thoughts in your journal as you go while they are fresh in your mind.

When you return home, make a list of all the different atmospheres you discovered on your scavenger hunt. Then take the time to imagine you are entering each of the atmospheres. It might help to write the atmospheres on separate pieces of paper and tape them about the room, creating the atmosphere for a particular area. Then slowly walk into that area and allow the atmosphere to affect you. Choose a simple task (tying your shoe, hammering a nail), and perform this simple task in each imagined atmosphere. Take note of what changes occur in the manner in which you do your task in each atmosphere. Does the tempo change? The duration? The intent? What sorts of images occur in your mind? Note down your thoughts in your journal.

Now choose a simple phrase, like "Hello, how are you?," "I love you," or "I hate you." Again, move about the room and enter each of the atmospheres you listed and say the line. How does this particular atmosphere affect the way you say your line? Is it louder? Softer? Faster? Does the motivation behind saying it change? What images flash through your mind? Be sure not to rush this exercise, and don't preplan how you will react to an atmosphere. The key is to let the atmosphere affect you and not to force a response. Try it with the different atmospheres you found, and record your thoughts in your journal.

Centers

To explore the concept of centers, first take some time to explore your own sense of center. Videotape yourself walking around the room, just as yourself. Watch the tape and try to determine your personal center. Now tape yourself again, this time playing with placing your center in different parts of your body. How does each new center (like your right knee or your left buttock) affect your manner of movement, or your sense of balance? Do you have emotional responses to different centers?

Now go on a center scavenger hunt. Walk around the neighborhood, or your favorite busy place, and take note of how different people lead with varied centers. What sort of judgments do you make about them and their character based on their center? What sort of education, class, money, or personality do you guess each person has, based on their center? How will their different centers affect the way they are perceived in society? Do you see behavior in these people that is consistent with the center you have identified? Take notes in your journal for later consultation.

Qualities and Sensations

Let's work with Chekhov's qualities and sensations next. Take a stroll and identify the different people you see with one of the qualities/sensations of movement discussed earlier. Do they mold? Flow? Fly? Radiate? Is their energy falling, floating, balanced, unbalanced? Do they possess a combination of them? For example, a waitress hurriedly serving customers might seem to flow easily from table to table, but her specific gestures of setting down full glasses and plates with care might suddenly mold. Note down your thoughts in your journal.

Get an actor and a camera. (Hint: Where you find one, you'll most likely find the other.) Play with the concepts of qualities and sensations. Choose a series of simple actions that a character must do, like getting dressed or eating dinner. Then ask the actor to perform them using each of the qualities and sensations. Note the many variations in which the same gestures are created. Which are more precise? Which are more pleasant to watch? What sort of emotional response do you, the viewer, have to them? What sort of images, types of people, situations come to mind? You can then set up the camera and record yourself performing some action with the given qualities and sensations. Are you as precise as the actor was? How does it feel to perform the action(s) with qualities rather than watch? How does it look to see the recording of yourself versus what you thought you looked like? What insights does it give you to do the exercise physically rather than direct it? Note down your thoughts in your journal.

For one final (and useful!) exercise, spend an hour doing all your chores around the house using qualities and sensations. A flyer, for example is going to vacuum, make a bed, and wash windows very differently than a molder.

Quality + Action = Emotion

To explore how action plus quality creates readable emotion, try the following: use simple gestures to create a series of equations and discover their outcome. For instance, start with a nice big yawn and full-body stretch (hey, you deserve it, and it will feel really good). The yawn is your action. Now add a series of qualities as you perform that action. Always take a moment to come back to a neutral position before undertaking the next quality. Here are a few examples you may want to try:

- Yawn/Stretch + Languidly = ?
- Yawn/Stretch + Erotically = ?
- Yawn/Stretch + Electrically = ?
- Yawn/Stretch + Cautiously = ?
- Yawn/Stretch + Painfully =?

After performing each movement, write down any emotional responses, memories, or images that may have come to mind. You will find that the body will unlock any emotion it needs if the proper stimulus is applied.

Psychological Gesture

As a warm-up to using psychological gesture, you must first also warm up the psychophysical connection. After doing some warm-up exercises (see Chapter 1), begin by moving about your room in large, abstract movements. Find a movement you enjoy doing and continue doing it for a few moments. As you perform this movement, become aware of your thoughts or emotions. If your thoughts or emotions change, change whatever motion you are doing to match the new emotion or thought. If after adapting this new movement your thoughts or feelings change again, change the movement again. Continue doing this for a few minutes as you become aware of the definite connection between your mind and your body.

Take the time to try out each of the psychological gestures as pictured in Figures 6.7 to 6.12. To effectively perform a gesture, adapt a neutral stance, take a breath, and with the exhale, involving as much of your body as you can, enact the gesture. Psychological gestures are not dormant statues; they are meant to be moving and connected to the breath. Remember to always return to a neutral stance before executing the next PG. As you perform each PG in its abstract form, take note of emotions, images, memories, or scenarios that might come to your mind, and write them down in your journal when you are finished.

After becoming familiar with the archetypal physical gestures, you can test how using a given PG affects line readings. Warm up using exercises from Chapter 1, then select a phrase like "I don't believe it," and simply say the line as neutrally as you can. Now say the same simple phrase while performing a gesture, such as wring. What happens to your emotional state when you say the line while contracted in the wring gesture versus, say, the open gesture? How does a given PG and the physicality of achieving that position affect how the line is said? What is the tempo of the line; what is its intent? What images or scenarios come to mind? Try saying the line over with different PGs and see how each affects the line reading in different ways. Note down your observations in your journal.

To begin to place psychological gestures on situations, think back to your superobjective of winning the Oscar for Best Animated Film. What would your PG be? Is it your will to be glorified? Exalted? Lionized? Is lift your PG? Maybe open? Perhaps embrace? Consider how character plus environment (qualities plus atmospheres) shapes which PG you select for this superobjective. Alternatively, how differently would you deliver your Oscar acceptance speech using an open gesture versus a smash one?

Next, use your imagination to create PGs for everyone you come into contact with. First determine what you think their superobjective in life is, and then apply an appropriate PG. Do it for people you know at work or home, characters from movies, or people on the street. Allow your observational skills to kick-start your imagination, and be sure to take notes concerning what you discover.

The Grotesque

To explore the concept of Chekhov's grotesque, let's use a fun exercise meant to free you from the constraints of reality and begin creating new characters simply and effectively. Find a picture of someone who has very defining physical or facial traits. Maybe it's your Aunt Maude who bears a striking resemblance to her Bassett hound; maybe it's a photo from a newspaper article about a soldier in wartime or an obituary photo of a leading corporate businessman. Spend some time looking at the picture and noting all the details of the face and body. Where are the wrinkles? How wide are the eyes? Is their weight shifted to one side? Is the nose wide or flat or pointed? What is the shape of the head—oval? Triangular? Square?

Now, as before in the incorporation exercise, get the image fully in your mind's eye, and then transfer it onto your own face and body. Keep checking the photo to be sure that you have applied all the characteristics. It can be helpful to have someone watch you do this and coach you to make sure you are not forgetting anything.

Once you have incorporated all the traits from the photo, take a breath, and overexaggerate them all to the point of grotesque—almost like a caricature you might see drawn at a twisted carnival. This creation will not be pretty and that's fine: the point is to feel your muscles responding to a new body. Once you feel comfortable in this grotesque, begin to move about the room, letting this body lead you. Eventually, allow sound to emerge from the body. Don't worry about the noise you make: the sound can be simple, inarticulate noise. Let this sound eventually connect with your breathing and let a voice emerge. Again, don't try to second-guess what type of voice will come based on the picture but allow the muscular contractions and sense of the character create the voice for you. As you move about the room, take note of emotions that seem to fill this "creature" and the atmosphere it seems to live in.

It may seem that you have essentially created a Frankenstein monster, and the initial movement may seem jerky and uncontrollable. At this point it often serves to apply the veil: gradually, start to soften the elements of this character's body and face and voice until it begins to feel more "natural." Don't let go of any of the idiosyncratic behavior that makes this character original—just blur the lines and smooth out the rough areas. You have now created a totally new human being without writing or drawing a thing.

The inspiration for creating a grotesque can be drawn from anything. Photos are a great place to start, but inanimate objects—things from nature, animals, insects, and so forth—are all fodder for character inspiration.

Polarities

To explore the concept of polarities, choose two polar-opposite PGs, such as open and close, and practice moving from one to the other. If you have a video camera, record yourself so you can go back and watch yourself change from one PG to the other. As you make the transition, continue to ask yourself, "At this moment how much am I going away from my starting position and how much am I moving to my ending position?" For example, how much throw is left halfway to embrace? Be aware of the subtle changes in your body needed to achieve the alteration. Play with adding a quality of movement to the transformation. Change in a molding manner, or in a flowing manner. What happens to the image?

Now think of the transformation as a tiny play: divide the change into a three-act structure. What is the movement's exposition, conflict, and climax? As you transform from one polarity to the other, what insight into the character is gained? How could you slow this transition down so that it takes the full length of a dramatic piece to happen? Be sure to take notes concerning your discoveries, and then try another pair of opposites and discover what new insights the transition between these two PGs brings to your understanding of polarities.

Using the Michael Chekhov Technique in Animation

Now that you have had the chance to incorporate many of Chekhov's techniques within your own physical body, you can transfer this visceral knowledge to use on a virtual character. As with other techniques covered in this book, these projects are merely a start into exploring Chekhov's techniques. Therefore, after doing these example exercises, you should apply what you learn here to something you are currently working on, using incorporation, psychological gesture, and other techniques to imbue your character(s) with heightened physicality and action that lead to clearly readable emotion and intent.

Psychological Gesture and Polarities

Let's begin by creating two polar opposite psychological gestures, and then animate the transition between them using one of Chekhov's qualities. By using and/or exaggerating photos of our actors in the PGs, we can start with a solid foundation and then build an animation atop this foundation as we wish. We have chosen push and pull for our example, as shown in Figures 6.14 and 6.15, but you can choose two others if you wish; just be sure they are polar opposites, like lift and smash, or open and close. From the accompanying DVD, load one of the psychological gestures from the included complete set into your animation package, and use it as a background element for a new camera view, naming it something like pushCam. (See Chapter 4 for more on how to do this in Maya.) As always, since the models are so big, be sure the far clipping plane is set large (like 10,000 in Maya) so both image and model appear in the view.

Figure 6.14

The push psychological gesture

Figure 6.15

The pull psychological gesture

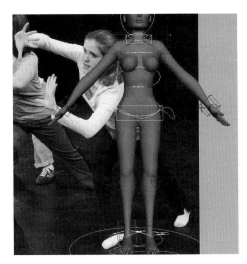

Figure 6.16

Importing the model into your scene

Figure 6.17

Creating the second camera view for the scene (from the Perspective camera's viewpoint)

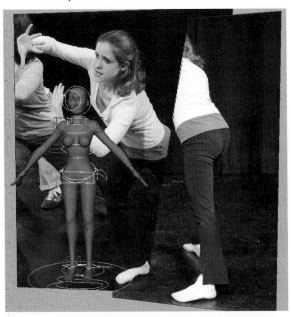

With the first image loaded, go to frame 1 in your animation timeline, and import either one of your models or one of the generic models included on the DVD. Figure 6.16 shows the Genna model in front of the actor creating the push PG. Once you have placed the model, create a second camera (name it something like **pullCam**), add the second image, and rotate the camera around until it is correctly positioned versus the first camera and image; this is made somewhat challenging by the differing angles of the two pictures but can be done, as shown in Figure 6.17. Note that when the position transition from push to pull is made, the easiest pivot point (for our example pictures) will be the left foot, so do a rough adjustment of the left foot in the pushCam view, then match that foot up in the second, pullCam image, as shown in Figure 6.18. If you are using other images, examine them to consider how the character will transition between the images, and then match the views accordingly. Now lock both camera angles so you don't accidentally change those views; then go back to the first view (pushCam) and adjust your model until it matches—or exaggerates—the pose the actor is creating, paying careful attention to posture, balance, and even facial expression if you wish. (See the sidebar "Using the Facial Animation Rig on the Included Models" in this chapter for more on using the facial animation system with the included rigs.) If you do facial animation, be sure to keyframe the facial poses so that they transition as well.

If you are using Maya, you can use the Attribute Editor for each camera's image plane to either enable or disable the visibility of the image plane for other camera views, which cleans up the scene when you are working with multiple image planes. Open the Attribute Editor with a camera selected, choose the imagePlane tab, and under Image Plane Attributes, select the Looking Through Camera radio button next to Display, as shown in Figure 6.19.

When you have finished posing the model in the first pose, keyframe all the model's elements, and then go forward to a later frame that you think will provide about the right amount of time for transition from one pose to another (we chose 4 seconds) and set your timeline there. You can always adjust this timing later; for now just choose something that feels about right. If you are using the included models, be sure to keyframe the character and subcharacter sets for the model.

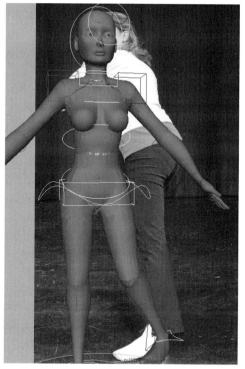

Figure 6.18

Matching the pivot point of the model to the actor's left foot

Figure 6.19

Setting the camera attributes to only show the background plane when looking through that camera

If you are using the included models (Genna and Marcel), which include built-in character/subcharacter hierarchies, you can have Maya automatically select the characters as you go. First, place the autoCharacterSelection.mel file in your home scripts directory (~Autodesk/maya/scripts on your home directory). Then copy the line of code from ACSEnable.mel into the Script Editor input pane, and drag it up onto your shelf. When you start Maya, simply click the ACSEnable button, and from then on, Maya will automatically select whichever subcharacter it needs based on what is selected in the scene. This makes selecting and keyframing characters far easier than having to remember to do so yourself.

Once complete, you will have two polar-opposite poses some temporal distance apart from one another. If you play back your animation now, you will see a transition, but it will look linear and awkward, without defining events in between the two key poses. First, save your scene at this state so you can go back to it later. Now consider one of the four archetypal qualities—molding, flowing, flying, and radiating—or possibly a sensation instead—floating, falling, and balance. For our example, we chose a flowing quality with a balanced sensation, where the character maintains balance throughout the motion, as it seemed to fit the poses well. Of course you can play against type and perform the motion with a flying quality and a falling sensation; do whatever strikes you as interesting or befitting your two poses. Once you have completed a roughed-out blocking of the animation, play it back and consider the timing of the animation. Do you want it to be quick, slow, languid, energized, or something else entirely? The archetypal qualities, the sensation, and the timing qualities will all interrelate to create the final motion. We ended up using "smoothly" as our motion quality, so the character proceeds between polarities smoothly, with a flowing quality and balanced sensation. If you find that your original timing is off, select all your keyframes and scale them up or down to get better timing for the motion. Figure 6.20 shows our model midway through her motion between polar-opposite psychological gestures; a playblast of this animation is on the DVD as pushPullPolarities.mov. The Maya file, pushPullPolarities.mb, is also on the DVD for your reference.

Figure 6.20

Changing from push to pull psychological gestures

Once you are happy with your first combination of quality and sensation, go back to your saved file and animate the character between poses again, this time using something very different for both quality and sensation. As you can easily see, even given the same starting and ending poses, Chekhov's techniques provide many, many ways to get from one to the other. Trying different ways of getting from push to pull (or whatever you choose) can help you understand the fundamental importance of quality, timing, and sensation to animation work. Try some other polarities, either using the images on the DVD or creating them yourself, and play with qualities and sensations for these as well. How does it look to transition between other polarities but with the same qualities and sensations you used for the push-pull poses? Do some qualities and sensations seem more natural for some polarities? Consider these and other matters as you continue exploring polarities and psychological gesture.

USING THE FACIAL ANIMATION RIG ON THE INCLUDED MODELS

The Genna and Marcel models, whose body rigs were discussed in the sidebar "Using the Included Maya Rigs for Body Animation" in Chapter 4, also include high-level facial rigs based on the Facial Action Coding System (FACS) and Maya's excellent blend shape implementation. If you are using the models for your work, this sidebar provides basic instructions on how to use this powerful yet relatively simple-to-use facial setup.

FACS was developed by Paul Ekman and others in the mid-1970s and was updated in 2002 as a means to code every possible human facial action based on musculoskeletal studies of people from across different racial and societal backgrounds. Ekman and his colleagues discovered that there are, in fact, a limited number of facial distortions, which they termed action units (AUs), that humans can produce, and that a combination of these AUs produces every possible facial pose. For our purposes, the import of these studies is that if you construct a series of blend shapes with all the relevant AUs (some, like head turns, are not included because they can be animated via the body rig), then you can re-create any human facial pose, and thus arrive at any emotion or other quality you wish.

Each of the two included rigs contains a set of blend shapes, each target shape of which is one of the AUs, often split into "left" and "right" for further control. AU 1, for example, is "inner eyebrow arch," and our rigs have a left and right version of this AU. Furthermore, the blend shape targets are labeled with both AU number and the feature distortion, for example, `InBrowRaiseLeft_AU01_LInBrRaise`, which makes it easier for you as an animator to know what the AU does (and what it is numbered, in case you want to do further research into that particular AU).

To facilitate control over such a large number of blendshapes, we devised a control scheme, shown in the following graphic, that places the controls on a set of NURBS curves that mimic the basic shape of a face. Most controls only operate in one direction (either up-down or side-to-side); controls that allow two axes of motion have an underscore between the controls. Thus `LCheekPuff` only allows motion on the X axis, whereas `RLipPuller_Depressor` allows motion in both X and Y, each axis providing a different control. In general, the controls are named and placed such that you should have a basic idea of what they do by looking at the "face" and reading the name of the control when selected. If a control doesn't make immediate sense, simply move it and see what happens.

(Continues)

USING THE FACIAL ANIMATION RIG ON THE INCLUDED MODELS *(Continued)*

To use the FACS AUs included on the DVD you should have the auto character selection script working (see the previous note). After that, simply move the facial controls until you are satisfied with the look at that given frame; then press the "s" key to keyframe the character controls on that frame. Then move to a different frame, adjust the controls, and keyframe the face at the new frame, continuing as you animate the model's face.

Creating a Virtual Grotesque

Now that you have created and animated between two (or more) psychological gestures, let's work with Chekhov's concept of the grotesque, constructing a virtual, rather than physical grotesque from an image at hand. First, select any image that provides an imagistic and emotional response in you. We are including on the DVD the image we used, shown in Figure 6.21, but if this image doesn't resonate with you, look through your old photos, in magazines, or online until you find something that provides a good starting point for you. Remember that you will not directly copy this image onto your model but will instead use it as inspiration for posing and distorting your model.

Now, just as in the acting exercise on grotesques in the previous section, concentrate on this (or your own) picture: write down all the details you see, as well as the emotional and imaginative responses that you feel coming from the image. The image we have chosen provides some humor as well as some pathos and is already "grotesque" in a sense, as the person (one of the authors' brother) is covered in a cream pie and trying to wipe the filling out of his eyes, giving him a mask-like quality. Further details we note are that the subject's spiky hair is accentuated due to the pie filling; the filling is very thick, which is especially notable around the eyes and on the cardboard "bib"; that it's bright and sunny outside; that the subject's arms are out and up, in something like a tear or even embrace PG; that his fingers pressing into his eyes could be a penetrate PG; and that, given that the subject is wearing a piece of cardboard around his neck, this was likely a staged event. Emotionally we react with some resignation, but also frustration or even anger in noting the way his head is down and the way the eyes look. Imagistically, the pie filling on the subject's face makes us think of the Joker or even Batman for some reason; the cardboard creates

Figure 6.21

A photograph from which to build a virtual grotesque

a shield but also a weight around the subject's neck, pulling him forward; we even get a sense of "coldness," as the pie filling is white like snow, though it's obviously summer when the photo was taken. You will almost certainly have other reactions, especially if you use your own image, but even if you look at our image.

Following the acting exercise again, fix the image that you see firmly in your mind; then incorporate it first by taking on the image yourself, exaggerating the form until you have a full grotesque created. Either videotape yourself or have someone take your picture while you are fully incorporated, and use this image as a guide to creating the virtual character. If you have drawing skills, you might want to draw a quick sketch of the character as well, as you can often find subtleties of character in sketches that you might not see in your picture. For our image, we discovered that a deep, growling voice accompanied the character; although we can't directly transfer this to the model, the deepness and anger in the voice are useful elements of the character that can help define what the character looks like to produce such sounds.

Figure 6.22

**The virtual gro-
tesque arising from
the picture shown in
Figure 6.21**

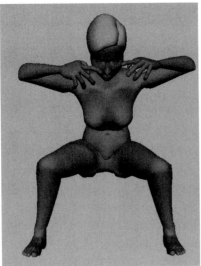
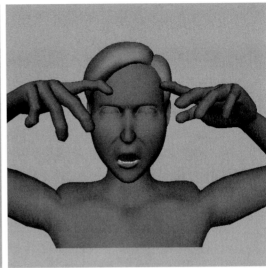

Figure 6.22

**The virtual gro-
tesque arising from
the picture shown in
Figure 6.21**

Now pose your character into the grotesque you have discovered, distorting its body and face into the vision you have in your mind. Use your photo (or sketch) as reference, but don't be constrained by it: explore the model's own potential to achieve what you have in your mind directly. It will likely become something related but different than what you created physically, which is just fine. The model might very well also become more distorted and grotesque than you were, because there isn't much pain in bending and stretching it beyond what most of us can do. Figure 6.22 shows the grotesque that we came up with after going through the exercise.

Once you have created your grotesque, save the file for later use, then keyframe the entire figure at frame 1. Move to some other frame, like frame 50, and reduce, or veil, the grotesque until it becomes somewhat realistic, but still exaggerated as if it were a cartoon character. When you are done, do you still see the original grotesque showing through the new pose? What details did you keep highly exaggerated and which did you reduce? Record your observations of your efforts for future work. Our veiling process revealed that the character looks a great deal like an angry ape, with a heavy body and symmetrical legs and arms. Figure 6.23 shows the resulting partially veiled pose. If you want to, you can again keyframe what you have, change to a new frame, and reduce the pose even more, down to a realistic veiling. Again, note what you keep, how much you reduce that, and what you discard, as well as whether the emotional and imagistic responses you had when looking at the photograph remain buried somewhere in this more veiled pose. Figure 6.24 shows our take on a well-veiled grotesque,

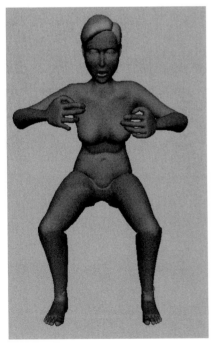

Figure 6.23

**Veiling the virtual
grotesque to
cartoon level**

which still has the ape-like qualities, but now looks a bit more downtrodden, the weight element taking hold via the hunched shoulders and downward trending body. While we dropped the character's arms almost to her sides, we did retain the tension in the fingers as well as the flared elbows, which match the still slightly flared knees and wide stance. Our version of this exercise, `grotesqueFromImage.mb`, is on the accompanying DVD for your reference.

After you finish this initial exercise, feel free to explore other grotesques you find, and try combining a grotesque with a psychological gesture. What does the PG do to the "raw" grotesque? How would you animate this combination of grotesque and PG? What physicality and physical limitations would this character have? Now animate your character through a walk cycle or simple action (like picking something up or sweeping) and see how the grotesque and PG combine to create a unique pattern of motion as well as pose. Continue working with your character by adding qualities of movement, atmospheres, sensations, centers, and polarities.

Figure 6.24

Veiling the virtual grotesque to realistic level

Quality + Action = Emotion

As a final exercise, imagine you are currently working on a character animation and want to explore your character's range of emotions. Animate the character performing a simple action in a neutral manner (such as waving a hand). Now make a list of ten words that describe what you know about this character; using adverbs or adjectives is best (for example, friendly, lonely, grieving). Then begin to try out these qualities by assigning them to the movement. What has to change for the hand waving to appear "friendly"? Is it tempo? Form? Is the emotion conveyed by the subtlety of a leading elbow, or something obvious like the heightened animation of the wrist? How does the movement of the fingers differ when the character is "grieving"? Does a lonely hand mold, flow, fly, or radiate? Work through many different combinations of quality and action and see if your friends or coworkers can easily tell what emotion you are trying to convey with each animation.

CHAPTER 7

Essences

An essence can be described as an intrinsic nature or indispensible quality of an object, either living or nonliving. For years, actors have been capturing essences of animate and even inanimate objects for use in their work. Constantin Stanislavski wrote about the use of animal essences as an idea for the foundation of character development. Since Stanislavski, almost every teacher of acting has spent some time with their students understanding and replicating essences as a productive tool in character development. Understanding essences or essential qualities of animals, elements of nature, and natural and man-made objects can be of great aid to the animator, especially since animators often animate these objects (or an anthropomorphic version of them) directly. Using an essence in the development of character can help the animator capture unique movement qualities and ways of interacting with other characters and the environment.

This chapter discusses:

- **A description of essences**
- **An exercise for using animal essences in acting**
- **Exercises for using essences of elements of nature in acting**
- **Exercises for using essences of man-made objects in acting**
- **An explanation of how essences can be used in animation**
- **Exercises to transfer essences to animation**

What Is an Essence?

An essence is an essential or main quality of some *thing*, as we perceive it. It is the intersection between the object itself (such as a giant sequoia tree) and a perceiver (such as a city girl seeing one for the first time), so the essence is any of a range of justifiable terms for the most fundamental nature of the object. According to practitioners, everything has an essence: a central feeling or abstraction of the essential nature of that object. Essences are something that most individuals will identify when thinking of or viewing the object, because it is the fundamental quality of that object. An essence of a snake might be "slimy" or "slithery" and connotes ideas of fluid, sustained, curving motion. The same term can also carry the quality of danger or even evil. An essence of a mountain might be "strong," "solid," "unmoving," or "rigid." An essence of a hurricane might be "turbulent," "whirling," "gusty," or "destructive." The essence of a sports car might be "sleek," "arrogant," "smooth," or "sexy." All things carry essential qualities or essences, but the exact one an individual will pick out from the list of possibilities has to do with that person as well as the object. Thus, while a poor high school student might decide a particular sports car is "arrogant," his father, in his forties, who is considering the purchase of said car might say that same car's essential nature is "sexy." Still, the term selected must be generally accepted as one of the central qualities of that object. Thus, "still," "wooden," or "foamy" would not fall into the category of possible words to describe the essence of a sports car.

Actors have long used essences in their work. For a given role, they will find the essence of an object or animal and develop their character based at least in part on that essence. The character will stand, sit, recline, and move using the essence of the object. He or she will interact with others using the essence of the object. The character will carry essential qualities of the object in their moods and feelings as they perform the role.

Most often actors work from the essences of animals or elements of nature rather than the essence of an inanimate object, but that is not to say that inanimate objects can't be used—especially when considering animation, where you might very well have to animate something like a candy machine. The essences of living things are easiest to grasp as they contain movement and are more easily personified, but pretty much every living and inanimate object can be used a basis for essence work.

The idea of finding essences in objects can and has been used very effectively in animation to discover character voices, movements and emotions. Pixar's *Cars* is a perfect example of an animation where animators need to find the essential qualities or essences of objects (different types of cars) and apply that to the voice and movement of that character. Lightning McQueen's modern sports car (voiced by Owen Wilson) is fast but reckless in its actions (a recklessness that gives way to more considered thought during the movie). Sally Carrera (voiced by Bonnie Hunt) is a flat-out sexy sports car who is comfortable being who she is. And Luigi (the little tire-changing vehicle, voiced by

Tony Shalhoub) is skittish but enthusiastic, as befits his small stature and job. For *Cars*, not only animators but also modelers and layout artists needed a solid understanding of essences, because they were creating a world of characters based on specific essences of given cars.

With animation that uses more human characters, essences become more arbitrary in their selection but can be just as important. To use another example from Pixar, characters in *The Incredibles* could have essences based on the superpower each possesses. For the character of Mr. Incredible (voiced by Craig T. Nelson), the essence of a mountain (huge, strong), or of a boulder (heavy), or even of an animal like a bull (big, aggressive) could be used to generate the qualities of his character. Elastigirl (voiced by Holly Hunter), on the other hand, could have the essence of a rubber band (stretchy) or an octopus (thin, fluid, stretchy, moldable). And Edna Mode (voiced by director Brad Bird), the costumer for the superheroes, has the compact, ill-tempered, and tough nature that could come from the essence of rock (solid, hard), wolverine (mean, protective), or even something like sandpaper (abrasive, rough). No matter whether an animation involves a character that declares its essence (like a variety of car) or it is something that must be sought out through reading the script, designing the model, or working with a voice-over actor, essences should be an important part of the animation process and can make a character come to life in ways that will resonate with the audience.

There are two main ways of going about or exploring essence work. One is to work from the actual object. The actor will interact with, view, and study the object at the beginning of his exploration and literally attempt to become the object. Then the actor will slowly transform himself from trying to *be* the object into maintaining the essential qualities of the object while behaving in a human manner, rather than literally being the object.

The other means of exploring essence work involves the imagination as the primary tool of exploration. Instead of working directly from the object, the actor will work from an imagined or remembered image of the object, never actually becoming the object but rather assuming the essential qualities so that she can immediately begin her work as character rather than object.

Both methods have their advantages and disadvantages. Working from the actual object can transform the object into the actor and thus into the character and doesn't leave much room for the imagination of the audience. It can also produce a character so enveloped by the literality of the essence that she becomes boring to watch. On the plus side, working from an object can help stimulate the imagination through the observation of and interaction with the object. The object itself also suggests guidelines for the exploration. Working from the imagination, however, might be too nonspecific and fail to provide enough detail for the actor to develop specificity in his character; this is especially true for less experienced actors, who might need more time with the actual object in order to get a sense of the specificity of that object. On the other hand, when working solely from the imagination, there are no boundaries, and anything becomes possible.

For the animator, it is probably best to begin essence work by studying real animals or objects rather than working from imagination. Not only will you then have a better idea of movement for the character, but since you are working with a nonphysical, imagined object in your character, the physical presence and nature of the actual object will help to ground you in a more physical reality when working with your virtual character.

Animal Essences

The idea of using the essences of animals for the basis of character development has been around since the time of Stanislavski (see Chapter 3). Animals are fun to explore because we, as humans, can easily see ourselves in animals, and them in us. We have close relationships with many different kinds of animals as pets in our homes, so many of us observe and interact with animals on a daily basis. Large numbers of animals like dogs, cats, birds, fish, reptiles, and rodents are truly a part of our families. We all know someone who treats their dog or cat as if it were a child. Perhaps this even describes you or a family member. Figure 7.1 shows the different essences house pets can have: a young puppy has qualities of energy and curiosity, while an older cat is sedate, relaxed, and calm.

Figure 7.1

The essences of a puppy and an older cat are very different.

We can easily imagine ourselves as land animals because our limbs can translate directly to theirs. In fact one, of the earliest games children with pets in the house play is one where they imitate that pet, often crawling around on hands and feet after the family dog. With a bit more imagination, we can feel our arms as wings and our legs as claws as we soar through the sky like an eagle or other winged creature. And although our bodies don't as directly translate into the animals of the sea, we can still find a fish's movement in our spines, or the motion of a jellyfish in our arms and back.

Due to our closeness in proximity and in evolution to animals, we easily place essences of basic human emotions onto animals and take the qualities of animals onto ourselves. We describe people as animals: she is mousy; he moves like a bull in a china shop; she laughs like a hyena; he is as slow as a turtle; she is as clumsy as an ox. Whether simply due to proximity or our shared heritage with them, we link animals and humans closely in our minds and imaginations.

Using an animal essence for the basis of character development starts with choosing an animal that has qualities we feel fit the character we are building, whether on stage, on the movie screen, or on a computer. Since we so closely relate to animals, this is not a particularly difficult task: we can sense differences in the essence of "dog" and "cat," and even more specifically we can distinguish the differences in essences within a species. It is not difficult to recognize the difference in essential qualities between a hound and a miniature poodle. The hound's essence might be "heavy" or "lazy" while the poodle is "quick," "light," and "yappy."

Although finding an animal essence to work with is not difficult, it is important that the actor and the animator make themselves familiar with the whole animal kingdom to have a wide variety of animals to choose from. For the simple reason that more knowledge of animal varieties leads to the ability to find just the right animal for a given character, the more kinds of animals we are familiar with the better. Watch National Geographic and other nature channels a lot, and if you have a particular animal you're interested in, look on the Internet for more information about that animal. Observe birds, rodents, bugs, and pets that populate your residence. Get out into nature. Take hikes. Visit farms and ride horses. Bird watch. Go to your local zoo and watch the lemurs, polar bears, and other exotic animals. Take a close look in the grass around your home, noting the way ants, crickets, grasshoppers, and other insects move. Or, as the animators for Pixar's *Finding Nemo* did, learn to scuba dive. The more you observe and become familiar with the animal kingdom, the broader your knowledge will be.

Of course, if you're given a particular animal as a character to animate, you should research that animal well, observing the real thing if possible, and if not, get your hands on as many video and picture resources as possible. If you have a fairly standard animal character like a dog, don't feel that you have to limit yourself to that animal for your essences work. Perhaps the dog is somewhat bear-like in his nature, or acts more like a wild wolf than a domesticated pet. While the clearest alternative is to use a dog essence, you might find a more intriguing and revealing essence by looking beyond the obvious choice.

Essences of Elements of Nature

Elements of nature might not be as straightforward to use as animals, but they also provide wonderful resources for essence work. Just as we naturally seem to personify animals, we extract human qualities from many natural objects and phenomena. "He is as dumb as a rock," "She is as slow moving as molasses," "She is as light as a feather," and "He blew through the room like a tornado," are just some indications of how much we associate ourselves with natural objects and events. Although natural objects and phenomena don't translate literally to our bodies, as animals do, they still carry a force that contains a perceptible essence.

There are two basic types of elements of nature: natural objects and natural phenomena. Natural objects are items that are or were once alive or that carry a life force.

Examples would be a tree, a leaf, a feather, a rock, a twig, a pinecone, tumbleweed, coral, and the like. Natural phenomena are big elements of nature that sometimes we can't actually see but can only observe the effects of. They can include lightning, thunder, volcanoes, tidal waves, tornados, avalanches, fire, geysers (see Figure 7.2), and hurricanes. It is interesting to note that we perceive most of these things as destructive because we place a value on the damage caused by these "acts of God." But there are also smaller and not as violent elements of nature as well: rain, clouds, wind, ponds, creeks, and, once again, fire, which has a crucial positive effect on our lives. No matter whether an object or a phenomenon, these varied elements of nature are excellent tools for essence work, as we can tap into the natural force within them.

Once again, it is important for both the actor and the animator to increase their understanding of and their attention to elements of nature through observation, both of nature and of our reactions to it. Look around; observe; feel the salt spray of a wave on your face; listen to the wind through the trees; taste wild blackberries; pick up sticks and stones and play with them, feeling their weight, texture, and movement. While you are out on your hikes, bird watching, or

Figure 7.2
The "Old Faithful" geyser erupting in Yellowstone National Park

scuba diving adventures, use all of your senses to experience and revel in the glories and miracles of nature around you. As an animator, you might well be called on to animate an object like a tree, a rock, or a cloud, so allow your imagination and feelings to interact freely with all around you, from the smallest grain of sand up to a massive mountain or an ocean. What do these elements of nature do to you? How do they affect you, both intellectually and emotionally? If you were asked to animate this thing (a leaf from a tree, say), how would you approach the animation? What qualities are inherent in this object or force that you can express through pose and motion? Don't get too caught up in the details of your answers, at least not while you're out observing up close; instead, concern yourself with the "big picture" aspects of how a given element of nature can inform a potential (or assigned) character.

Essences of Inanimate Objects

Although we may not find working from inanimate objects quite as fascinating as working from living things, inanimate objects still provide a wealth of opportunity for essence exploration. Furthermore, in animation man-made objects have been used time and time again, often in starring roles. From the classic *Pinocchio*, to Pixar's iconic lamp, *Luxo Junior*, to Disney's household objects (teapot, candle, clock, etc.) in *Beauty and the Beast*, to the unforgettable robot, Wall-E (although many will argue that he is indeed sentient), objects from our daily life have populated the screen in countless animations.

What is important when dealing with man-made objects is specificity. An actor should not work with the vague and general idea of "a chair," for example, but rather pick a specific chair—ideally one that they have at hand and can observe closely. The specificity of a particular chair is crucial to creating a solid character from it. For example, one can immediately feel the essence of the old, green, duct-taped, Lazy Boy chair belonging to Frasier's father in the TV series, an essence that is very different from the elegant leather sofa Frasier has right next to it, or from a delicate dressing table chair or a rustic wooden rocking chair. While "chair" is unspecific and uninteresting, each of the four chairs here have specific, and different, essential qualities. For another example, imagine what a difference the essence of an expensive blown glass bud vase has as compared to an earthenware piece of pottery. The pocket watch from your great-grandfather will provide a remarkably different essence from the digital sports watch used by your kid brother. Consider how different the essential qualities of the watches are in Figure 7.3.

Figure 7.3

Different watches provide different essences.

In Chapter 3, we gave you some exercises to help develop your observational and sensory skills. This heightened awareness can come in handy when you're exploring the essences of man-made objects, so you might want to review those exercises now. Additionally, it is helpful when working with objects if you can see, touch, smell, listen to, and in some cases taste the object that you will be working with. The more you can interact with any given object, the more you will understand it from both an intellectual and (more importantly) an emotional point of view. If you are assigned a pre-modeled character that is a man-made object, like a toaster in a movie, a slice of pizza in a TV series, or even a bug spray bottle for a commercial, locate the previsualization artwork, then try to locate a real object that matches this art as closely as you can, and interact with it as much as you can to get a real sense of its qualities. You can even ask the artists who designed and modeled the character, as, more than likely, they based their work off real objects that they will likely loan you for research purposes. And if you are working on a project where you're both designer and animator, then find your research object(s) before you go through the design phase; then, as you design and model your character, consider how this creature will move, and what other essential qualities you are discovering from the object(s) you are using to design and model the character.

Exercises for Understanding Essences

Using the following essence exercises, we will explore taking an essence into your body and voice and then applying it to an improvised character. All of the exercises are based on observation and interaction with an animal, object, or natural phenomenon and thus can be applied directly to the animator's work in creating a CG character.

When working with essences of animals, you should first study the animal you intend to use. If possible, watch it live for several hours. If not, you should watch video of it. As a last resort, you can look at pictures.

When working with an object, either natural or man-made, it is best if you can have the object in front of you to feel, move, and interact with. Objects that you find, discover, and choose yourself tend to carry more meaning or emotional weight than something someone gives you. Perhaps you even collect objects from journeys in your life. You might have a shell from a particularly memorable beach, rock from a volcano you climbed, a feather from a hawk, or a pinecone from a forest you visited or even from your backyard. Using an object that has personal meaning for you, whether it is natural or man-made, will enrich your work. While this can cause some trouble for animators asked to animate a provided "object" character, it is best to follow these exercises with a "found" object so that you have the best understanding of how the process works; then, when you are given an object to animate you will hopefully understand the process well enough to follow along with an object you have not selected yourself.

When working with a natural phenomenon, you may be able to view it live or, more likely, view a recording. If you can find neither, you can use a remembered event in your life or even your imagination—for example, imagining a hurricane even if you've never lived through one.

Before doing any of the following exercises, it is important to warm up and center yourself so that your body, voice, and imagination are ready to respond. Refer back to Chapter 1 if you need a reminder of different warm-ups.

Animal Essence Exercises

In this section it would be wise to do the exercises three different times. Do each once with a land animal, once with an air animal, and once with an animal from the sea. Hopefully you can spend some time viewing, either live or in media, a specific animal that you have chosen. (An Internet video repository like YouTube.com is an excellent resource for video of animals.) If you are not able to watch a given animal, at least spend some time remembering or imagining a specific animal.

After viewing a land animal, first warm up, then lie on your back on the floor with your arms about 45 degrees from your body and your palms facing the ceiling. Your legs should be uncrossed and relaxed with your feet falling slightly open toward the floor. Take several minutes to center yourself by focusing on your breath. Now let your attention travel from your breath to your animal. Spend some time seeing your animal in your mind's eye. Picture it in its most natural environment; if you watched a lion in the zoo, try to picture the lion in Sub-Saharan Africa rather than its caged enclosure. This will give you a better sense of the animal in its most natural state. In your mind, watch it move. Watch it interact with its environment. How does the animal interact with other animals of the same species? What about other species? Pay particular attention to its limbs and spine. How does the spine work? How does the animal hold its head? How does

Figure 7.4

Tiger the cat relaxing

it move through space? What leads its movement? What is the tempo and rhythm of the animal? Do the limbs move together or separately? Does the tempo of the animal's "arms" differ from that of its legs? Does the movement of the animal suggest to you any qualities? Do those qualities bring up any feelings or emotions?

For an example, say you were working with a house cat, like the one in Figure 7.4. Consider not only how this cat rests but also how it moves. First, spend some time watching the cat. Pay particular attention to the movement of the spine. Watch how the head always leads or begins the

movement of the entire spine. Notice the fluidity of the spine as it arches up toward the ceiling in a stretch. Notice once again how the head leads to movement of the spine as it comes out of the stretch.

Watch the cat as it slowly walks around the room with its legs and especially rear hips sort of rolling from side to side. Notice how the tail sways in counter-rhythm to the body while the animal walks. Watch the cat when it is studying a fly on the window. How does it sit? What happens to its energy as it begins to stalk the fly? What happens when it pounces on it? And don't forget about sound: when does your cat make sound? What kind of sound does it make?

When you can clearly see, feel, hear, and sense the cat in your mind's eye, lie down and focus on your breath, and begin to transfer the movement of the cat first to your imagination and then to the movement of your own body. Start with your spine. Imagine that your spine is just like the cat's. You don't have a tail but imagine, sense and feel a long tail extending off of the tip of your tailbone. Make your arms and legs the cat's four legs. How do your paws grip the floor and use it to push off? Feel your body as if it were a cat's.

Next begin to explore this cat body and see what it can do. Move your spine as the cat. Arch your back. Stretch out long. Let your head lead the movement. How does the long fluid spine make you feel? What essence or quality does it suggest to you? Make sure you connect with the long tail on your backside. How does that tail make you feel? How does it make your rear end move? What kinds of essences or qualities do these physical changes suggest to you?

Now begin moving through space as the cat does. How does your body roll from side to side as your cat/body moves around the room? How does this make you feel? Interact with objects in the room. (As in previous chapters, it is useful to scatter props or objects around the room to play with.) How does this interaction make your feel? What qualities does it suggest? Do you find that a long piece of string suddenly is much more interesting now?

After you have explored the space and objects in the room, let your animal being interact with other animals. If you are working with other people, you can interact with them as the animal that they are investigating. If not, use imagined animals. How does your cat/body react to other animals, such as a dog, another cat, a mouse, a bird, a squirrel? Is it afraid? Is it aggressive? It is playful? Is it inquisitive? What feelings, qualities and essences do these interactions suggest to you?

Does the cat communicate with sound? If so, don't be afraid to investigate your voice. What kind of sounds does your animal/body make? What is the pitch of the sound? The length? The quality? When does the animal make sound? Why does the animal make sound (what purpose does the sound serve)? Is it to intimidate? To comfort? To mate? Go ahead and make the sound of the animal. Where does this sound tend to resonate in your body? How does the sound make you feel?

As you continue to explore your cat/being, begin to consider the following question: What do you feel is the central quality or essence of this cat? As you move from imitating the cat itself to retaining its essential nature, the answer to this question will serve to keep you on track in your further work.

After you have fully explored the movement, voice, and personality of your cat/body, you can begin to abstract the cat into the essence of the animal. Slowly try to move your cat essence into an upright body. Instead of literally crawling around on the floor as the cat, transfer yourself to a standing posture. Continue, though, to think of your spine as the cat spine with the long tail and your arms as paws. Now start to move through space on two feet instead of four, but continue to think of yourself as the cat all the while. Allow your head to lead the movement. (This is actually the way all animals, including humans, move.) Keep feeling the fluidity of the spine. Keep thinking of your arms and legs as the cat's four legs. Pay particular attention to the essential quality or essence that you discovered when you previously explored your cat/body on the floor. Make sure that you retain the essence of that movement and posture in your upright body. Your goal is to become a cat in a human's body.

Explore space, objects, and other upright animals/people. How does this exploration make you feel? Is it different from how you felt when you acted as the "real" animal, on all fours? Slowly begin to move and interact with your surroundings, letting go of the actual animal body but retaining the essence or essential quality of the animal's movement. Keep moving as a human but with the same feelings and sensations of the animal. Keep the same tempo and rhythm that you had as the animal. You are now fully human but moving and responding with the essence of the animal.

As you move with the animal's essence, what qualities of personality or type of character does this movement suggest to you? Is your cat essence seductive? Playful? Sly? Lazy? Do you stalk and prey on others? Do you toy with or bait others? Do you want to touch or rub against them? As you move, begin to create an imaginary character from the essence of this movement, a character with motivations, a past, and goals to achieve. Allow this cat essence to take on a life of its own.

If you are working with other people, start to interact with them as your cat essence character. Imagine that you are at a party and don't know anyone. You need to react to others in the room with the essence of your cat character. Your cat might be curious and want to get to know certain people or it might be afraid of other people (a scaredy-cat). Move toward someone and introduce yourself. What happens to the way you move as you approach and then interact with someone unfamiliar? Also note how the essence of this character is reflected in your voice. What happens to your pitch, volume, diction, tempo, or even dialect? Improvise stories about your cat character to share with other people at the party. If you are working by yourself, you instead can imagine other people that your cat character can interact with.

Now place your cat character in a more uncomfortable situation. Say that you are in an elevator and the power goes off. As your cat essence, improvise the situation with other animal characters, either real (working with others) or solo (working alone). How does your cat character respond in a situation that is confined and stressful?

Then try another situation, this time even more stressful: place your cat/character in a bank that is being robbed. How would your cat character respond when threatened? Would it be a hero or would it try to hide? What if instead your cat character were the bank robber? How would the essence of the animal transfer into the situation?

There are countless scenarios that you can play out with your animal essence. Try a few of the following and note how your character interacts with the place and the other characters within it:

- A nightclub
- A job interview
- A nude beach
- An amusement park
- A church

Or try some of these solo exercises. Have your cat character:

- Dress for a party
- Sing in the shower
- Sit by the grave of a friend
- Eat alone in a crowded restaurant
- Clean the house

Always try to retain the essence of the cat even in extreme situations. After you have explored a land animal, repeat the exercise for an animal of the sky and for a water animal. Although the exercise is essentially the same, the movement will transfer differently to your body, and thus your character should interact with the world in very different ways physically, emotionally, and vocally. We can't literally fly or swim (at least not on dry ground), so the movement will begin in a more abstracted and less literal place.

BOTTOM: A CASE STUDY IN ANIMAL ESSENCE WORK

In Shakespeare's *A Midsummer Night's Dream*, the character of Bottom the weaver is transformed into an ass by the mischievous fairy Puck. Many actors have felt that the character of Bottom needs to contain some qualities of an ass even before he undergoes the transformation, since the "punishment" Puck applies to Bottom is then appropriate to his character traits.

In a 2008 production of the play by the University of Georgia's Department of Theatre and Film Studies, actor Brandon Wentz was cast as Bottom and applied animal essence work to the development of his character.

BOTTOM: A CASE STUDY IN ANIMAL ESSENCE WORK *(continued)*

Wentz began by studying an actual donkey at a farm at the university. He watched the animal off and on for several days and also looked at pictures of donkeys online, gleaning the most important qualities of the donkey through this research.

He then began to explore the actual movement of the animal in the studio, first moving as a literal animal, and then transforming the essence of that motion, posture, and voice into his developing human character.

(continues)

BOTTOM: A CASE STUDY IN ANIMAL ESSENCE WORK *(continued)*

At the beginning of the play, before he is transformed, Wentz already used qualities of the ass he discovered during his explorations. When Puck transforms him into a "real" ass, the character has an ass's head added to his costume and works with this costume element as if it were his actual head. After exploring the movement of the ass and the essence of the animal in the studio, Brandon added on his costume head and further explored the attitude, movement, and posture of using this essence.

In the end, he created a character that contained the essence of the ass, and later in the play, after his magical transformation, moved as the literal ass. The following graphic shows Wentz as the transformed ass, playing opposite Amy Roeder as Titania, who worked from the essence of a jellyfish to create her character.

Exercises for Elements of Nature Essences

We will undertake two different exercises to explore the essences of elements of nature. One will be for a natural object and one will be for a natural phenomenon. For the natural object, you will need to find an object and work with it. For the natural phenomenon, you will work from your memory or imagination. The exercises are similar to the exercises for animal essences, and just as with the animal essence exercises, these exercises can be used over and over again for different objects or phenomena. Also they can be done solo or with a group.

Natural Objects

Select a natural object such as a flower, a rock, a branch, a nut, or a leaf and bring it into your working space. After warming up, sit on the floor in a comfortable position and place your object in front of you. Take a few minutes to center yourself by focusing on your breath; then pick up your object and use all of your senses to begin to examine and explore that object.

Start with your sense of touch. Keep your eyes closed and examine the object with your hands. How does your object feel? Is it rough? Smooth? Soft? Hard? Slimy? Scaly? Prickly? Is it a combination of any or all of these things? How much space does it take up? Is it long? Short? Wide? Flat? Round? Pointy? Thick? Thin? Is it a combination of any of these things? Does it have edges? What are they like? Is it rigid or flexible? Feel the object's weight. Is it heavy or light? Is it dense (like lead) or not (like a feather)? Can you easily balance it on a point or is its weight unequally distributed? Explore this object with the sense of touch for several minutes.

As you explore your object, pay attention to any sound that the object might make. What happens as you move the object to touch it? Does it crinkle or squeak? Does it crack or scrape? What kind of sound can your object make as you move it? What kinds of sounds can your object make as it brushes against your skin, or your fingernails, or the floor? What kinds of sounds can it make as you move it quickly or slowly through the air? Finally, before you open your eyes, smell your object. Is it sweet, musky, rotten, fresh, clean, or citrusy? Does its smell remind you of something else, or some memory from your past? Spend several minutes exploring the sound and smell of your object.

Now open your eyes and repeat all of these steps, but this time observe the object as you explore it. What new information do your eyes tell you about the object? As you continue to explore the object with your eyes, start to pay attention to what you would call the essence of the object and the essence of the object's movement. Obviously an object does not move on its own, but as you move it through space what is the essence of that movement? What happens when the object is dropped, thrown, or rolled? If the object is flexible, how does it bend when being moved about smoothly? When moved more violently? What qualities does the object have and what qualities does the movement of the object have?

Stand up and continue to explore the object and the movement of the object with your whole body. Allow your body to become an extension to the object so that you *are* the object. Become one with the object so that as the object is moved, your body moves and responds as the object would. Of course you are not a feather or a rock or a seedpod, but allow your body to be infected with the essence and quality of your object and move with it.

Now put your object aside and allow your body to move and explore space as your object. Take the essential qualities or essence of your object and allow it to overtake your body. Allow it to affect your interactions with the space. The shape your body takes and its movement will not be human in any way. What you are discovering is not the literal object in itself, but the essence of that object.

Figure 7.5
An actor explores the essence of a feather.

Don't forget about your voice. Does your object make sound, and when does it do so? If so, how does the essence of that sound transfer into vocal qualities? If you were exploring a feather, would the voice take on a light, airy, breathy quality? Would it be raspy or smooth? Don't grab onto the first thing you think of; instead, try many different sounds and movements until you feel you have captured the essence of the object. Figure 7.5 shows an actor exploring the essence of a feather object.

Now just as you did in the animal essence exercises, slowly start to translate the essence of the posture, movement, and vocalization of this object into the essence of a real human being. What qualities does the essence of your object suggest? How can you abstract the movement of the object into a human body, a real human voice? Take your time and slowly translate the essence of the object into the movement and voice of a character.

Often characters created from natural objects are more extreme types of people than those created via animal essences. Therefore, natural object essences can be a great help for animators who need to create characters with more exaggerated qualities, movement, and voice. The ages of these characters will vary greatly from children to very old characters. They might have interesting characteristics like a broken leg, a humped back, or other deformity. Their voices might be very different from your own. Let these characters surprise you and lead you to the exaggeration that is often so valuable for animated characters.

After you have established your character's body and voice from exploring your space, go back to the exercises in the animal essences section and allow your character to interact with others in different situations. Use any of the situations listed in the animal essences section, or invent your own. The possibilities are limitless. If you are working alone, you can do the solo exercises or imagine other people to interact with. If you are with a group, try having your natural object character interact with other natural object characters, and then with characters with animal essences instead. Are there differences in the way you interact with object/characters versus animal/characters?

Natural Phenomena and Large Natural Objects

Natural phenomena, such as tidal waves, hurricanes, or lightning, or large natural objects, such as mountains, the ocean, or giant sequoia trees, can offer wonderful possibilities for essence exploration. Because these phenomena and large objects cannot be taken physically into a studio and worked with, your imagination will be your primary tool when exploring these essences. You can also use one or more pictures if you want help to get you started. Working with these essences requires a more imaginative connection, so we recommend you do some exercises with animal and small object essences before doing these exercises; those experiences will help ground you in the technique and let you encounter these natural phenomena essences more easily.

Part of the challenge and excitement of using a large element of nature for essence work is that the element itself is immense. It is quite literally beyond us. We can't take on its shape, as our human bodies do not transfer to their shapes. We cannot take on their movement as many of them don't move. A mountain, for example, doesn't move (at least not in a manner we can perceive); it simply exists. A cloud doesn't move of its own volition. It can be moved by the wind but it doesn't move itself. When working with a natural phenomenon or large object, we are truly finding an essential quality as opposed to copying or abstracting movement.

Begin by warming up. Then lie on the floor on your back as in the previous essence exercises. Take some time to center yourself by focusing on your breath. If you have a picture, you might study it here for a minute or two. If not, don't worry: your imagination will do just fine.

As you lie on the floor, concentrate on your object. If you are using a mountain, put all of your focus on the mountain in your mind's eye. Your goal here is to sort of fuse with or become one with the mountain. You are the mountain—not literally, but your energy, body, and voice will take on the energy and essence of the mountain. Do not think about a time when you were on a mountain or develop a character or scenario for your mountain, as this would lead to confusion about which essences or experience you are capturing. Instead, simply become the mountain. Figure 7.6 shows several images of the same mountain range, indicating the range of different essences that can arise from the same natural object.

Figure 7.6

The Grand Tetons mountain range provides a number of possible essences, including serenity (top left); imposing or massive (top right); aloof, powerful, or wise (bottom left); and even threatening or terrifying (bottom right).

Lie on the floor and concentrate on the mountain until you feel that you and the mountain are becoming one and that the mountain demands that you take on its life. Only then, once you feel the mountain occupying your presence, should you begin to move. You might move quickly or slowly. You might find yourself rolling, crawling, or leaping. Do whatever your impulses tell you to do; there is no right or wrong. Your own imagination is determining how the essence of the mountain has become your essence and moves your body.

You might have impulses to make sound either vocally or with some other part of your body. If so, go ahead and explore the vocal nature of your object or phenomenon. Remember what you are creating is an essence, not a literal sound. A mountain might demand that you roar or "crack your cheeks," as King Lear so famously put it. That will depend on the essence that you sense as you fuse with the mountain.

Spend at least 15 minutes exploring the essence of the mountain. Then stop for a minute or two to rest and think about all of the qualities that this essence suggested to you. Was it old? Heavy? Large? Powerful? Gnarled? Broken? Wise? Removed? Terrifying? Now get back up on your feet and begin to translate these qualities to real human movement.

When you were the mountain, you might have rolled or squirmed across the ground, but a human doesn't move that way. Take the quality of weight and transfer that into a walk. Take the other qualities you discovered and transfer them into your human body. How do these qualities affect your spine? Your tempo? Your focus? Your expression? Your gait? How do the qualities that you discovered with sound transfer into a real human voice? How do these qualities affect your thoughts? Emotions? Personality?

Consider how you could exaggerate these qualities even more for an animated character. Would you have this character walk with an exaggerated limp, or possibly even drag itself over the ground from the weight of the mountain essence? How could your animated character behave in ways that you can't?

As in the animal essence exercises, slowly start to translate the qualities you have discovered into a real human character as you move through and explore the space. Give your character a name and begin to interact with other characters, real or imagined, as if at a party. Introduce yourself to others. After this, try putting your character into some of the different situations we've listed and see how your mountain responds to other characters and situations.

Exercises for Man-made Object Essences

When working with man-made objects, feel free to adapt and use any of the exercises described earlier. If the object is small and you can take it into the studio with you, you can use the exercises from the natural object section. If the object is too large, like a pickup truck, or too dangerous, like a syringe, you can use a picture or your imagination as in the natural phenomena exercises.

Some man-made objects are harder to work with than natural objects, as they aren't as easily personified as living things or natural objects and events. But remember, your imagination can create almost anything, so let it be free to explore. To help ensure that these exercises are successful, make sure you choose an object that immediately suggests an essence to you. Again it is best to work with a specific and not general item: a Dodge Viper is very different than an old GMC Pacer, though both are under the umbrella of "car." A picture can aid you in your exploration but is not necessary. Your imagination can work fine. If you are hired to animate an actual man-made object, like a portable MP3 player for a commercial, then your choice becomes more obvious: get ahold of the real object you will be animating a virtual version of (or something very similar if the real thing isn't available), and work through your essence exercises using this object.

After you have chosen your object, complete the appropriate exercises from the previous sections. Let this object speak to you and tell you what its essence is, and then transfer this to your body and feel the quality of the posture, movement, and voice of this object. Next, have the character you have created from the essence of that object interact with other characters, real or imagined, in different situations. Have fun. Surprise yourself. Figure 7.7 shows the image of an actress (one of the authors) who used the essence of an old, wet dishrag to help her find her character for the opening scene of the third act of Edward Albee's *Who's Afraid of Virginia Woolf?*

Using Essences with Animation

After having explored animal, natural object, phenomenon, and man-made object essences using your body and mind as your tools, it's time to transfer your work to character animation. The world of essences is (as you probably figured out from the acting exercises) nearly infinite, so we will only point the way to start working here, rather than try to be exhaustive, which could be the subject of an entire book on its own. Fortunately the methodology of working on essences is pretty much the same for anything, so once you have a handle on a couple of examples, you should be able to explore on your own fairly easily. We will work up a pose using a natural object (a mountain), create an animal essence (a donkey) using video reference footage, and finally create a bit of animation of a man-made object (a pen) that you might have to do for a commercial or even as a character in a full-length animation.

Using a Large Natural Object Essence to Create a Character Pose

When using a large natural object like a mountain, it is important to research the object first. If you recently took a trip to the mountains (or have the good fortune to live near some), recall as precisely as you can what the mountains looked, sounded, smelled, and felt like. Remember this isn't you *on* a mountain—it's what the mountain itself was like. If you took pictures of the trip, find one or two that show them in their full glory, preferably without people in the shot. If you don't have any pictures of mountains, or have not recently taken a trip to some, then use a book or the Internet to find some good pictures for your research. Study the pictures, or relax and remember the feel of the mountains for yourself. Remember, here it is your imagination that is connecting with the mountain to find its essence, so let it have free rein to recall what it will.

For our work, we will be using the lower-left image from Figure 7.6, but use whatever image (either pictorial or imaginative) that suits your wishes. Look closely at the picture, then close your eyes, breathe deeply, and let the mountain and you merge into one. Let your mind float freely until you light upon the true connection you have with the mountain. Is it grand, or aloof, or frightening, or massive, or cold, or something else entirely? After relaxing and focusing on the image, we arrived at "grim" and "grandiose" as the essence of this mountain for us. We impulsively created a rigid finger-pointing gesture, and had the idea of a stern orator gesturing during an impassioned political speech in which dire warnings were being made.

We then took this conceptual work and created a rough gestural sketch to guide our work in posing the character. This sketch revealed that our character is rigidly on tiptoes, right hand raised up in a rigor mortis–like gesture, upper body extended up but hunched over, and left arm crossed in front of the body (as if the arm were resting on a podium), left hand balled into a fist. The face as well is stern, eyes looking down and mouth scowling. We then posed our character into a posture like that we imagined and sketched out, exaggerating the effect somewhat since we are dealing with an animated character. The result is shown in Figure 7.8, and our Maya file, `mountainPose.mb`, is on the DVD. If we were to animate our character, she would speak angrily and haughtily to the crowd, admonishing them to do better in some time of crisis.

Obviously you will (and should) have a different interaction with our picture, or your own (or your imagination), so your character's pose will be different. The secret for an exercise like this is to let the connection come to you—don't force yourself to find some predetermined essence (like "big" or "rocky"), as that will only reduce the imaginative and creative response you will have, and thus reduce your ability to create something striking and unique from the essence of the object you are studying. Later, when you are working on discovering the posture and movement of a character for some animation you are working on, this freedom of imagination will come to your aid: you will be able to see beyond the obvious posing and movement choices to something more unique using your essence work.

Figure 7.8

A "grim," "grandiose" character posed from the essence of a mountain

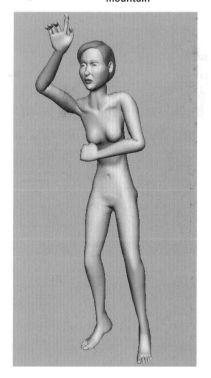

Creating an Animation of a Character with an Animal Essence

For this exercise, we will utilize video reference footage of Brandon Wentz exploring the donkey/ass essence for his work creating the character of Bottom in *A Midsummer Night's Dream* (see the earlier sidebar "Bottom: A Case Study in Animal Essence Work"). As with other animation work, it can be valuable to use video reference of a person—an actor, or you—to help with creating a character. The file donkeyEssence.mov on the accompanying DVD has about 4 minutes of work on the character, from initial work on the ground as a "real" donkey, to transforming this into a human character, to creating the magically transformed "ass" (with the head costume piece) after Bottom is transformed by Puck. For our purposes, we will use a short segment (donkeyEssenceShort.mov on the DVD) where the actor is creating a very animalistic version of the character: he is bent over, slack jawed, and stiff-legged in his motion. The segment, while too exaggerated for realistic acting, is wonderfully exaggerated, and thus great for animation.

First, open a new scene file in your program of choice. (If you are using Maya, feel free to use the Genna or Marcel rigs on the accompanying DVD.) Be sure you have your animation preferences set to NTSC/30 frames-per-second (since the video footage is at that frame rate); then import the donkeyEssenceShort.mov file and use it as a background plate for your character. Next, do an initial matchup of your character to the first frame of the background image, as shown in Figure 7.9.

Figure 7.9

Matching the character to the background plate to begin creating the donkey animation

See Chapter 4 for more information on importing images and using the book's included rigs in Autodesk Maya.

If you are using the DVD's models (Genna and Marcel), which include built-in character/subcharacter hierarchies, you can have Maya automatically select the characters as you go. First, place the autoCharacterSelection.mel file in your home scripts directory (~Autodesk/maya/scripts on your home directory). Then copy the line of code from ACSEnable.mel into the Script Editor input pane, and drag it up onto your shelf. When you start Maya, simply click the ACSEnable button, and from then on, Maya will automatically select whichever subcharacter it needs based on what is selected in the scene. This makes selecting and keyframing characters far easier than having to remember to do so yourself.

Now look through the video footage to determine the key poses in the animation. We found that frames 1, 10 (completion of his head turn), 22 (high point of right foot passing position), 26 (right heel contact), 34 (right foot down fully), 46 (head about to turn), 55 (turning, left foot up), 63 (foot down), 72 (right foot passing), 76 (side heel strike), 82 (foot down), 90 (left foot passing), 96 (left foot strike), 99 (left foot down), and 106 were good starts for a pose-to-pose animation. While this is a fairly dense set of key poses, there is a good deal of action occurring in the video—specifically several steps—and the actor is very expressive and exaggerated here, so it seemed prudent to create more poses at the outset.

Once you have blocked out the basic poses, go back and fill in the subtleties of motion that happen between the key poses, being sure to note and mimic the weight that Brandon gives to this character—the shifting heaviness and lumbering nature of this donkey-esque character. As his facial expressions are so important, be sure to do another pass where you animate your character's facial features to match the video reference footage. Feel free to exaggerate your character beyond what the actor is doing, but in this case, the motion is fairly exaggerated to start with so you might not find it necessary to do much beyond what is given. Figure 7.10 shows a frame from the final animation, which is on the DVD as donkeyEssenceAnimated.mov. The Maya file, donkeyEssence.mb, is also on the DVD for your reference.

There is more reference footage of Wentz creating his character on the DVD, so feel free to use this other footage to explore this character more. As should be obvious from working on this exercise, having video reference footage can be a wonderful tool when animating essences, especially when a good actor is doing the work. As you create essence-based work of your own, be sure to use video reference footage—of you or an actor who knows this technique—to help you feel out the character. This can be especially useful when you are just getting to "know" a new animated character, as the reference work can help you figure out how and why this character moves.

Figure 7.10

A frame from the animation using a donkey animal essence

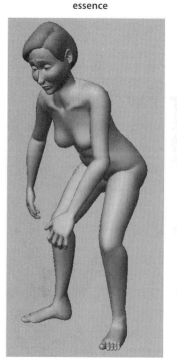

Animating a Man-made Object Using That Object's Essence

In this final exercise, we will consider how to work from a man-made object that is given to you to animate. In this case, we will consider that you have been assigned to animate a pen for a commercial. The client has asked for 10 seconds of animation showing off the wonderful nature of their new product. Here you have been given an object, rather than being able to select it for yourself, so you need to be able to find the essence of this particular object. We have created a simple pen model and rig, shown in Figure 7.11, that has been handed off to you to animate.

Figure 7.11

The ball point pen character, modeled by Josh Kundert-Gibbs

The first thing to do is to find a similar pen to study, as per the object essences exercises outlined earlier. Use your sense of touch first, eyes closed, to feel the weight, texture, temperature, hardness, and other attributes of the pen. The main body of the pen we used has a soft, slightly tacky exterior that stays fairly cool to the touch. Contrasting this, it has a hard upper area and push button for extending and retracting the ball point. This tackiness gave a sense of some flexibility for the main body of the pen, though not a huge amount.

After exploring the pen with touch, open your eyes and look at the pen. What color or variety of colors is it? What shape? How does it reflect the light, and how does that vary over the body of the pen? Our pen is a medium gray over most of the body, with black top and bottom (similar to the model, but black instead of blue at the top), giving it a fairly neutral feel overall: this is a pen for professional use, not a play toy.

Also use your senses of smell and hearing to get more information about the pen. Does the pen give off an odor? If so, what is it, a new "plastic" smell, or something else? Does the pen make a clicking sound when you extend the ball point? Or does it have a cap that clicks into place? How does the pen sound when you drop it or tap it on a hard surface like a desk?

Once you have fully explored your pen, close your eyes again and let all the information flow freely. What stands out as you imagine this pen? What is its most essential quality? Take your time, but eventually come up with one or two qualitative words that describe the pen to you. For us, the essential quality we latched on to was "purposeful": the pen is designed to do what it does, and do it well. While not the most obvious quality, this was the essence we discovered in our pen. Obviously you will discover some other essential quality for your pen, so your animation work will be different.

For our actual animation work, we will consider that we have been asked to produce an animation test, rather than some specific action. Thus we need to show the manner in which our pen character works. If you have Maya, open the pen file (pen.mb on the accompanying DVD); if not, create a simple model and rig setup. Due to the relatively inflexible nature of our pen's essence, we created only a few control points: one "foot," a "hip" translation control, a "low back" rotation control, and a "head" rotation control. There is also a main control that can move the pen as a whole, with its pivot at the ball of the pen. Figure 7.11 shows the control curves wrapped around the model. If you wish, feel free to adjust the rig as you desire.

For our animation test, we will have the pen walk (or hop, rather) up to look at the camera, and then begin writing on a sheet of paper. As our pen's essence is "purposeful," it has a forceful, almost aggressive movement, with each beat of the animation (the movement forward, looking at the camera, and then beginning to write) well defined and intentional.

Figure 7.12

**Animating the
pen character**

For our work, we blocked out the main movements to get a sense of timing and motion, and then went back and added extra keys to give the pen personality and make it move more naturally and with more weight. Figure 7.12 shows a frame from our final animation, which is available on the DVD as penAnimationTest.mov. The Maya file, penAnimationTest.mb, is also available on the DVD for your reference. Use the movie and/or scene file as reference, but as your essence will be different, so should your animation work.

One of the most interesting aspects of essence work for both actors and animators is how differently you can enact or animate a character based on different essences. After you finish animating your pen character using the first essence you found, try animating it using one or two very different essences, like ponderous or playful, and see what significantly different characteristics even a simple character like this can portray.

CHAPTER 8

Laban Effort Analysis

Rudolf Laban was a dancer and movement theorist who developed a means of analyzing movement that has been used in many different movement disciplines and even in industry. The element of his work that has most direct application to actors and animators is his focus on "effort," which analyzes the intention and quality of a movement through the examination of weight, space and tempo/rhythm. Laban has identified eight different Effort shapes that describe different combinations of these movement qualities. It is useful for the animator to study and learn to embody these Effort shapes as a means of developing character, as these different types of movement can be mapped to characters, giving them distinct, easily understandable patterns of motion.

This chapter discusses:

- Laban's life and work

- Laban's eight movement categories, or Effort shapes

- Exercises for using the movement categories in acting

- How Laban analysis can be used in animation

- Exercises to transfer Laban Effort to animation

Rudolf Laban

Rudolf Laban was born in 1879 in Austro-Hungary. His father was a high-ranking military official and had intended for Rudolf to have a military career. But Rudolf was more interested in the arts and went to the École des Beaux-Arts in Paris to study architecture. It was there that Laban became interested in the moving body in space and the relationship between humans, objects, and the space surrounding them.

He then began a transition from the study of architecture to the movement arts. He moved to Munich at age 30 and began to develop his movement vocabulary. His ideas were influenced by social and political strains of thought. He believed in movement for the masses and created opportunities for all people to experience dance.

While in Germany he established himself as a major force in the field of dance. He ran a dance company and opened over 25 schools of Laban dance. He established choreography as an art and designed a system of choreographic notation called Labanotation.

In 1937 he rejected Nazism and fled Germany for England. In retribution for his flight, the government propaganda office in Germany destroyed all of his work. In England, Laban continued teaching with his close friend Lisa Ullmann, and they founded the Laban Art of Movement Guild, which still exists today as the Laban Guild for Movement and Dance.

While in England, much of Laban's work focused on movement in industrial settings. He studied patterns of movement in the workplace and helped employers design jobs that used movement in the most economical and constructive means possible. He also published a book of his research called *Effort*. He continued teaching and researching until his death in 1958. His work lives on today in many disciplines. Not only is Labanotation used in dance, but his research into movement and movement types are used in theater, industry, and even physical therapy.

The Effort Shapes

When Laban studied movement, one particular aspect of his analysis centered on what he referred to as the Effort shapes. He divided the study of effort into three continua: strong versus light, which examines weight; direct versus indirect (we will refer to indirect as flexible, as the word more clearly describes the movement), which examines space; and sustained versus quick, which examines tempo/rhythm. Additionally there is an overarching category called flow. For the sake of the effort analysis, we are only concerned with the three movement continua.

According to Laban, all movement can be examined through the lens of the three continua. Thus a movement can be either strong or light, and direct or flexible, and sustained or quick. Of course, since these categories are continua, a movement can also fall somewhere between light and strong, direct and flexible, or sustained and quick. In order to analyze a movement and determine its Effort shape, the observer's task is to determine if a movement is more strong or light, more direct or flexible, and more sustained or quick. When we have defined where on the continua a movement is most closely aligned, we will be able to determine the Effort shape of that motion.

Let's take a look at these continua. The first continuum is strong versus light. This category focuses on the movement's weight and energy. Is the movement a strong movement or a light one?

We'll use the normal walk of a human being from point A to point B to dissect this category. Say a person is walking with intention from point A to point B. The person is not late or rushed, but does have a definite purpose in moving between these two points. Now look to the energy and weight of the person's foot meeting the ground. Does the person sink into the ground? Does the person roll through their whole foot? Does the person push off the ground? Do the feet make sound when they walk? If so, the movement would be categorized as a strong movement.

If the movement were a light one, it would be very different. Does the person hardly seem to touch the floor? Do they walk only on one part of the foot: the toe, instep, or outside? Does the whole foot lightly hit the floor all at once? Does it appear that they aren't sinking into the ground or drawing any energy from the ground to help propel them into their next step? Do their steps seem to glide across the top of the earth rather than sinking into it? If so, their movement would be considered light.

When you are examining this continuum, do not become confused by the size or weight of the person. A very large person, animal, or even object (when thinking of animation) can be light in its movement. Think about the ballerina hippopotami in Disney's *Fantasia*. Although large and somewhat cumbersome, their movement would be considered light (which is, of course, the basis of the humor in the scene)—that is, of course, while they are dancing; when the lead ballerina falls asleep on her settee, she becomes very heavy, nearly breaking the furniture beneath her. Meanwhile the Road Runner, although small and feathered, which could easily be thought of as light or delicate, is strong in his movement.

Next look at the continuum of direct versus flexible, which pertains to a movement's space. A direct movement happens in a straight, unwavering line. A flexible or indirect movement has twists or turns to it. In looking at a person moving from point A to point B, consider the movement in the spine. Look at the person from either the front or the back (not the sides) and observe what happens with the movement of the spine. Does the spine stay somewhat straight and rigid? Then it would be a direct movement. Does the spine twist from side to side or roll up and down or forward and back with the movement of the hips or shoulders? If so, the movement would be more flexible. Cats generally have very flexible movement. Often this flexibility will translate into gross motion as well: when moving from one place to another, a flexible person will meander, not traveling in a straight line, while a direct person will, as expected, move in a direct manner between points A and B. This could be something as small as foot placement—the flexible person taking steps that cross and move around each other, while the direct person's feet step directly in front of each other—to larger motion—a flexible person will actually wander back and forth in a serpentine-like walk, while the direct person will walk in a very straight line. In animation, Bowler Hat Man, from *Meet the Robinsons*, is a very flexible character, while the Road Runner is direct.

The final continuum is sustained versus quick. This is the hardest continuum to dissect. It deals with the tempo/rhythm of the movement, and thus is something that exists only in time, not in space. If a movement is sustained, it happens in one continuous even tempo or rhythm; it is consistent and equal. If the motion is quick, the tempo can change. It can start slightly faster and then slow down, or it could be faster in the initiation and the culmination of the movement but slower in the middle. It could also start slower and then speed up. Quick movement contains bursts of energy while sustained tends to evenly spread the energy throughout the motion. As animators, you should have a better sense than the general population concerning the timing of motions, so use your skills to observe people and animals moving around, looking to see whose motions are quick and whose are sustained.

If you are considering a person moving from point A to point B, watch him or her from the side. Does it appear that the person has one even, fluid energy of motion, as if a rope were tied to the person's chest, slowly reeling the person in? If so, then the movement would be sustained. Or does it appear that the movement has short bursts of energy that alter tempos within each burst? If so, then the movement would be quick. An extreme example of quick would be Steve Martin dancing and snapping his fingers in *The Jerk* as he is trying to find rhythm. Elaine's famous jerky dance in *Seinfeld* is another great example of quick motion. In animation a sustained mover would be Crush, the "surfer dude" turtle in *Finding Nemo*, while Dori, the forgetful fish from the same movie, would be quick.

When a movement or mover (person, animal, or object) is analyzed for these three continua, one can determine the Effort shape that the movement carries. Different combinations of these continua lead to different Effort shapes, which Laban categorized. Different Effort shapes suggest different qualities that in turn suggest different personalities or characteristics for a person (or animal, or cartoon character). Laban has named the different Effort shapes carefully, suggesting the precise quality of movement with the name. Using his categories, we can specify the qualities of movement and use those specifics to suggest qualities of a character. Furthermore the Effort shape, when applied to a particular gesture, can carry an intention or objective for a character. Sometimes a character will generally follow one Effort shape, but a specific motion will clearly be another, and this difference indicates some different intention for the character. For example, if a generally laid-back character, whose movement is continuous, suddenly begins to move in a quick, darting manner, one would understand that something has changed in his circumstances: perhaps he is lying to his girlfriend, or thinks the police might be after him. Motion can carry intention as well as character, so the better we understand Laban's Effort shapes, the more precisely we can craft both overall characteristics for an animated character and also specific intention for a given moment in the animation.

There are a possible eight combinations of the three sets of two variables, so there are eight Effort shapes: wring, press, slash, punch, dab, flick, glide, and float. Let's discuss each one in more detail.

Wring

The wring Effort shape is composed of the strong, flexible, and sustained qualities. Thus a movement that is strong, flexible, and sustained would be a wringing movement. To

Figure 8.1

Wringing out a towel

get a better idea what a wring is, think about basic gestures that we call wringing. When squeezing the water from a towel, we are wringing out the towel, as shown in Figure 8.1. Think about this gesture: to wring water out of the towel, you use a lot of force (strong) to twist (flexible) in a continuous manner (sustained) water from the towel. Sometimes when people are anxious or concerned, they wring their hands to alleviate stress. Again, this is a strong, flexible sustained motion.

Gestures can be wringing gestures, such as the ones just listed, or people themselves can be wringers. Wringers move through space, gesture, and interact with others in a strong, flexible, sustained manner. In animation many moustache-twisting villains would be wringers; a recent example is the Bowler Hat Man in *Meet the Robinsons*.

This type of movement suggests certain qualities. Obviously since the movement is strong, a shy, retiring, or weak character could never be a wringer. Because the movement is flexible it suggests, on one extreme, a looser, easygoing type of character, and on the other extreme, it could mean a more sly, conniving, and manipulative one. Because the movement is sustained, it is always going to be more fluid and thus would not work well for someone who is easily startled.

A wringer is a complicated character to animate—especially for hand-drawn animation—due to the twisting and heavier motion, so you will tend not to find wringers frequently in low budget cartoons. Instead, these characters more frequently populate full-length movies with the budget and animation talent available to create them. Fortunately 3D character rigs make creating wringer characters easier than ever before, so creating this kind of character is not as difficult as with pencil or ink animation. However, even with good rigs you will find this type of character tends to take longer to animate than some of the direct ones.

Press

A press is determined by a movement that is strong, direct, and sustained. To get a better idea of this combination, think about when we use the term "press" in our daily lives. We press flowers in a book. We press our clothes. We press metal into sheets. All of these movements require strength. They must be direct and sustained or the pattern or object will be destroyed. Think about when you press your clothes, as shown in Figure 8.2: the movement is strong, sustained and direct to press out the wrinkles. If the movement were light, flexible, or quick, one would do a poor job pressing clothes.

Figure 8.2

Pressing clothes

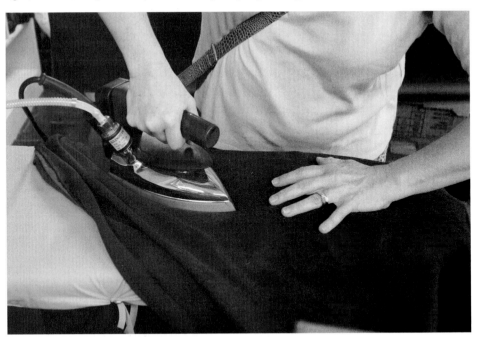

This movement suggests character qualities that are similar to that of the wringer. It is still strong and sustained so it will be inhabited by a dominant, fluid character, but since it is direct as opposed to flexible it will often not have the easygoing or conniving qualities that a wringer would possess. The intentions of this character would be more direct and not as hidden. A character like Mr. Incredible, from *The Incredibles*, could be seen as a presser: he is strong and direct, and his movements are sustained rather than quick, like when he lifts a heavy object over his head.

Due to the more direct nature of a presser's motion, these characters are easier to animate than wringers. The major difficulty with them is to imply the correct amount of weight for the characters, who are often weighty. Since their motion is continuous, one must be aware of creating weight without sharp stops and starts. On the other hand, the motion is fluid and straightforward, which helps with the sense of weight.

Slash

The slashing movement is created by a strong, flexible, quick gesture. If you think of Indiana Jones slashing his way through a rain forest jungle with a machete, you will see a slashing movement. For another example, any of the pirate battles in the *Pirates of the Caribbean* series exhibit lots of slashing movement with the slashing of the swords. Look at the position of the wrist in Figure 8.3: as the arm and wrist move to strike with the sword, the wrist must lead the sword, which is flexible, and the motion must be strong or it will have no affect. Finally, the motion must be quick to block a surprise attack or to strike without one's enemy anticipating the motion.

Figure 8.3

Slashing with a sword

The slashing movement demands alertness and agility in a character. It suggests qualities of boldness and bravado, and perhaps also recklessness. A slasher is poised to strike a deathblow in any direction. In animation we can observe slasher qualities in Bugs Bunny while he is conducting (to death) the opera singer in the cartoon, *Long Haired Hare*. As Bugs conducts, he slashes his arms up and down to make the singer change notes, and you can actually see the drawings of his arm turn into solid sheets for a few frames during the motion, which shows just how much of a slashing motion the animators were after.

To animate a slasher, you want to be sure your motions are quick, but also that there are moments of near stillness between the movements. If you don't create those contrasting still moments, the slashing ones won't read as well, and the movement will become muddied and look like other types of movement.

Punch

Figure 8.4

Throwing a punch to break a board

A punch is fairly easy to recognize, probably because we have all delivered or received a punch. At the very least, we have seen punches thrown in a playground fight or a classic western or kung fu movie. Seeing, delivering, or receiving a punch leaves a lasting image in our minds: punches deliver damage in a strong, unexpected manner. An effective punch (unlike the unwieldy roundhouse punches often thrown in drunken brawls) is a strong, quick, direct movement that packs a great deal of power in a very small space. Think about a martial artist breaking a board, as in Figure 8.4: in order to break the board, the movement must be strong or it will have no effect. It also needs a direct, quick burst of energy to break the board.

A person who moves like a puncher is very easy to recognize. She seems to throw a jab with every step she takes. Punch. Punch. Punch. Punch. The punching movement suggests wonderful things character-wise. It is strong, decisive, and aggressive. In animation you can observe a puncher in the movement of the Road Runner when it eats bird seed: the "bam-bam-bam-bam" motion of its beak whacking into the pile of bird seed.

Animating a puncher is a great deal of fun, and due to the quick motions, is relatively easier to animate—though one generally generates a lot of keyframes to create all of the motion involved. Punchers walk and move in quick, but purposeful motions (not spastic motion, which is a different type), so animating them is all about driving motions and fairly sharp changes in direction.

Dab

The first four Effort shapes were all strong and therefore all carried some similar qualities of weight and power. The next four are all light and thus will suggest very different character types. The first one to consider is the dab, which is the exact opposite of the wringer, who is strong, flexible, and sustained. As shown in Figure 8.5, a dab is light, direct, and quick. Think about when we dab in our daily life. We dab paint on to a wall to create a sponge effect. We dab on makeup or something like acne cream. We dab up a small spill.

Light, direct, and quick movement suggests wonderful things in terms of character. A dabber will automatically be a slightly weaker character, given the light quality of its motion. Because these characters are direct and quick they can be somewhat erratic or easily startled. They can also be somewhat rigid, repressed or intellectual. Dot, from *Animaniacs*, is a nice example of a dabber, especially when she does her "I'm cute" business.

Figure 8.5
Dabbing a hand dry

Animating a dabber can be a bit challenging, as the motion has to be direct and quick but at the same time light. The tendency will be to make the character look a bit heavy, or alternatively to make it look too floaty for a dabber. The secret is to round out the peaks and troughs of the animation curves just a bit to keep the character light. Characters with this type of movement are a bit underrepresented in animation, but they are a great type to animate, and really have a distinct look on screen.

Flick

A great example of a flick that almost everyone can relate to is flicking a towel at someone. A flick, which is light, flexible, and quick, is the opposite of a press, which is strong, direct, and sustained. Try flicking some water across the table at your dining partner and you will observe a flick firsthand: in order to make the water travel through space, the movement of the arm, hand, and finger must be light, flexible, and quick. Look at the movement of the tie in Figure 8.6 to observe a flick captured in motion.

It would be difficult for a flicker to be anything but fun, so they tend to be comic relief–type characters. A flick suggests airy, frivolous, and easygoing. A flick can't really do a lot of damage; rather, it is ineffectual or playful. Flicking can be observed in animation in characters like Dori in *Finding Nemo*. Her motion is light, quick, and flexible, and she is definitely airy and frivolous in her mannerisms.

Creating a flicker's motion takes a bit of work, but the classic animation technique of "breaking" joints (so that they bend backwards) during a motion is a great way to create this type of character. Of course plenty of overshoot after the main motion is also called for, as is a good deal of offsetting of keyframes for differing body parts. The goal is to create a looser character that's a lot of fun to animate and to watch.

A great reference guide to animation that speaks at length about breaking joints in (hand-drawn) characters is *The Animator's Survival Kit* (Faber & Faber, 2002), by Richard Williams. Williams, who directed animation for *Who Framed Roger Rabbit?*, learned from the best of the first-generation Disney animators, and his insights are very beneficial for any animator.

Figure 8.6

Flicking a tie

Glide

You will recognize a person who is a glider right away. They seem to move as if they are gliding on a pair of ice skates, as in Figure 8.7. A glider almost doesn't contact the earth and the top of their head is always at the same level as they move. A gliding movement is light, direct, and sustained, which is the opposite of a slasher, which is strong, flexible, and quick. A glide is a very smooth, fluid, and even motion with purpose and direction.

Figure 8.7

A skater (Mariah Behm) gliding across the ice

Gliders exude grace. They seem relaxed and controlled at the same time due to their lightness mixed with sustained, direct movement. While in motion, Eve in *Wall-E* is gliding. She will often initiate her movement or switch directions in a quick manner, but while in motion she is gliding. Another place where many people recognize gliding motion is in marching bands as they make formations or in a color guard as they take the field. The members' heads are always on the same plane and their feet roll lightly across the top of the earth.

This light, direct, sustained motion can be a challenge for animators, not because it is difficult to animate—in fact, in CG animation this is about the simplest movement to animate—but because a character can come across as being too unearthly, too light, or too "CG-like." If you consider the qualities of a glider, you get a sustained, direct motion, which can be achieved as simply as setting two keyframes at differing times and letting the object move consistently between them in a gliding motion. (Consider a simple box or sphere moving between two points in a linear manner.) If you add in the quality of lightness, then your goal is to keep weight out of the animation as well, which means your character shouldn't bounce too heavily while moving (e.g., the head and hips will remain on more or less the same plane during a walk), furthering the possibility for creating motion that is "too smooth." Thus, while gliding seems to be an ideal type of movement for animators to create, they shy away from it normally, with notable exceptions like Eve and Frollo from Disney's *The Hunchback of Notre Dame*, who carries himself in a gliding manner in order to put on the façade that he is above all earthly concerns. Instead, gliding is usually reserved for special circumstances: when a character goes skating, or slips and slides on an icy pond—as in Peter Jackson's 2005 remake of *King Kong*—or is wearing socks on a hardwood floor. In these instances, characters don't move in their normal mode, taking on gliding for a specific scene and to show a specific interaction with their environments.

Float

Figure 8.8
A balloon floating on air

David Letterman once had a segment on his late-night show called, "Will It Float?" where he would place objects in water to see if they would float. Ideally he wanted to surprise the audience about what could actually float. One thing that this segment illustrated quite clearly was that size is not the determining factor in floating. We all recognize what something is like when it is floating. It is light and continually moves in an irregular manner. Soap floats. Balloons float. Clouds float. Boats float. Many different things, in many different sizes, float.

All things, regardless of their size or shape, have the potential to move with a floating motion. The movement of float is light, flexible, and sustained, the opposite of punch, which is strong, direct, and quick. One of the best ways to observe a floating motion is to watch a balloon as it is released outside on a calm day, as shown in Figure 8.8. As the balloon gently glides along, it will twist and turn as it bobs and weaves in the breeze. The motion is light and constant but with flexibility (as opposed to gliding, which is direct).

We often can observe floating in animation—and often during special circumstances (as with the glide). One classic bit is for a character to suck on an air hose and suddenly fill with helium or air; they then float away, often helplessly, until they release the air or are "popped." As they are set under water, many of the characters in *Finding Nemo* and *The Little Mermaid* spend time floating. Due to their being suspended, in these movies animators created gentle back-and-forth motions due to waves, and allowed the characters to move vertically as well as horizontally, all creating a floating movement quality. Internally, floating suggests qualities of ease or sometimes aloofness. A floater can be peaceful but not necessarily. The Queen of Hearts in *Alice in Wonderland* and Ursula in *The Little Mermaid* both spend time floating, but are by no means peaceful, nice characters. Thus floating can present character qualities of ease and calm, or arrogance and superiority, depending on other traits the characters have.

Animating a floating character is easier to achieve well than is animating a gliding character. The flexible nature of a floater allows you to create "eddying" motions on the character, which helps sell the weight (or momentum, to be more precise) of the character as well as its interactions with the world. Consider a beach ball's movement: while the ball itself drifts along, it is susceptible to air currents, gravity (albeit slowly), striking a wall or table, and of course being hit by someone. The fact that the beach ball can rotate slowly and eddy (drift back and forth about its center of gravity) as it moves, as well as the fact that it can change directions quickly upon striking (or being struck by) another object, creates a much more lively motion than does gliding, which perforce must continue on in a direct, uninterrupted manner. The really fun thing about animating floating characters is that they can (and often are) very large. If you are a fan of the *Dune* books, consider how much character you could impart to Baron Vladimir Harkonnen, who is so heavy that he is held up by floating devices attached to his body. The contrasting nature of a very large, heavy body buoyed up by these devices so that he weighs almost nothing could make for some fun animation.

Exercises to Use Laban's Movement Categories in Acting

The following exercises are designed to help you both mentally and physically understand Laban's Effort shapes. All of these exercises can be done by yourself, but it is quite useful to have at least one outside observer to give you feedback. If you don't have an outside eye, a full-length mirror will be helpful. Even better than a full-length mirror would be to work in a dance studio that has a complete wall of mirrors. You can also videotape yourself and watch the playback, but this is less efficient since you can't see yourself as you actually do the exercises.

Analyzing Walks

A good way to begin your personal exploration of Laban's Effort shapes is by analyzing different walks. This will give you a basis for understanding the different effort shapes and then a tangible means of changing your personal movement. For this exercise, when analyzing your own movement you must have either some kind of an outside eye looking at you or a group of people. If you are not working with a group, you may record your own movement, then play it back and watch it in order to analyze the motion.

Bear in mind that motion study is not an exact science. Because we are examining continua, some people can and do fall very much in the middle between the extremes of particular motion types. It may then be more difficult to determine which end of that continuum they are closer to. Also, when a person's movement falls very close to the middle of a continuum, it is relatively easy for the individual to subconsciously change his or her movement to either side of the continuum. In fact, they might even do this naturally depending on the circumstances.

Say a person falls very much in the middle of the continuum from direct to flexible. He might change his movement subconsciously from flexible to direct without even thinking about it. When relaxed and hanging out with friends, his movement might be more flexible, as opposed to when he is in a formal business meeting giving a presentation, where he would be more direct.

Some people are much more difficult to analyze than others, so it is really helpful to have a group of at least 12 to compare and contrast when doing this walk exercise. If you get stuck with a particular person, you can skip ahead and analyze another individual, then come back to the initial person when you have others to compare him to.

To analyze a walk, examine each one of the continua separately. Pick a point A and a point B and instruct the individual being analyzed to walk between those points. The walk needs to have intention or purpose and be as close to the walker's natural walk as possible. The walker should imagine that he is walking to meet someone at a restaurant for lunch. He is not late or rushed to get there, but he has an intention for his walk: he knows where he is going and that he should be there on time. The walker should keep walking from point A to point B, then reverse course and walk from B to A. It is a good idea to continue this walk for several minutes. At first the walker will likely be self-conscious, but as he continues to walk, he will relax into what is his more natural stride, allowing the observer(s) to get a better sense of his natural motion.

For the remainder of this exercise, we will assume you are the observer, either watching a tape of yourself or watching another person and analyzing their movement. First consider the continuum of strong versus light. Watch the walk from the side and take note of how the body interacts with the earth. Does the walker sink into the floor? Does the whole foot roll from heel to toe and push off the earth as it moves to the next stride? Do the feet hitting the floor make sound? If so, this walk would be categorized as strong. On the other hand, does the foot seem to avoid or only make slight contact with the earth? Does the walker only contact the ground with part of the foot—the toes, the outside, or the instep? Does the foot land lightly on the ground and then does it not push off strongly into the next stride? If so, the walk would be categorized as light. Strong versus light tends to change a lot as a person relaxes, so be sure to allow the subject to walk for a minute before trying to analyze this continuum.

Next let's look at the continuum of direct versus flexible. For this continuum, it is necessary to observe the walk from the front and back as opposed to from the side. If you are working with a group of people, change the position of your point A and point B so that you are walking toward and away from your classmates. If you are taping yourself, change the position of the camera and tape yourself for several minutes walking toward and away from the camera.

Observe the movement within the torso and of the spine to analyze this continuum. Does the spine remain fairly straight? Do the shoulders and hips remain relatively stable? Does it appear as if a rope is tied to the sternum or belly and is continuously pulling the torso forward? If so, the walk would be more direct. On the other hand, does the spine twist and bend from side to side or front to back with the rolling of the hips? Does the torso flex back and forth or around the hips? This type of walk would be more flexible. Do not allow the movement of the arms to confuse you. Some people can be very direct within their torsos but their arms swing wildly.

Finally, look to the continuum of sustained versus quick. It is necessary to examine this continuum from the side, so return your point A and point B to the original starting position. If using a camera, you can move the camera back to your first taping position. This is the most difficult continuum to analyze, as it relates almost solely to timing, so comparing a large number of walks to others will help you determine if a given one is sustained or quick. If all else fails, go outside on a busy street during lunch hour and watch the passersby, taking note of whose motion is sustained and whose is quick.

To determine quick versus sustained, first consider whether the energy of the walk is consistent throughout. Does the tempo remain the same from the initiation to the completion of a stride? Does it appear as if the walk is being controlled by a rope pulling the person at an even tempo? If so, the walk would be considered sustained. On the other hand, does the walk have quick bursts of energy? Does the tempo change within each stride? Is the tempo inconsistent from one step to the next? If so, the walk would be considered quick.

After dividing yours and others' walks along the three continua, you will have determined to which extreme you are closer within each of the continua. Referencing the earlier list, you can now tell what Effort shape your natural movement corresponds to. If you have a group, it is wonderful to watch everyone that is one certain shape moving at the same time, so try this if you are able: for example, have all of the wringers come to the front of the room. Have them line up shortest to tallest and, beginning at point A, have them move to point B. They shouldn't try to copy anyone else's movement, but they all should start on the right foot and continue to move left, right, left, right at the same time. If you have analyzed the movement correctly, you will be amazed to see that all of these disparate people look alike as they move. It will surprise you how people that you view so differently and who look very different physically can all move the same way. If you have had difficulty analyzing anyone's movement, having the person walk with a possible Effort shape group is a good way to compare them to several different Effort shapes and see what shape they most closely resemble. Try this group walk with all of the different Effort shapes you have in your group.

Changing Your Walk

Now that you know your own Effort shape, try to change to another shape. To do this, take a walk. You can just walk around in a circle in a classroom, but it is much more fun to take a walk outside and cover some territory. It would be useful to have the chart in Table 8.1 with you on your walk so you can note what your new shape is.

Table 8.1

Laban's Effort Shapes, Grouped into Opposing Pairs

WRINGER	DABBER
Strong	Light
Flexible	Direct
Sustained	Quick
PRESSER	**FLICKER**
Strong	Light
Direct	Flexible
Sustained	Quick
SLASHER	**GLIDER**
Strong	Light
Flexible	Direct
Quick	Sustained
PUNCHER	**FLOATER**
Strong	Light
Direct	Flexible
Quick	Sustained

To change your walk, begin by looking at each continuum separately. First, start walking your own natural walk. After you have sunk into your natural stride, turn your attention to the continuum of strong versus light. Remember what you are naturally and then try to change it to the opposite. For example, if you are strong, attempt to walk lightly. If you are light, attempt to move strongly. To help change this category, think about shifting your center to different positions in your body. A higher center in the upper torso, say your sternum to clavicle, will create a lighter motion. A lower center from your belly button down to your pelvis will create a stronger walk. Once you have adjusted yourself to your opposite, note what new Effort shape you have become.

Now go back to your natural walk; relax for a moment (so that you fully return to your normal stride) and then try the same thing for the continuum of direct versus flexible. If you are direct, try to move flexibly. If you are flexible, try to move more directly. To move directly, think about keeping your torso very rigid. Don't allow your spine or sternum to flex. If you wish to move more flexibly, roll as you walk. Allow your spine to twist and turn. After you have achieved this other movement, note what new Effort shape you have become.

Lastly, examine the continuum of sustained versus quick. After returning to your natural walk, try to switch your movement within this continuum. If you are sustained, try to become quicker. If you are quick, try to become more sustained. Changing your tempo can help a bit here: literally move at a faster pace for quick and a slower pace for sustained. If you want to be more sustained, try walking as if you are in waist-deep water and every step is fluid. If you want to be quicker, imagine that your feet are stuck in mud and that you have to pull your foot free, and as soon as it frees itself from the mud it moves faster. After you have changed the rhythm of your walk, note what new Effort shape you have become.

Now let's move on and try to change two of the continua at once. This will become much more difficult, as you have to concentrate on changing two facets of your walk simultaneously. Begin walking with your own natural walk, and then switch the continuum of strong versus light. If you are strong, go light. If you are light, go strong. After you have that established, add in the continuum of direct versus flexible. If you are direct go flexible, and if you are flexible go direct. After practicing the new motion, note what new Effort shape you have become.

Return to your natural walk and try changing another pair of continua. First, focus on the continuum of strong versus light. If you are strong, go light, and if you are light, go strong. After you have that established, add in the continuum of sustained versus quick. If you are sustained, go quick, and if you are quick, go sustained. Once you have those two changes established, note what new Effort shape you have become.

Return once again to your natural walk. Now focus on two new continua. First change the continuum of direct versus flexible. If you are direct, go flexible, and if you are flexible, go direct. Once you have that established, add in the continuum of sustained versus quick. If you are sustained, go quick, and if you are quick, go sustained. Once you have established these two changes, note what new Effort shape you have become.

At this point you will have explored all of the Effort shapes except one: the shape that is the complete opposite of your natural walk. This, of course, will be the most difficult to achieve, and you might feel very awkward doing it, which is perfectly natural. In order to walk in your complete opposite you must change all three movement continua. As always, begin in your natural walk. Then focus on the continuum of strong versus light. Next add in the continuum of direct versus flexible. Finally, focus on the continuum of sustained versus quick. Now you will be walking in the Effort shape that is the complete opposite of your natural walk.

Different people have very different responses to the different Effort shapes. Generally speaking, it is easier to change if you are more in the middle of a given continuum. If you are on a far extreme of one of the continua, it can be very difficult for you to change that particular continuum, so be patient with yourself. Thus, some people might have great difficulty changing light versus strong while others might have difficulty changing direct versus flexible. One thing you will discover in this exploration process is just how comfortable your natural movement is, and how much effort it takes for you to change it to something else.

Exploring the Effort Shapes with the Entire Body

The next set of exercises will help you explore taking an Effort shape into the entire body and translating that into gesture and movement and finally character. The process will be the same for each of the Effort shapes. It is helpful but not necessary to have mirrors to observe yourself in these exercises, and also helpful to have a group so you can observe as well as enact each exercise. Make sure that you warm up first so that you are prepared to begin the explorations. Additionally, as in exercises from previous chapters, it will be useful to place props and objects around the room to work with as you become comfortable with each Effort shape.

Wring

After warming up, stand in a neutral position. Think about the Effort shape of wring. Remember that it is strong, flexible, and sustained. See if you can move your entire body into a wring, as shown in Figure 8.9.

Figure 8.9

Actors exploring wring in the extreme

As you explore this Effort shape, don't settle on the first position that you come up with. Try ways in which you can make your whole body strong, flexible, and sustained. Note how this position makes you feel. Observe if this position suggests any qualities or characteristics.

Now try to wring in this body: maintaining your physical position, try to move and wring. Try to wring this whole body through space. Again, note if you feel anything or if any qualities or characteristics present themselves to you.

Now slowly make this very abstract wringing movement that you have created to a more human place. Try to translate the movement into the body and gestures of a real person. To do this, continue to move slowly, distilling the movement into a more upright position. Keep the wring in your torso in a way that is more upright. Allow the wring to become gestures that you might use in real life, as shown in Figure 8.10.

Continue to wring around the room, interacting with props and people. See how this wringing makes you feel and interact with others. Note any qualities or characteristics that present themselves as you interact in the wring. As you have done in previous chapters, see if you can create a character based on the feeling and qualities suggested by the wring Effort shape. Come up with a name for this character. Begin to introduce yourself to others in the room. How does that wringer sound? How can the wring become a part of the voice? Does the shape affect your pitch, tempo, and/or rhythm? Allow your voice to wring as well as your body.

After you have introduced yourself to other people in the room, go back and speak to one of your group-mates. Find out three things about this person's character, and share three things about your character with him. Then go on to another person and tell the new person three things about the first person you met. While you are doing all of this, make sure that your walk, gestures, and body continue to wring. Allow this wringing to create the character.

Figure 8.10

Wring in gesture

Press

Follow the steps above for a press, which is strong, direct and sustained. First create the press in your whole body, as seen in Figure 8.11. Then transition the movement into a human being that has the gesture and qualities of a press, as seen in Figure 8.12. Finally, use the feelings and qualities of the press to create a character that interacts with space, objects and other pressers. Don't forget to take the press into your voice.

Figure 8.11

Actors exploring press in the extreme

Figure 8.12

Actors exploring press in gesture

Slash

Repeat the same sequence for the slash Effort shape. Create a slash, which is strong, flexible, and quick, with the whole body and slash around the room, as shown in Figure 8.13. Distill the slash into real human movement, and note how this movement makes you feel as you interact with the space and objects, as shown in Figure 8.14. Now create a character from the slash. Allow the qualities and feelings that accompany the movement of the slasher to create a character that you share with others. How does this slasher relate vocally and physically to other people?

Figure 8.13

Actor exploring slash in the extreme

Figure 8.14

Actor exploring the slash Effort shape

Punch

Once again, repeat the sequence for the final strong Effort shape, punch. Try to feel the whole body as a punch: strong, direct, and quick. Figure 8.15 shows an actor in a punch. Now distill the punch down to real human movement, as Figure 8.16 shows. Finally create a character from the punch. Allow the feelings and qualities of the punch movement to dictate the character and how he interacts with the world. What kind of tactics does a punch employ when interacting with others?

Figure 8.15

Actor exploring punch in the extreme

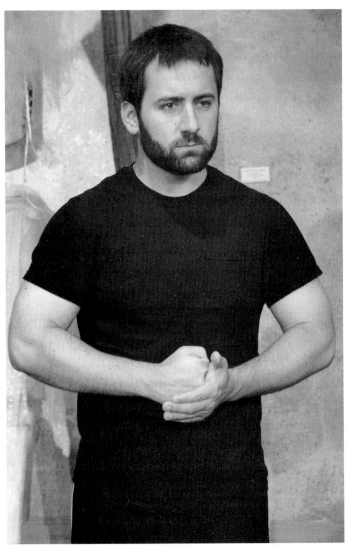

Figure 8.16

Actor in punch

Dab

Now move on to the light Effort shapes and create movement and characters from these. Start with dab: light, direct, and quick. Find a dab in your entire body, as illustrated in Figure 8.17. Once again, allow this shape to distill down into real human movement, as shown in Figure 8.18. Finally, repeat the process to develop a character from the dab Effort shape and have it interact with objects and other people.

Figure 8.17

Actor exploring dab in the extreme

Figure 8.18

Actor dabbing

Figure 8.19

Actors exploring flick with their full bodies

Flick

The flick Effort shape is light, flexible, and quick. Find a flick in the extreme in your whole body. Figure 8.19 shows actors doing this. Next, distill the movement down to gesture, as shown in Figure 8.20. Now allow the qualities and feelings that come from the flicking motion to help you create a character based on the Effort shape flick, and have it interact with the people and objects in your space.

Figure 8.20

Actor flicking

Glide

Begin to explore glide with your whole body. A glide is light, direct, and sustained like an ice skater or marching band member. The actor in Figure 8.21 is exploring glide. Reduce the shape so that you can find glide in a gesture, as shown in Figure 8.22. Create a character from the glide. What sort of a person glides? How does a glider sound and interact with others? What sorts of tactics would a glider use to get what they want? Play around with this.

Figure 8.21

Actor exploring glide in the extreme

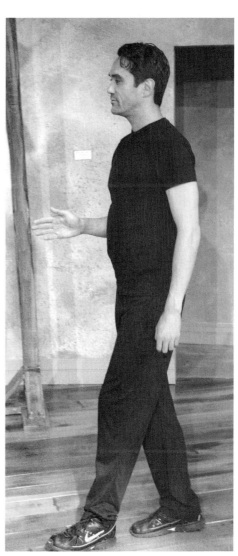

Figure 8.22

Actor gliding

Float

The last Effort shape is float, which is light, flexible, and sustained like a balloon floating through the air. Explore and find the float in your whole body, as shown in Figure 8.23. Now allow the float to translate and distill down to real human movement and gesture, as seen in Figure 8.24. Finally, create a character from float. Interact with the space, props, and other people as your float character, and take note of the way this shape adjusts your interactions with others.

Figure 8.23
Actor exploring float with her entire body

Figure 8.24
Actor floating

Creating Laban Effort Shapes in Animated Characters

Now that you have a solid, physical conception of the eight Laban Effort shapes, let's work through some exercises to transfer this knowledge into animated characters. There are myriad possible exercises based on the differing Effort shapes; we will present three examples using specific Effort shapes, which should serve as starting points for you to explore the other Effort shapes using the same format. On the accompanying DVD are several video files (`WringWalkFront.mov`, `SlashWalkSide.mov`, etc.) that contain reference video for walk cycles done with each character type, taped from the front and the side. Be sure to utilize these files as you work with Laban's Effort shapes in your animation work.

Creating a Wring Pose

First, we will create an Effort shape pose based on the characteristics of the wring Effort shape. We will first distort our model into an extreme wring shape, and then reduce this pose somewhat so that it might fit an animated character: more exaggerated than a realistic human, but still able to interact well with its animated environment.

Open a new scene file in your 3D software of choice and import a character. (If you are using Maya, feel free to use the Genna or Marcel rig included on the DVD.) Then create a new camera, import the `WringPose.jpg` file from the accompanying DVD, and use it as a background image for the camera. Figure 8.25 shows the model placed against the background image. Note that due to the pose, the actor's left foot is to the right of the right one in the photograph, so your model should be placed with her left foot on the appropriate foot, as in the image.

Figure 8.25

Placing the Genna model against an actor creating an exaggerated wring Effort shape

> Please see Chapter 4 for more information on importing images and using the book's included rigs in Autodesk Maya.

Using the background image as a guide, pose your character into a solid, full-body wring shape. Don't feel that you have to mimic the actor's shape; just use it as a general guideline to get you started creating your own shape. You might find that you wish to twist your character around more, past the bounds of physical possibility (and what looks good with the model!), and this is fine for now: you are exploring the limits of this Effort shape, not creating a pose that would actually be used in production. Figure 8.26 shows the results of posing our tortured model into position.

Figure 8.26

Twisting the model into an exaggerated wring shape

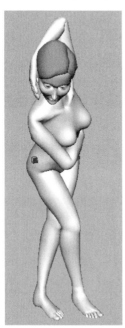

Now save your scene file with a new name, and then keyframe your first pose and move forward in the timeline, then create a pose that is reduced from the exaggerated pose. This pose can still be exaggerated from the realistic but should now be ensconced in character, allowing the model to move about in space (perhaps in a distorted manner), and interact with other characters in a unique fashion. Figure 8.27 shows the results we came up with for our character-based wring Effort shape; yours will almost surely end up different. For reference, we have included our Maya file, `wringerPose.mb`, on the DVD.

As you are creating this second pose (and potentially after you finish it), consider how the physicality of this character will force it to move and interact with its environment. Will the character walk sideways, or with a limp? Will it be an evil, or sad, or timid character? Will the character be aggressive or shy in its relationships with other characters? Will it like to reach out and touch objects or keep itself wrapped up and protected from the outside world? In what sorts of situations would this character be comfortable, and (more amusingly) in what situations would it be uncomfortable? Use these observations to help build a character; give him or her a name and a past and goals. By the time you finish, you should have a distinct and unique character that can provide humor or pathos in an animation. Our character is timid, protecting herself from the outside world, but also angry about something, generating a quality of cautiousness and fear in the character that could be used in animation work going forward.

Figure 8.27

Distilling the wring Effort shape to something an animated character could use

Creating a Punch Walk Cycle

Now let's create a walk cycle based on the punch Effort shape. For this exercise we'll base the walk off of video reference we have on the accompanying DVD. Later, you can explore this and other walks in a more exaggerated fashion if you wish, using the included walk cycles as a basis for your work.

If you are using the included models (Genna and Marcel), which include built-in character/ subcharacter hierarchies, you can have Maya automatically select the characters as you go. First, place the autoCharacterSelection.mel file in your home scripts directory (~Autodesk/ maya/scripts on your home directory), then copy the line of code from ACSEnable.mel into the Script Editor input pane, and drag it up onto your shelf. When you start up Maya, simply click the ACSEnable button, and from then on, Maya will automatically select whichever sub- character it needs based on what is selected in the scene. This makes selecting and keyfram- ing characters far easier than having to remember to do so yourself.

For this walk, since we have front and side views, we created two cameras rather than one, and attached the front and side views to the cameras. Then, as the actor doesn't actu- ally get well on screen in the side view until frame 9, and gets near exiting at frame 78, we cropped the timeline to fit this. We then used frame 48, where the actor is in the middle of the screen from the side, to match the model to the actor, as shown in Figure 8.28.

Next, in the side view, starting at frame 12, when the actor's hips are visible, we key just the hips into position in Z and Y, hiding the geometry so that it's easier to see where the body lines up. As the arms and legs would drag otherwise, we also pull them into a

Figure 8.28

Initial matching of the model to the video sequence at frame 48

basic position that matches the hips. At frames 12, 16, 22, 29, 36, 42, 47, 54, 59, 67, 72, and 78, we set keys on the heel strike and passing positions of the walk cycle. (Frames 12 and 90 are not properly passing positions but are ini- tial and final frames, so received keys.) After adjusting the hips, arms and legs into basic positions in the front view, we use the front view to adjust frame 90 and add a keyframe at frame 4 (the first frame of the animation) as well as at frame 9, which is a heel strike. Figure 8.29 shows the control rig overlaid onto the video sequence.

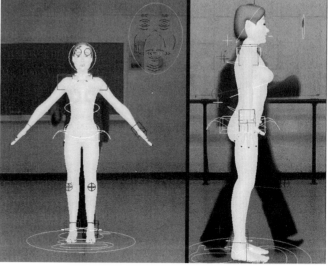

After this initial work, our rig follows the front and side motions with the hips. The rest of the work involves adjusting the feet and arms so that they match more precisely, add- ing foot roll to the walk, twisting the torso and neck a small amount (since the punch is a direct walk, there is not much torso motion), and adding a basic facial look to the walk (most easily done from the front view near the end). In the end we get a nice punch walk with some good pop to it—a basis for exaggeration or further exploration of this walk. Figure 8.30 shows a still from the animation, which is on the accompanying DVD as punchWalkAnimated.mov. In addition, we have included puncherWalk.mb on the DVD should you wish to look at how we animated the character.

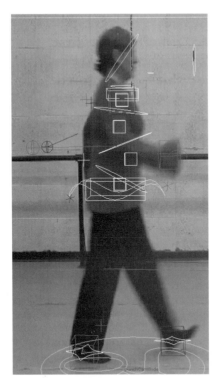

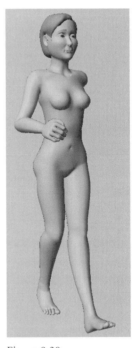

Figure 8.29

Matching the hips to the video sequence

Figure 8.30

The final punch shape walk cycle

The included DVD contains walks by various actors from front and side views. (These views were recorded at different times, so they will not match up precisely.) The movies are listed with the name and view on them; for example, `dabberWalkSide.mov` and `dabberWalkFront.mov`. Use these video sequences to get a better understanding of the sometimes subtle differences between the Effort shapes involved in these walks, and also to explore animating the different walks.

Wiping Tears Using the Flick and Dab Effort Shapes

As a final exercise, we are going to animate a simple gesture—wiping away tears—using two distinct Effort shapes: the flick and dab shapes. Using this exercise, we will get a better sense of how a gesture can be quite different when done with differing Effort shapes. For reference, we have `flickWipe.mov` and `dabWipe.mov` on the accompanying DVD. On looking over the files, you can easily see not only that the action of wiping tears is very different using these two distinct Effort shapes, but that the two shapes carry with them very different emotional qualities. The flick wipe is quick and shows something like frustration or annoyance at crying: the actor is trying to get rid of the tears quickly, and the flick of her finger is a little bit aggressive. The dab wipe, on the other hand, is much slower and contains more self-pity: the actor here dabs at her eye with a tissue, and is perhaps asking the viewer to take pity on her sad state. Figure 8.31 shows still frames from each sequence next to each other, showing how different this motion can be.

For this exercise, you can either load in the video sequence and use it as a guide for your animation or you can look at it a few times and then create your own motion. If you choose to load in the video sequence, we found that placing the character beside, rather than in front of, the actor video, as shown in Figure 8.32, makes it easier to create the animation.

> Note that the actor here is using the Alba breath technique to create sadness (see Chapter 9). This is just one example of the crossover between techniques described in the book.

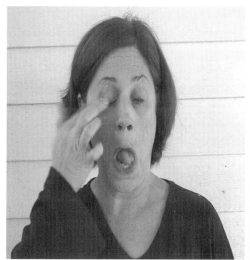 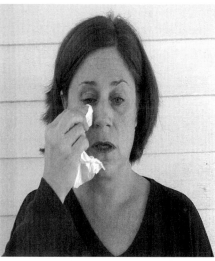

Figure 8.31

Wiping away tears with a flick (left) and a dab (right)

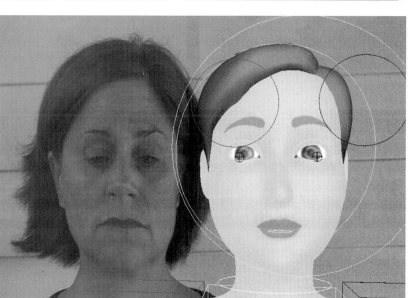

Figure 8.32

Placing the model beside the actor's head

First, we'll create the flick Effort shape. We will set a basic sad look on the model's face, and then animate the right arm and hand to create the wiping motion. As we are only animating the arm, upper chest, and head, we will leave the rest of the body alone for this animation—after all, there's no reason to animate what you can't see! Since this is a close-up on the hands and face, we set the fksdk setting of the right RtHandConfig node to 1 (forward kinematics), for better control over the fingers. The most crucial part of this short animation is about frames 30–39 of the video sequence, where the actor swipes her hand across her eye and "flicks" the tear away. As this is a flick Effort shape, the most work to make this animation pop should go into these frames. Aside from that, it's all about the subtlety of motion of the head and upper body, and the reaction of the face to the finger wiping across it. Figure 8.33 shows a frame from the resultant animation, flickWipeAnimated.mov, which, along with the Maya file, flickWipe.mb, is on the accompanying DVD.

On completing the flick version of the wipe, open a new scene and create a second, dab, version of this gesture using dabWipe.mov as a reference. This animation will be slower, and also gentler than the flick version. In addition, the head moves toward the hand as each dab is made, creating a back-and-forth motion to both the head and hand. While the actions are slower, there are still a number of keys that have to be set on the hands and head as each dab is made.

Start once again by getting the model's face in generally the correct pose, then animate the arm and fingers (once again, we did this with the forward kinematics setting on the fingers for more control), and then adjust the shoulders, neck, torso, and face to finesse the animation. Figure 8.34 shows a frame from the final animation, dabWipeAnimated.mov, which, along with the Maya file, dabWipe.mb, is on the accompanying DVD. When finished, note how differently the two animations you have made read, and how differently your audience would react to the two motions, even though both would be described as "wiping away tears."

Obviously there is a great deal more you can do to create different gestures using differing Laban Effort shapes. Videotape yourself, or grab a mirror and watch yourself performing different

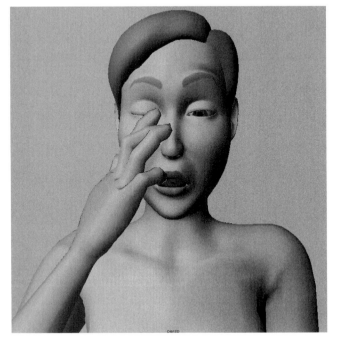

Figure 8.33

The model, wiping her eye with a flick gesture

motions and animate your characters to match or exaggerate these motions. Given the wide variety of Effort shapes, you can create just about any look you like for any gesture or walk, so animate away!

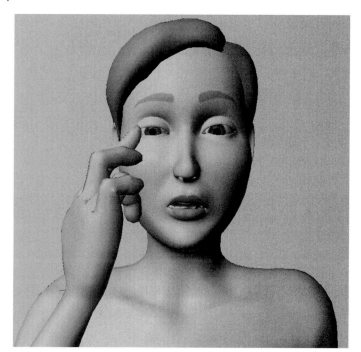

Figure 8.34

The model, dabbing at her eye

CHAPTER 9

Alba Emoting

Alba Emoting is a technique for exploring an emotional state in a purely physical manner. It allows an actor to release and control emotions in a safe and effective way. The key to the technique is the breath. An actor learns a breath pattern for an emotion and then adds in a series of tensions or relaxations and a postural attitude. When breath, tension, and posture are mastered, the actor will experience the emotion. This technique is particularly useful for animators for two reasons. First, it helps animators understand and experience the changes in breath and muscular tensions or relaxations that occur when experiencing an emotional state. Second, as this is an "outside-in" technique that generates emotions purely through physical effects (as opposed to having an emotion and then having a physical reaction to it), this technique can create highly convincing emotions in a nonliving character without the animator having to guess at what looks correct for that particular emotion. Thus, Alba Emoting is an effective technique for creating emotion when a director (or you) says something like "I want the character sad right here."

This chapter discusses:

- An explanation of Alba Emoting

- A look at the neutral breath

- A look at the six effector patterns

- Exercises to help you understand the patterns

- Exercises to transfer the emotions to animated characters

Development of Alba Emoting

Dr. Susana Bloch, a Chilean neuroscientist, after years of studying emotions in human beings, developed a psychosomatic theory of emotion that she termed *Alba Emoting*. Although there are varying opinions on exactly how many primary emotions there are, Bloch, through her research, claimed that humans experience six primary emotions: tenderness, anger, sexual love, fear, joy, and sadness. Other emotions (like guilt) are combinations of these primary emotions.

The key to her work was the discovery that all humans, no matter from where or from which cultural background, exhibit the same breath patterns, series of tensions and relaxations in the body, and postural attitudes when experiencing a particular emotion. Bloch called these responses *effector patterns*. She also identified a pattern of emotional neutrality. All of these patterns were the same regardless of gender, race, age, or background.

For the actor, emotion has always been a problem. How does one experience emotion? What, in fact, is emotion? Is it mental? Is it physical? Is it a mind-body combination? Actors are always searching for a means to experience genuine emotion reliably on the stage. Countless acting theories have been developed to capture, control, and maintain emotion. For the animator, this trouble is compounded by the fact that they must create the sense of emotion in an inanimate object, imbuing something nonliving with the subtle signs of human emotion.

Like an actor, whose work is highly creative, Bloch saw her work as a scientist to be equally artistic. She had many good friends in the arts, and she began to wonder, if she taught these effector patterns to her actor friends, could they experience genuine emotion at will? If so, she knew that this could be an invaluable tool for actors, who often struggle mightily and even cause themselves great personal emotional pain in their pursuit of honest emotion on the stage. She began teaching her actor friends the patterns while they were in rehearsal for a production of Garcia Lorca's play *The House of Bernarda Alba*, and the name Alba Emoting developed from that relationship. Bloch also liked the name because *alba* means pure or white in Spanish, and this represents the purity of the emotional experience.

Through work with these and other actors, she did indeed find that an individual could experience at will an emotion and also release that emotion by moving to the neutral breath, all without the need for an emotional context or psychological difficulties. Working with the actors, she refined her system and began to teach it internationally. Although Alba Emoting was designed as an acting technique, psychologists, therapists, and sociologists now are exploring the technique for its possible therapeutic benefits. The ability to utilize breath and tension patterns to replicate emotional response is ideally suited for animators as well, as one can almost follow a recipe to create external signs of an emotion in the character, removing all of the guesswork of creating emotions in animated characters. Of course, this ability comes at some cost: it takes time and effort to become proficient in the patterns.

For a full discourse on the subject of Alba Emoting, there is no better book than *The Alba of Emotions: Managing Emotions Through Breathing,* by Susana Bloch. This is the first (and only) English translation of Bloch's work and is available only via special order. Go to `http://facstaff.unca.edu/lfaccipo/`.

The Patterns

There are six basic effector patterns used in Alba Emoting for the six primary emotions, and additionally a seventh, very important pattern called neutral breath. Each pattern has three components: the breath, the tensions and/or relaxations of the body, and the postural attitude. Mastering these patterns takes a great deal of time and energy. Different patterns come easier to different people or at different times in life. Because these patterns have been scientifically identified as the way individuals experience emotion, you will find that you can observe them all the time in your daily life as you watch others experience emotions.

In fact, you should make a habit of watching people and observing what emotion they are experiencing by regarding their breathing, tension, and postural signs. It is also very interesting to look at pictures of celebrities and politicians to see if you can identify what they are feeling at the moment the picture was taken. Most individuals have several patterns that they spend the majority of their time in. When you understand and can identify the patterns, you will often observe that the patterns exhibited by an individual will belie what their words say; this can be especially true for politicians, who often feel one thing but must say another.

Within the Alba Emoting system, there are levels of emotion, ranging from 1 to 5. The lowest level, 1, is a weak emotion that occurs with some frequency—for joy, for example, joy 1 might be a slight happiness at getting a card or email from a friend. Level 5 is the other extreme: complete, all-out emotion that comes fairly rarely in our lives—for joy, this might be a moment of supreme religious intensity, when one feels a direct connection to their deity. In between are levels that range between these extremes.

Neutral Breath

The first pattern learned in Alba is that of neutral breath. This is the most important pattern as it allows you to release any emotion that you may experience, whether is be small or enormous. This pattern is practiced and returned to continually. It becomes a safety mechanism for the work, allowing you to escape from whatever you are feeling simply by changing your breathing and tension pattern.

Just as the name would suggest, this is a neutral pattern, void of any emotion. Thus, moving from an intense emotional experience into this pattern allows the emotion to be cleared away. The body is in a neutral stance, free from tension. It is important that the face is also free from tension in this pattern. The breath is an equal inhalation to an equal exhalation, for example, 3 seconds in, 3 seconds out. The inhalation comes through the nose, and the breath is expelled through straight-line lips. The breath should be deep, relaxed, and easy. Inhalation and exhalation are always the same length of time. The eyes are focused on a point on the horizon. The focus is soft and relaxed. The breath is drawn in easily from the point on the horizon and expelled purposefully to this point. If you have practiced yoga, you will recognize the even, relaxed breathing that is a goal of that art form within the neutral breath in Alba. Figure 9.1 shows an actor in the neutral breath pose, while neutral.mov (on the accompanying DVD) shows this pattern in motion.

Figure 9.1

Actor in neutral breath

Tenderness

Tenderness is the emotion of love that is not sexual. It is experienced between a parent and child or two very close friends. It could be called *agape* love.

Like the neutral breath, it is also relaxed and easy. Tension in the face or body can make it impossible to achieve this pattern.

The breath for this pattern is inhaled and exhaled through the nose. There is a slight pause between the inhalation and the exhalation, and the exhalation is slightly longer that the inhalation. The breath must be deep, relaxed, and easy.

The head is tipped slightly to one side, and the chin is tucked slightly in or down. The eyes are focused gently on the horizon and seem to twinkle. The muscles on the outer corners of the eyes are drawn back to meet the ears. The corners of the mouth turn up into a slight smile as if trying to meet the corners of the drawn back eyes. This smile broadens and grows as the emotion grows. The postural attitude is relaxed, slightly forward and in. Often the arms even reach out to draw another person in to an embrace. This pattern creates feelings of goodwill and precipitates the desire to share it with someone else. Figure 9.2 shows an actor doing the tenderness pattern, while tenderness.mov (on the accompanying DVD) shows this pattern in motion.

Figure 9.2

Actor experiencing tenderness

Anger

This pattern is fairly self-explanatory. Interestingly, low levels of this pattern are experienced while in deep concentration or focus on one subject. A high level of this pattern is experienced in intense rage.

Like tenderness, this pattern involves breathing in and out through the nose. The breath for this pattern is tense and sharp. The inhalation and exhalation are equal in time and both through the nose. They may be long or short but the inhalation and exhalation always remain the same: sharp and tense. At lower levels, like seething anger, the breath is usually longer, while at high emotional levels the breath is quick, short, and sharp.

This is a very tense pattern. The body is tight and tense. The lower eyelids rise to narrow the eyes. The forehead remains flat and is displayed prominently. The lower jaw is tense and moves forward so that the top and bottom front teeth line up inside closed lips that are pursed together. The postural attitude for this pattern is forward and tense, an aggressive display that clearly says, "Don't mess with me!" This pattern may be very frightening both when experienced and when observed. Figure 9.3 shows an actor doing the anger pattern, while anger.mov (on the accompanying DVD) shows this pattern in motion.

Figure 9.3

Actor experiencing anger

Sexual Love

Susana Bloch originally called this pattern erotic love but later renamed it sexual love. Apparently some of the Alba instructors were concerned that the word "erotic" might suggest too much of a pornographic connotation for Americans, who are not comfortable with their sexuality as compared to many other parts of the world.

The inhalation and exhalation for this pattern are both through the mouth. The breath is deep and full, in fact undulating the spine from the pelvis all the way up through the skull. Once again the inhalation and exhalation are equal, but they can vary from shorter to longer breaths and often are erratic in the length.

In this pattern, the jaw is opened and relaxed. There is a slight smile on the face. The head is gently pulled back so that the neck might be exposed. The focus of the eyes is soft, in fact almost unfocused toward a higher point like the corner of a wall with the ceiling. The eyes are partly closed as if you were looking through the veil of your eyelashes. The postural attitude for this pattern is relaxed, open and receiving with the body relaxing slightly backward in expectancy.

This is the only pattern that has a small variation depending on whether you are the giver or the receiver. What is described above is for the receiver of sexual love. If you are the giver, your body and focus is slightly more forward and your upper teeth are slightly exposed. Figure 9.4 shows actors doing both versions of the sexual love pattern, while sexualLove.mov (on the accompanying DVD) shows this pattern in motion.

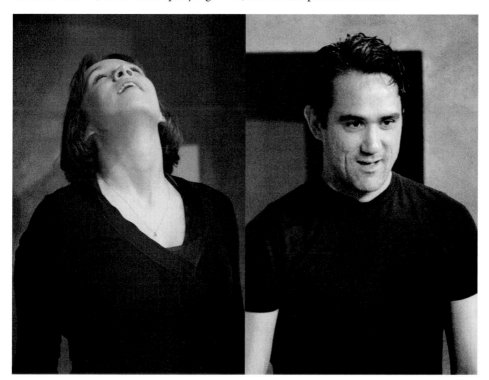

Figure 9.4

Actor experiencing receiving sexual love (left) and giving sexual love (right)

Fear

This pattern is, interestingly enough, similar in ways to the breathing pattern of sexual love. It too is inhalation and exhalation through the mouth. The fear pattern is very different from the other patterns, though, because the breath is held tightly in the chest. All of the other patterns take breath deep into the body, but the tension in fear holds the breath in the chest and won't allow it to drop down into the lower body.

The breath for fear begins with a large sudden inhalation through the mouth that is never completely exhaled. At the same time that the inhalation occurs, the stomach muscles tense and suck in so that, rather than take breath into the stomach (or lower lungs to be precise) all of the breath remains in the chest (or upper lungs). After this initial breath, the pattern continues with quick and erratic small inhalations and exhalations through the mouth without the breath ever fully leaving the body until the emotion is expelled and the tension released.

There is a big drop of the jaw, the mouth remaining open through the whole pattern, forming a big round "O." The chin tucks in, and the eyes bulge out. This pattern is dependent on the eyeballs almost bugging out of the head without forehead involvement. The eyes seem to almost lift out of their sockets to see better, get more light, and provide better peripheral vision.

The body is incredibly tense in this pattern. All of the muscles are rigid and pulling back. The postural attitude is rigid with tension, ready for retreat. Figure 9.5 shows an actor doing the fear pattern, while fear.mov (on the accompanying DVD) shows this pattern in motion.

Figure 9.5

Actor experiencing extreme fear

Joy

Joy is a pattern that is contagious and, like tenderness, produces warm feelings that want to be shared with others. It is open, relaxed, and silly. This pattern is inhaled through the nose and exhaled through the mouth. The breathing partner to joy is sadness, which is also inhaled through the nose and exhaled through the mouth.

The breath for joy starts with a short inhale through the nose that still needs to be big enough to drop down into the belly. Even though the inhale is short and fairly quick, it still needs to remain relaxed and easy. The exhalation is actually a series of short exhales through the mouth with stops in-between each of the exhales. The series of short exhalations with stops progresses to the point where your abs are squeezing out the final remnants of breath in the body to less than what you would normally consider empty, or out of breath. It is best to begin this pattern with the exhalation and then progress to the inhalation instead of starting with the inhalation as in all of the previous patterns.

The body is very relaxed in this pattern. The eyes look more levelly, ready to connect with others. The forehead needs to stay relaxed and uninvolved. The postural attitude for this pattern is relaxed, open, and floppy. Try not to collapse at the sternum in this pattern, rather keeping your posture upright, or you will end up mixing joy with another pattern. Figure 9.6 shows an actor doing the joy pattern, while joy.mov (on the accompanying DVD) shows this pattern in motion.

Figure 9.6

Actor in joy

Sadness

This pattern, like its partner, joy, begins with the exhalation, which is through the mouth, and then progresses to inhalation through the nose. It is a very internal, withdrawn sort of pattern that is difficult to share or connect with someone else.

The breath is a long slow exhalation to the point where you are completely out of air and the diaphragm goes into spasm. The inhalation follows as a series of short sniffs through the nose. The sniffs are quick and fairly tense while the exhalation is slow and relaxed.

The body in this pattern needs to remain relaxed. The eyes are in a soft focus toward the ground. The jaw drops, and the corners of the mouth turn down on the exhale. On the inhale, the space between the eyebrows is pinched up and together. Once established, this pinch remains through the entire pattern. The postural attitude for this pattern is relaxed, with the chest collapsed forward toward the ground. Figure 9.7 shows an actor doing the sadness pattern, while sadness.mov (on the accompanying DVD) shows this pattern in motion.

Figure 9.7

Actor experiencing sadness

Secondary Emotions

Alba Emoting is concerned with pure, primary emotions and not the mixing of emotion. In life, however, we often experience secondary emotions or feelings that in reality are a mix of several of the primary emotions. For instance, let's examine the feeling of jealousy. Jealousy comes from the mixing of emotions. It can come from a mix of sexual love and fear or sexual love and anger. Or it could have all three of these with a little bit of sadness thrown in. According to Bloch, the secondary emotions, unlike the primary ones, are not an exact science, and thus she doesn't study them herself. However, since you will likely be called on to create these mixed emotions it's best to consider how to create them as well.

Secondary emotions are always mixes of the primary emotions, but the exact mix depends on the person experiencing the feeling as well as the situation that person is in. Guilt could come from fear mixed with anger or fear mixed with sadness, or even sexual love mixed with fear. It all depends on the person who is experiencing that feeling and why they are experiencing the feeling, so analyzing what is going on in that character's life is crucial to knowing how to create these secondary emotions.

Consequently, there aren't exact patterns for any of the secondary emotions. But this does not mean that they are off limits for the actor or the animator. In fact, with secondary emotions the animator can have more creativity in expressing the emotion: the animator can look at the specific character and the situation that they are in to determine what combination of primary emotions the character is experiencing. Then the animator can simply mix some of the tensions from one pattern with some of the tensions from another pattern and alter the breath accordingly. Secondary emotions are a wonderful opportunity to play with and combine the different primary patterns. To find these secondary feelings, try to break down any given feeling into its constituent primary emotions. You can even think of these secondary feelings as a kind of emotional "lighting setup": mix red and blue and you get a certain shade of purple light; mix fear and sadness and you might get a certain shade of guilt. Emotions aren't as simple as combining lights, so there is no one "correct" answer, but it is still valuable to think of how the primary emotions blend together to create a final secondary one.

Alba Emoting for Inanimate Characters

As revealed through descriptions of different emotional patterns, Alba Emoting focuses breathing, tension, and bodily posture to create an emotion within a practitioner of the technique. What happens, then, when the "practitioner" is an inanimate group of pixels or lines on a piece of paper? Obviously an animated character cannot feel anything, but since specific breathing, tension, and posture are, according to Bloch, inextricably intertwined with a given emotion, we can reproduce those elements to provide a convincing replication of a given emotion, making an audience buy into the illusion that your character is a living, feeling being. If done well, your audience (and even you) should emotionally connect with your character as if it were a person they were interacting with.

Since Alba, like other techniques described in this book, reveals internal motivations and feelings via external signs and patterns, the goal of the animator is to create the most realistic—or exaggeration of realistic for more stylized characters—replications of these patterns as possible. If done properly, the character should express the desired emotion to an audience of any culture or background, which is hugely important to films, television, and gaming today, all of which have international distribution and audiences. Although creating the basic patterns might seem a bit mechanical, once your characters have to interact with one another and their surroundings, variability and artistic expression come very much to the fore, and having a straightforward way to create readable emotional responses to given situations will aid in the overall objective of animating scenes that audiences can connect with.

One area worth exploring is what to do about nonhuman characters. It would seem we would need a whole different set of Alba Emoting patterns for dogs, cats, dragons, space aliens, robots, and such. If we consider animated characters, however, we realize that most of these characters, even small square trash compacting robots like Wall-E in Disney/Pixar's eponymous 2008 animation, are anthropomorphized a great deal to make them more appealing to the human audience. Thus, while a character like Wall-E has no mouth or legs, he has very large, expressive eyes, the ability to bend his "back" (the box that makes up his torso), and a long neck that can create a great number of silhouettes and poses. Wall-E even "breathes," after a fashion, by raising and lowering his body and arching his torso and neck back and forth. Not only do Wall-E's eyes express recognizable human emotions, but he clearly tenses and relaxes imaginary muscles throughout his body as his eyes move around. The apparent tensions and relaxations that move his eyes, neck, torso, and even his tractor treads around are the same as the tensions and relaxations in Alba Emoting, so we the audience recognize human emotions in this virtual mechanical object. Thus, even with a character as supposedly nonhuman as Wall-E, we can apply Alba breathing, tension, and posture patterns, creating readable human emotions in this nonhuman but still highly anthropomorphic character. As you proceed through the exercises for the actor in the next section, consider how you can transfer the physical feelings as well as the observable externals to an animated character.

Exercises to Create Alba Emoting Patterns

Exercises for this chapter begin with exploring and practicing the individual patterns. Then we will progress to shaking things up by exploring one pattern after another, and finally use the patterns to explore space and relationship.

We must issue a huge note of caution on this work: this is a very advanced technique, and when exploring emotions through the Alba technique, an individual can and eventually will experience intense, deep, powerful emotions, even though there is no context for them during the exercises. Your emotional core is not something to be played around with. We explain the process here so that you can intellectually understand it. The instructions and pictures will help you, as an animator, to be able to copy and create the emotional state in your work. However, due to the intense and unpredictable reactions you might have while doing these exercises, we recommend that you not attempt these exercises yourself (excepting the neutral breath exercise) without the aid of a certified Alba instructor. At the very least, you need an experienced acting teacher to oversee the exercises so that they can monitor and guide you if you encounter an emotionally overwhelming situation. Do not attempt this on your own.

Neutral Breath

Begin by lying on your back on the floor in the relaxed position described in Chapter 1. For this pattern, it is important to begin with a neutral body. This means that you need to let go of tensions that are blocking you. You might want to do some of the relaxation exercises described in the first chapter. Now release any tension that you are holding in your face. Check for tension in your jaw, tongue, forehead, brows, and all around the eyes. It often helps to gently stroke your face to release tension if you find any.

Next, look to a spot on the horizon; since you are on your back on the floor this means that you will pick a spot on the ceiling at your eye level. Softly focus on this spot. It is important that the spot is at your eye level and not above or below it, as this will take you to different patterns. Also your focus must be soft, light, and easy. Now switch your attention to your breath. You should inhale through your nose and exhale through straight-line lips. The inhalation and exhalation should be of equal time, so count both and make sure that they are matching. Your breath should drop deep in your body, all the way down to your lower belly. You should feel the space between your belly button and your pubic bone (the front, lower portion of the hip bones) increasing first. Your breath should be deep, smooth, and regular. Work to eliminate any roughness or inequality in your breath.

Breathe in good, clean air from your soft focus spot on the horizon, and purposely blow out your breath through straight-line lips. It is important that your lips are in a straight line or very close to a straight line without becoming tense. There should be little to no sound on this exhalation. If you are hearing a lot of noise as you blow out, relax a bit more but still make sure that the exhalation is very purposeful. Practice this breath pattern often. It allows you to clear emotion and frees you from any lingering elements of another pattern.

After you have mastered this pattern lying on the floor, you need to master it on your feet. Again, it is important to begin with a neutral body. This means that you need to let go of tensions that are blocking you. Focus on your alignment. Begin by letting your upper body collapse over your legs, then roll up the spine as done in your warm-up. Your feet should be parallel, one foot distance apart. Your knees are soft, and your pelvis is centered with your tailbone pointing down between your heels. Your chest and back should be spread wide, with your shoulders dropped down and back. At the same time, make sure that your spine is long with your head floating on top.

There are several images here that might help you. First think of the vertebrae in your back as pearls that are delicately strung together. Gently stack your vertebrae on top of one another as a string of pearls beautifully comes together. Next think of zipping up the front of your body as if you had a jacket on and were zipping it up. These images will help you lengthen and align your torso without adding in any tensions.

When you feel comfortable, relaxed, and aligned, pick a spot on the horizon on which to focus. This should be at your eye level, and you should softly keep your eyes on this spot. Then start practicing the neutral breath pattern: equal inhalations through your mouth to equal exhalations through straight-line lips. The breath is deep in your relaxed body, easy yet purposeful, with no rough edges. Breathe in good, clean fresh air from your spot on the horizon and purposely breathe away any tension or emotions through your straight line lips to your spot on the horizon. Figure 9.8 shows an actor doing the neutral breath. (A movie showing full breathing in a standing position, `neutral.mov`, is on the accompanying DVD.)

Figure 9.8

Actor doing neutral breath

The Step-Out

After you have mastered the neutral breath, you need to take the pattern into a step-out. The step-out is designed to further release and clear any emotion that will come from the patterns. The step-out adds physical movement that meshes with the neutral breath pattern. The movement is designed to break any physical tensions that might be lingering from the breath patterns to help you shed the emotion. After practicing the neutral breath and the step-out, you will find that it becomes easy to release even intense emotional experiences quickly, effectively, and consistently.

To begin the step-out, start in the neutral standing position. Begin by achieving the neutral breath pattern. Then, on an exhale, bring your hands together in front of you and clasp your hands. Slowly, on your next inhale, raise your arms (hands still clasped) up over your head. When your clasped hands are directly over your head, bend your elbows and drop your clasped hands behind your head. You should be continuing the inhale as you do this. When your elbows are bent above your head and your clasped hands are behind it, hold your breath while you squeeze your hands together. Continue holding your breath as you release the squeeze but keep your hands clasped. Then begin an exhale while you straighten your elbows so that your clasped hands are once again above your head. Continue the exhalation as you lower your arms to the starting position. Just as in all neutral breaths, the length of time for the inhalation and the exhalation while raising and lowering your arms should be exactly the same.

To complete the step-out, the sequence needs to be repeated two more times for a total of three times. Then gently stroke your face to remove any lingering tension. Finally you need to move or shake out your body and make sound. It is important to flex or bend your spine in this move and to release sound from the body. This completes the step-out and, with practice, will allow you to come to a balanced and neutral emotional place. Figure 9.9 shows an actor in five phases of the step-out. stepOut.mov on the accompanying DVD shows the complete process in motion.

Figure 9.9

Actor doing the step-out. 1: Hands clasped. 2: Hands over head. 3: Hands behind head, squeezing. 4: Hands back over the head. 5: Hands back down.

Tenderness

Figure 9.10

Tenderness

As you begin to learn Alba, you need to move into all of the breath patterns from a good neutral breath. Advanced practitioners are able to move from one pattern to the next without the need for the neutral breath.

To begin tenderness, lie on your back on the floor in neutral breath. Start by shifting your inhalation and exhalation to your nose only. This inhalation and exhalation should be easy, smooth, relaxed, and gentle. Allow a slight pause before you begin the exhalation and extend the exhalation a little bit longer than the inhalation. There is no prescribed count to use here. Simply do what is comfortable for you.

After you have established this new breath pattern, allow your head to tip slightly to one side and your chin to tuck slightly in. Keep your soft focus on the same spot on the horizon as you had in your neutral breath. Since your chin is now tucked, keeping this focus will make it seem as if you are looking up slightly. This process needs to be done with ease and relaxation as tension in this pattern will make it impossible to achieve tenderness.

Next allow a small smile to come to your lips. Draw the muscles on the outer corners of the eyes back to meet the ears. Allow the smile to grow and the corners of the mouth to reach up to meet the corners of the pulled-back eyes. The postural attitude for this pattern is drawing in, as if you wish to embrace the world. Both breathing and body need to remain relaxed and easy. You might actually want to move your arms to draw someone into you.

After you have mastered this pattern on the ground, rise to a standing position and repeat the process. Be careful not to add in tensions when standing or to collapse in the area of the sternum. Do not become frozen. You might move your head from side to side and the smile can change from smaller to larger as the emotion grows. To release the emotion, shift your body and breath to neutral and then perform a step-out.

When you are doing this pattern correctly, you will feel calm, kind, and open. It is as if you are looking at a sleeping lover, child, or pet. It is a feeling of love that does not contain a sexual quality. Figure 9.10 shows an actor performing the tenderness pattern. (The pattern in motion, `tenderness.mov`, is on the accompanying DVD.)

Anger

Begin by lying on your back on the floor in neutral breath, then shift your inhalation and exhalation to the nose only. The breath for this pattern is tense and sharp. Put tension in your nose to accomplish this. The inhalation and exhalation are equal in length. They may be long or short but always remain the same. At low level or seething, the breath is usually longer while tense, while at high emotional levels the breath is quick, short, and sharp.

Now tense up your body. The lower eyelids rise to narrow the eyes. The forehead remains flat and displayed, which is to say that it is placed prominently forward so that it is the part of the face that is most easily observed. The lower jaw is tense and moves forward so that the teeth line up. The postural attitude for this pattern is forward and tense. This is harder to accomplish on the floor, but you will find it easier when you move to your feet.

After you have mastered this pattern on the floor, move to standing. Your whole body should be tight and tensed, as if preparing for a fight. Your focus is still on the horizon and is very intense, almost piercing. Because of the postural attitude, you will probably be leaning slightly forward. Be careful to leave the forehead without tension. The tension in the eyes comes from the lower eyelid and not the upper. You will feel angry or enraged when you have mastered this pattern, so be sure you can do the step-out effectively before working on this pattern.

To release this emotion, do a step-out. Due to the extreme tension in this pattern, it is sometimes difficult to release. If you do a step-out and feel that you have not released the tension or are still feeling the emotion, do another step-out. Continue to do step-outs until you have completely returned to a balanced and neutral emotional place. Figure 9.11 shows an actor performing the anger pattern. (The pattern in motion, anger.mov, is on the accompanying DVD.)

Figure 9.11
Anger

Sexual Love

The sexual love pattern has two variants: giving and receiving. We will work on receiving. Begin by lying on your back on the floor in neutral breath, then shift your inhalation and exhalation so that they are both through the mouth. The breath needs to be very deep and full. Allow this deep breath to undulate your entire spine from the tip of your tailbone up to the skull. The breaths may vary from shorter to longer and often are erratic in length.

Obviously since you are breathing through your mouth, the jaw needs to be dropped. Make sure that it is relaxed. There should be no tension in the body for this pattern.

Now bring a slight smile to your face and tip your head back so that the neck is exposed. Don't allow tension to come into your neck with this movement; it should be free and relaxed. The exposed neck can move and roll the head. As the head tips back to expose your neck, the focus of your eyes will rise to a higher point. It needs to be a very soft focus, sometimes even unfocused. Now allow your eyes to partly close as if you were looking through the veil of your eyelashes. The postural attitude for this pattern is relaxed, open, and receiving with the body relaxing slightly backward as if in expectancy. When you are fully engaged in this pattern, you will be filled with desire and anticipation.

After mastering this pattern on the floor, move to standing and repeat the process. Be careful when standing that you don't bring tension into the body. To achieve the openness of this postural attitude, your chest will open and be broad. Your spine continues to undulate, and your head will rock around across the back. Do not be surprised if there is a lot of fluid, physical movement with this pattern. To release it, move to the step-out. Figure 9.12 shows an actor performing the receiving sexual love pattern. (The pattern in motion, sexualLove.mov, is on the accompanying DVD.)

Figure 9.12

Sexual love: receiving pattern

Fear

Lie on your back on the floor and begin the neutral breath. When this is firmly established, suddenly drop your jaw and open your mouth in a large "O" as you inhale. As you do this, you need to pull in your stomach muscles so that all of your air is held in a big expanded chest. Do not completely exhale. In fact, try to continue to inhale into your chest. Keep your mouth open the whole time. Small amounts of air will be released through this open mouth, but you need to quickly replace it with even more air. The exhalations and inhalations through the open mouth are small, quick, and erratic. Never fully expel the air until you release the pattern and move to a neutral breath.

Figure 9.13

Fear

Your whole body needs to tense in this pattern. Tuck your chin in to help facilitate the drop of the jaw but more importantly to protect your neck. Try to bug your eyeballs out of your head as if they need to see everything at once. Open your eyes very wide and lift the eyeballs up and out so that they can get more light and have better peripheral vision. You might also even allow your eyes to look around to find the danger, but don't move your head, just your eyes. The postural attitude for this pattern is tense retreat, so on the floor you will find yourself pulling back sharply into the floor.

When you move this pattern to your feet, you might find that you take steps backward. Your body must remain tense. This pattern does not have a specific focal point. Instead, your bugged-out eyes will be darting around and looking for danger. When doing this pattern properly, you will feel scared, and even perhaps paranoid, terrified of your surroundings. As this pattern is particularly intense, do not stay in it for very long. Several step-outs may be required to release this pattern at the beginning of your training. Figure 9.13 shows an actor performing the fear pattern. (The pattern in motion, fear.mov, is on the accompanying DVD.)

Fear is (as you might expect) the most dangerous of the breathing patterns: you can actually experience a full-blown panic attack if you are not careful. For this pattern especially, be sure to have a trained acting coach—or at the very least a good friend—watch you to be sure you don't get lost in the pattern.

Joy

Begin on your back on the floor in neutral breath; then, to shift to joy, allow your inhalation to come through the nose and the exhalation to drop out through the mouth. The inhalation is short but not tense. It needs to be relaxed and big enough to fill you all the way to deep in the belly. The exhalation is actually a series of short exhales through the

Figure 9.14
Joy

mouth with stops in-between each of the exhales. (Imagine yourself laughing in a relaxed, slow-motion fashion.) Allow the series of short exhalations with stops to progress to the point where your abs are squeezing out the final remnants of breath in the body to below what you would normally consider empty, or out of breath. It is best to begin this pattern with the exhalation and then progress to the inhalation instead of starting with the inhalation as in all of the previous patterns.

As you do the series of short exhalations, allow a smile to grow on your face. The eyes try to connect with others. The forehead needs to stay relaxed and uninvolved. Make sure that your body is relaxed. It needs to be loose and sort of floppy. The postural attitude for this pattern is relaxed, open, and floppy. Try not to collapse at the sternum in this pattern, or you will end up mixing joy with another pattern like sadness.

After you have mastered this pattern on the floor, move to standing and repeat the process. When standing, be especially careful not to collapse in the sternum area or you will have great difficulty achieving the pattern. This pattern is particularly contagious, and it helps to have other people around when learning it. Gales of laughter will erupt. You will feel that life is hysterical and quite wonderful.

This pattern can feel so good that you might not want to release it. It is important, though, to move to the neutral breath and step out so that you know that you are in control of your emotions. Figure 9.14 shows an actor performing the joy pattern. (The pattern in motion, joy.mov, is on the accompanying DVD.)

Sadness

To begin this pattern, lie on the floor, but instead of lying on your back, begin on your side slightly curled into a fetal position. Start your neutral breath in this position. Then

shift to a long, slow exhalation through your mouth to beyond where you are completely out of air. The inhalation that follows is a series of short, tense sniffs through the nose. Continue this pattern of long, slow exhalations through the mouth and a few short, tense sniff inhales through the mouth when drawing in breath.

Once you have established this breathing pattern, begin to make physical changes to match. The body needs to be quite relaxed. Drop the focus of your eyes toward the ground (near your feet when you're lying on the ground) and keep the focus fairly soft, almost unfocused. On your slow exhale, make sure that the corners of your mouth turn down. On your inhalation, pinch the space between your eyebrows up and together. Once you have this pinch, maintain it even through the exhalation. Allow your body to curl into a fetal position.

Once you have mastered this pattern on the floor, move to standing. You might find it difficult to stand in this pattern because all of your energy needs to be collapsed forward and down. Keep your knees soft. Collapse at the sternum. Your gaze is dropped down. Your shoulders are rounded forward. The body is released down with no energy or tension. When doing this pattern correctly, you will be overcome with feelings of great sorrow. Figure 9.15 shows an actor

Figure 9.15
Sadness

performing the sadness pattern. (The pattern in motion, sadness.mov, is on the accompanying DVD.)

To release this pattern, do a step-out. If you experience the emotion very deeply, you might need to do several step-outs.

Drilling

After you have learned all of the patterns individually, you can progress to moving from one pattern to the next. In a standing position, start in a neutral breath and then move to the first pattern that you learned, tenderness. After you have spent some time in tenderness, return to a neutral breath. Once you have completely released into the neutral breath, you can progress on to the next pattern. It might take you only one or two neutral breaths to release the pattern, or you might have to do an entire step-out. After the next pattern, anger, return to neutral breath and continue through the patterns in this manner.

As you continue to work this way, try to minimize the number of neutral breaths that you need to do between each pattern. As you become more adept at the patterns, try to progress to the point where you can move directly from one pattern into the next without a neutral breath in between. For tenderness, anger, sexual love, and fear, always begin the pattern on an inhale. For joy and sadness, begin on an exhale.

Space

After you can move through the patterns in the manner we've described, you can start to explore space with the patterns. Within your practice room, drill the patterns while interacting with the space around you. This time do not drill the patterns in any particular order. Allow the interaction with your space to lead you to the next pattern. You might find that you repeat one or two patterns often. That is absolutely fine. For the sake of learning the patterns, make sure that you do each one at least once, but aside from that, whatever your interaction dictates is fine. Allow the patterns to move you physically. Some patterns will take you to your knees, others to your back. Still others will send you across the room. The interaction between the pattern and the space will guide you without you having to plan what to do.

After you are comfortable with interacting with the space around you, try it outside. Susana Bloch loves the patterns to be a part of the natural world. You will find that often nature can move you very freely to deeper emotional places. Just be sure you find an outdoor place where you can feel comfortable displaying these patterns: the tension of worrying about others watching will make it difficult to achieve the patterns.

Interrelating with Others

After you are comfortable exploring space, you can share the patterns with other people. Start by sitting or standing directly across from another person. Both of you should start by progressing through drilling the patterns in the same order so that you are always sharing the same pattern. Then try mixing it up so that you are on different patterns at the same time. Don't plan what you think a response should be; just respond on impulse to whatever pattern is presented to you.

Finally, you should explore space and others at the same time. This works best with a group of people. Everyone picks a starting place where they begin neutral breath. Then they simply allow the interaction with others and the space to move them from one pattern to the next. It is quite amazing what happens during these sessions.

Exercises for Creating Alba Patterns in Animated Characters

In some ways, creating Alba patterns via an animated character is easier than doing so in person: you can observe the character from the "outside" as you animate it, and you don't have to go through the sometimes uncomfortable experience of feeling these emotions yourself when animating the character. However, as with most art, the truest creations will come when you, the artist/animator, "feel" along with the character, so the more you understand the patterns both physically and internally, and the better you can create them in your own body, the more adept you will likely be at creating them in a virtual character. That said, you can do the following exercises without having gone through the previous acting exercises, much less mastered them. At the least, however, you should carefully read through the acting exercises and walk through the patterns and tensions to better understand what should happen within your character. As we work through these exercises, our goal is to create fairly realistic animations: the point of the work is to produce "emotions" that an audience will understand and believe, so starting at a realistic point is valuable in this instance. Once you have the more realistic animation work down, you can then work to exaggerate certain aspects of the patterns to create more exaggerated emotions, or emotions in a more exaggerated type of character.

Creating a Single Primary Pattern

We will begin by creating a single breathing pattern, using the video reference files we have on the accompanying DVD to help. For our example, we have chosen the Sexual Love pattern, and will use the sexualLove.mov file as reference for re-creating the pattern in our animated character. Note that this is the "receiving" pattern, which is different from the "giving" pattern.

First, open your model of choice in a new scene file. (If you use Maya, feel free to use either the Genna or Marcel models on the accompanying DVD.) Be sure your animation timeline settings are set to NTSC/30 frames per second, since our video footage is shot at that speed. (In Maya, choose Window → Settings → Preferences → Preferences; then on the Settings tab, set Time to NTSC [30 fps].) Next, create a new camera, create a background plane, and attach the sexualLove-Short.mov file (on the DVD) to the plane. If you are using Maya, don't forget to move the image plane back to around 1,000 units, and set the far clipping plane of the camera to a large value like 10,000. Because this video sequence is about 6 seconds long, we set our timeline to 190 frames in order to see the entire movie. Finally, match up your character to the person in the video as closely as possible, paying special attention here to the placement of the waist and shoulders. (Since the feet don't move in this sequence, they are less important for matching.) Figure 9.16 shows the initial placement of Genna over our video footage.

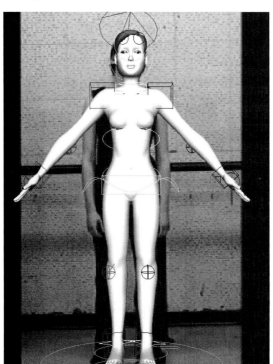

Figure 9.16

Placing the model over the video footage

If you are using the included models (Genna and Marcel), which include built-in character/subcharacter hierarchies, you can have Maya automatically select the characters as you go. First, place the autoCharacterSelection.mel file in your home scripts directory (~Autodesk/maya/scripts on your home directory), then copy the line of code from ACSEnable.mel into the Script Editor input pane, and drag it up onto your shelf. When you start up Maya, simply click the ACSEnable button, and from then on, Maya will automatically select whichever subcharacter it needs based on what is selected in the scene. This makes selecting and keyframing characters far easier than having to remember to do so yourself.

Now match up the posture of your character with the video; feel free to use other portions of the sexualLove.mov file to see what the character should look like from a side view, and more closely focused on the face. To create our first poses, we keyframed the character on the "top" and "bottom" of the inhale-exhale breaths: frames 1 (exhale), 49 (inhale), 64 (end of pause after inhale), 103 (exhale), 117 (end of pause after exhale), 165 (inhale), 170 (end of pause after inhale), and 190 (partial exhale). These are, of course, observations from the video—we focused mostly on the shoulders, as they distinctly rise and fall during her breathing—so you might find you set your keyframes slightly differently. When keying these poses, note that (from the side view in the longer version of the movie) the pelvis is tilted forward and the upper back is tipped backward, with the head following this motion, being tipped very far backward and up. The arms (and head to some extent) hang loosely, the shoulders on the exhalations are very much dipped, coming up on the inhalations, the eyes are half closed, and a big smile is on the face. (See the sidebar, "Using the Facial Animation Rig on the Included Models," in Chapter 6, for more on working with the facial blend shapes in the included rigs.) Also, as we are working with breathing, we have included two "breath" blend shapes: one for the chest, the other for the belly. Feel free to incorporate those blends into your work to fully replicate the breathing pattern for sexual love: deep breathing through the mouth, with erratic lengths and the jaw dropped to take in lots of air.

Once you have finished blocking out the main poses, go back and fill in the details of the animation. Note in particular the eyes, hips, and shoulders, and also how flowing the animation is. Look for any hard transitions in your animation and try to smooth them out; using a graphical curve editor (like the Graph Editor in Maya) is particularly useful here, as you work to smooth out the animation. Figure 9.17 shows the character posed with the video reference for this pattern. A complete animation, `sexualLoveCharacter.mov`, as well as the Maya file we created, `sexualLove.mb`, are on the accompanying DVD. Once you have this pattern animated, try copying the included videos of the other Alba patterns. Which ones are easier for you and which more difficult? Is it easier to do the looser motions or the ones with more tension? How does breathing affect the look of the patterns? How important are the facial expressions to each one?

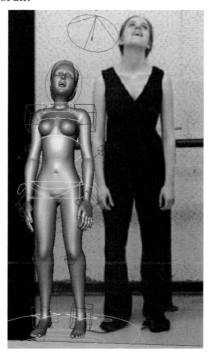

Figure 9.17

Character pose for sexual love pattern

Creating a Secondary Emotion by Mixing Patterns

Next, we will create a secondary emotion by combining two primary Alba patterns to create one "shade" of frustration. In this instance, imagine that our character has just discovered that she has been laid off at work. In this case, her frustration could be a combination of the primary anger and sadness patterns, as she is sad about losing her job and angry at her company for laying her off. (She might also be afraid for her future, but we will just focus on a combination of two here.) After reviewing the tensions and breathing of the two patterns, we need to figure out how the two can work together to create this intermediate pattern and emotion. After trying a few experiments, we found that a combination of the anger breath and sadness tensions, plus a posture that combines some of both, worked best to create the feeling of frustration (and it actually did create that feeling!). Thus we will work to produce these combinations in our character.

Create a new scene and import your model of choice (or Genna or Marcel) into it. If you have a reference video, import that and use it as a background plate for a new camera. (See the previous exercise for more on how to do this.) If not, then time yourself to see how long things like inhalation and exhalation take, then observe yourself performing this combination and look at where the tensions are in your face and body, as well as the general posture you are holding. We did two inhalations/exhalations for our example, and discovered that the inhalation is quick, filling the chest in particular, but the lower

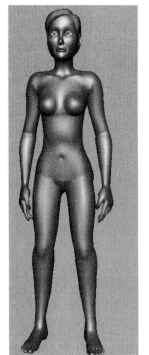

Figure 9.18

The pose for complete exhalation for the combination frustration pattern

stomach as well; there is then a slight pause at the "top" of the breath, followed by a slower exhalation of about 1 second. Finally, there is a pause at the "bottom" of the breath before we took in another breath. In terms of posture, we stood fairly erect, but with slightly sagging shoulders; during the breaths, we were fairly rigid, though our body moved side to side a bit. The biggest motion was in the chest, and our arms moved out to the side to make way for the expanded chest.

The face contains some of the anger pattern, due to the fact that the character is breathing entirely through the nose, but the downturn of the mouth and soft, distant gaze are indicative of the sadness pattern. We also found that our eyebrows were raised on the outside, and the creases between the nose and outer edges of the lips were well defined in this pattern. Figure 9.18 shows the frustration pattern while fully exhaled, while Figure 9.19 shows our character at the fully inhaled position. The pattern took about 2 seconds per breath, so we created a 120-frame animation to contain the two breaths.

Once you have blocked in the breaths, go back and add in the detailed motion of the hands, body, and face that will make the animation come alive. The arms are especially important here: while the body is very rigid and the face moves little with this combination pattern, the arms do move slightly due to the tension placed on them. Our example movie, `frustration.mov`, as well as the Maya file, `frustration.mb`, are on the accompanying DVD for reference if you wish to look at them.

After working through this example, consider some other combination patterns like fear and anger, anger and sexual love, tenderness and sadness, or even something as complex as joy and sadness (laughing through the tears). Consider what these combinations feel like when you try them out, and then see if you can get your audience to "read" that emotion when they look at your animation. There are obviously many, many possible combination patterns, but if you step back and analyze what is happening to your character at a given point in your animation, you should be able to determine what one, two, or even three patterns make up what that character should be feeling at that point, which will enable you to create a combination pattern to suit the needs of any given scene.

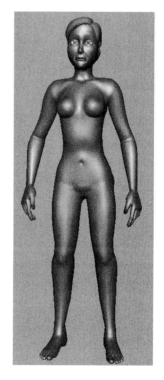

Figure 9.19

The frustration combination pattern when breath is fully inhaled

Creating a Transition Between Two Primary Patterns

As a third exercise, let's create a transition between two patterns (akin to the drilling exercise in the acting exercises). Let's imagine our character comes home to her apartment, opens the door, and a whole bunch of people yell out "Surprise!" and "Happy Birthday!" Our character will at first be shocked, or afraid, followed closely by a reaction of joy at having a surprise party thrown for her.

The first thing we need to do, beyond reviewing the fear and joy patterns, is to determine how the two patterns can transition. As the fear pattern is one that begins on the inhalation (deep inhale, tension across the body, eyes bugging out) and the joy pattern begins on the exhale (relaxed body, floppy appendages), and since the fear reaction is short-lived, we can simply have one inhale with the appropriate posture and tension for fear, followed quickly by an exhale of joy with its loose posture and (lack of) tension. As these two patterns contrast in so many ways, it should be fun to watch how quickly and dramatically your character can transition between them. If you wish, you can record yourself or someone else doing the fear-to-joy transition; if not, try enacting the motion a few times just so that you can feel it within yourself before beginning.

Figure 9.20

Posing the character in a neutral position to begin the animation

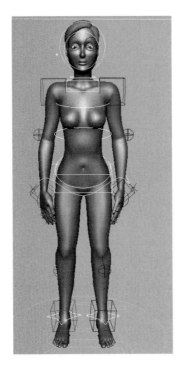

Figure 9.21

Posing the character at a full fear inhale

Create a new scene file and import your model into it. (Feel free to use the Genna or Marcel rigs on the DVD if you use Maya.) If you have a video recorded, you can attach that to a new camera (as per the sexual love exercise earlier) and use that as a basis for creating your animation. If not, time yourself going through the two patterns so you have a basic idea of how long the animation will take. We found that ours timed out to around 9 seconds, so we started at 270 frames for the animation.

Begin by posing your character in a neutral stance pose (or at the least something very different from the fear pose you will move to after this). Figure 9.20 shows our character in the neutral pose.

Next, move to the full inhale of the fear pattern, posing your character to reflect the full fear pattern. We figured this would take about 0.5 seconds, so we posed the character in this position at frame 16, as Figure 9.21 shows. Note that the character is very vertical, even up on her toes slightly, that she has her upper back bent backward (and pelvis thrust forward some to compensate for the balance), and that she has a fully indrawn chest breath. Her head pulls back and in, protecting her chest; her mouth is in a wide open "O" shape; her eyelids are fully open; and she is looking around to take in as much information as possible.

After achieving the full in-breath, our character needs a moment to process her surroundings, taking in the scene and determining whether or not to flee (or fight) in fear. We moved forward nearly a full second, to frame 42, and reposed the character in a "moving hold" pose that is very close to that from frame 16, adding just a little more backward motion, rocking her back on her heels and tucking the chin in even a bit more. We also darted the eyes around some so that she can take in the scene. Next comes the moment of relief and happiness (joy) when our character discovers it's a surprise party for her. From a very rigid body posture and full in-breath, we move quickly to a floppy, loose body and a laughing exhale. The end of the initial transition should take a little time, so we moved to frame 80, about 1.3 seconds after the end of the fear pause; obviously once the main motions are blocked out, frames will have to be inserted into this area to refine the motion. As this pose is much looser, we can also introduce much more asymmetry into the poses from now on. While the mouth stays open, the tension in the face changes significantly at this point: the eyes close, the eyebrows relax, and the tension shifts to the edges of the mouth and deepening creases between the edges of the lips and the nose. Figure 9.22 shows the character after the initial transition to the joy breath pattern.

After the initial collapse into laughter, consider how the joy exhalation pattern continues: there are "ha ha ha" hitches to the exhale, and a general loosening of the body. After some experimentation, we blocked out keyframes at 123, 191, 220, 244, and 262. After completing the blocking, go back and insert frames where needed to create more motion; in addition, be sure to offset some of the controls (arms for example) from the main keyframes you have set, so that the character looks looser. Also, from observation, the joy pattern involves floppy arms, so we put in lots of arm swinging to help with the notion that the body is loose after the character shifts to the second pattern. Figure 9.23 shows a frame from later in the joy pattern. A movie with the complete transition, fearIntoJoy.mov, as well as the Maya file, fearInto-Joy.mb, are on the accompanying DVD.

Once you have worked through this example transition, try a few more on your own for more practice. What would it be like to go from joy to tenderness (or vice versa); from fear to anger; from sexual love to fear? Consider different possible combinations, act them out on your own, and then animate those patterns. Do some combinations flow better from one to another? Does this have to do with the way the emotions might be connected? Consider the possibilities as you work through other combinations.

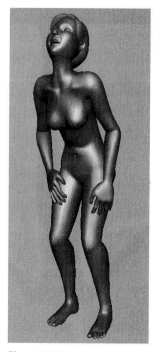

Figure 9.22

The character after the initial transition to the joy pattern

Figure 9.23

The character in the joy pattern

CHAPTER 10

The Voice and Voice-Over Acting

Professional actors, or those specializing in voice-over acting, usually perform voice-overs for characters in large-budget animated movies. Often, however, animators or other "in-house" talent will voice a temp track to begin the initial work on the animation. Sometimes the temp track voice will become so much a part of the personality of the character that the animator will be asked to voice the character in the film. (PIXAR, for example, is famous for having many smaller characters voiced by their own staff.) Additionally, for small-budget productions it is often up to the animator, director, or even friends to perform voice-overs for the project. It thus becomes beneficial for the animator to understand the mechanics of voice-over work, as well as the fundamentals of achieving a quality voice-over. (Chapter 11, "Creating Lip Sync and Facial Performance for Voiced Characters," is a companion chapter to this one and focuses on the technique of creating lip sync as well as using lip sync with facial performance.)

This chapter discusses:

- ■ **An explanation of the voice-over process**

- ■ **A description of how the voice works**

- ■ **Information on how to develop your voice**

- ■ **Methods for creating character voices**

- ■ **What to expect in a voice-over session**

What Is a Voice-Over?

A voice-over is the voice that you hear behind the commercial on TV or the radio; it is the voice under the infomercial or behind the CD; it is the voice of recorded messages on phone systems or reading books on tape; it is also the character voice of animations for film, TV, and video games. For the animator, it is not necessary to understand how to use the voice for selling products (unless the sale is being done by an animated character) or how to interpret ad copy; instead, we will focus on the development of the voice for character animation work.

Voice-over work for animation is acting, plain and simple. Everything that is necessary to bring a character to life for the stage or film is also necessary in voicing an animated character. The only difference for the actor is that the audience gathers all of the information about the character from the voice; therefore, the actor must pay particular attention to how and what his or her voice communicates. A voice-over is basically using your voice to bring a character to life, and as the term *animation* is based on the Latin word *anima*, meaning breath or life, there is an obvious connection between the two.

The voice-over actor must possess a flexible voice capable of expressing emotion and character easily. The voice must be clear, without any impediments to articulation or dialects that stand out. The voice actor must command a mastery of acting technique as well as vocal technique. This combination of technically difficult skills is probably why most animated characters in big-budget movies or games are voiced by professional actors.

When voicing a character for animation, the actor must do all of the same initial work that he would do for a role in a play. He must study the text and determine the super-objective of the character. He must then determine all of the smaller objectives that lead to the super objective. He will note all of the obstacles standing in the way of obtaining those objectives and determine the tactics that he must use to overcome those obstacles. He will also do any research necessary to fully understand the character. Then, using the "magic if," he will begin to develop his character. (See Chapter 3 for more on creating a character.)

It is important that the voice actor use his body in the development of the character, just as he would in the development of a character for the stage. The body's alignment, tension, and gestures greatly influence the voice. Therefore, in the development of a voice character the actor cannot separate the body from the voice. If you have ever watched Tom Hanks and Tim Allen voicing Woody and Buzz in PIXAR's *Toy Story*, you will note the high degree of physicality they use behind the microphone. In addition, you can look on this book's accompanying DVD, which contains audio/video recordings of actors repeating simple lines as different characters. Note in Figure 10.1 how much these actors use their bodies, and how different the body is for varied characters speaking the exact same lines. We will work with these files later in Chapter 11.

Figure 10.1

Actors creating voice-over characters use their bodies to help make the character voice.

The voice actor must first understand basic acting techniques. She must then be able to create a physical character. (Any of the techniques studied in this book would help do this.) And she must pay particular attention to the voice. She must know her voice inside and out. She must have a strong mastery of her voice. She also must understand and have a clear knowledge of microphone technique—how to use the microphone to help define the character—in order to translate her character to recorded sound waves.

Most of this book has been dedicated to the physical creation of character because that is what is most applicable to the animator. In dealing with voice-overs, though, we need to devote some attention to the voice. How does the voice work? What can you do to develop the voice and create character voices? How do you act in front of a microphone? These are some of the issues that are important to a voice-over actor.

How the Voice Works

A need to communicate is the very foundation of why we speak; from infancy, we have a need to communicate our needs and thoughts verbally with the society around us. This need to communicate translates into electrical impulses in the brain that are sent through our nervous system to our vocal apparatus. The entire process involves complex science, but we will attempt to describe it in terms that can be understood by someone other than an M.D.

Upon feeling the need to communicate verbally, our brain sends impulses to our diaphragm, which contracts and pulls down into the lower half of the torso. At the same time the intercostal muscles (the muscles between the ribs) expand and pull apart. This causes a vacuum in our chest cavity, pulling air into the lungs. The diaphragm then relaxes and releases back up, causing air to be released from the lungs in a pattern similar to a normal breath.

The air from our lungs travels through the trachea and continues up through the larynx and out of the mouth. The larynx, which is often referred to as the voice box, houses the vocal membranes or cords. As breath passes between the vocal membranes, it forces them apart, causing vibrations. The more tension placed on the vocal cords, the faster the vibrations and thus the higher the pitch of the sound. These vibrations then resonate and are amplified in hollow spaces in the body, including the chest, throat, mouth, sinuses, and nasal passages. The final stage of speaking occurs when our articulators, which include the lips, teeth, tongue, and palate (the roof of the mouth), break up the sound waves into small bits, making intelligible speech from the sonic vibrations in the throat.

For the most part, the speech process occurs without our conscious thought or concentration. Except for those times when we are nervous about speaking in front of people, or if we have sustained a head injury, the method via which we produce voice and speech is almost as unconscious as breathing, and yet there are innumerable ways in which this process can be sent awry or manipulated.

Interference in the vocal process can occur anywhere in our body and brain. If all of the electrical signals from the brain are working properly, the next place where the vocal process can be hampered begins with the breath. If you don't breathe freely, the voice will be affected. In order for you to breathe freely, your spine must be aligned properly and your whole body needs to be free from tension. This means that your entire torso, including your pelvis, back, and abdominal muscles, must be relaxed. Many people carry tension in these areas, and any tension will affect the breath and thus the voice. You only have to think of a nervous teenage boy trying to ask a girl out in a squeaky voice to understand just how much tension in the body can affect the voice.

If your breathing process is free from tension and is functioning properly, you can still have other tensions that undermine your voice. Tension in your throat or tongue will place tension on your larynx, which in turn affects the proper functioning of the cartilage and muscles that operate the vocal folds. If you carry tension in your jaw or facial muscles, your diction will be affected as the tension filters back to your larynx.

The palate and sinus cavities can also drastically affect voice production, especially if the soft palate (the back of the roof of your mouth) carries tension, or if the sinus cavities are blocked somehow—by a cold, for example. Singers, actors, and other vocal professionals spend years perfecting the way the vocal cord vibrations travel through the mouth and sinus cavities to produce the most pleasing, or most interesting, sounds possible.

Although it appears that our speaking process should be easy, there are roadblocks to the proper functioning of the voice at every turn. In fact, the ability to speak naturally and freely is an amazingly fragile process that we—most of the time—take for granted. For voice-over actors, the layers of tensions can become a playground as long as they understand how to control them: overtightening the vocal cords and pitching the voice well forward into the frontal sinuses, for example, can produce a high, nasty, squeaking sound that could be wonderful for a particular character. Thus, not only is it good to understand your voice in order to relax it to its most natural state, this knowledge can also become a powerful tool in vocal character creation.

Working On Your Voice

Since the voice is one of the main ways in which an actor communicates his character and there are so many potential problems within the vocal process, actors spend years training their voices. Even if you are blessed enough to have a naturally supple, powerful, and interesting voice, you will not be guaranteed success with voice work unless you train your voice. Many actors train as part of a college or conservatory degree, and others take private voice lessons from a vocal coach.

After developing a strong voice, many actors have a daily physical and vocal routine that they practice in order to keep their voice in shape. Just as an athlete needs to exercise to keep her body in top physical condition, the actor needs to continue to practice vocal exercises in order to keep his voice ready to communicate intention, character, and emotion. Because the voice is completely dependent on the body's health and alignment, voice and body work go hand in hand.

Work on the voice comes in three parts: alignment working in tandem with relaxation and freedom, development of resonance and power, and speech work. Thoroughly training and developing a strong voice can take years, but we will investigate some basic exercises to help you better understand and strengthen your vocal apparatus.

One of the best vocal teachers in the United States is Kristin Linklater. Her book, *Freeing the Natural Voice* (Drama Publishers, 1976), is an invaluable tool for any student of voice.

Relaxation and Alignment: The Alexander Technique

In Chapter 1 we developed a warm-up to place the actor in a proper state to begin training. The first part of the warm-up involved relaxation and alignment. Relaxation is absolutely crucial to proper vocal functioning. Any tension almost anywhere in the body will somehow affect the voice in a negative way.

The first step in finding true relaxation is by rediscovering the proper alignment of the spine. We say rediscovering because most children learning to crawl and walk have properly aligned spines. Over the years and as we grow, we develop bad alignment habits from stress, emotional tension, and repeated physical activities. Our skeleton is designed to hold our body upright without muscular tension. Unfortunately, most humans do not allow the skeleton to do the work it was designed to do. Instead they begin to use muscular tensions to hold up the spine. These tensions become chronic and result in what many people call bad posture.

To undo the muscular tensions, we must first align our spines. F. M. Alexander, an actor who chronically lost his voice, developed a system of coming back to natural spinal alignment called the Alexander Technique. In searching for the cause of his vocal problems, Alexander discovered that he was putting tension on his larynx and throat from improper spinal alignment. He then set out to discover a means to properly align his spine. In doing so, he saved his voice by eliminating muscular tension. He went on to teach his technique to others.

One of the best books on the Alexander Technique is *How to Learn the Alexander Technique: A Manual for Students,* by Barbara and William Conable (GIA Publications, 2008).

Alexander discovered that by properly aligning the spine, our muscles are free to do what they were intended to do and the resulting movement is free, easy, and graceful. His system is used by dancers, musicians, and actors. It is taught all over the world, and classes are usually open to anyone. Indeed, the classes are often attended by nonperformers suffering from chronic muscular tension that has resulted in pain such as carpal tunnel syndrome, tennis elbow, or lower back pain. The Alexander Technique is now even being used by physical therapists and chiropractors to help heal chronic muscle pain.

For proper spinal alignment, the head must float on top of the spinal column, moving forward and up. When you think forward and up, don't think about the front of your face. Think about your whole head. Right now, allow your whole head to float forward and up, freeing tension from your neck. As you look at the skeleton image in Figure 10.2, note that the weight of the head rests on top of the spinal column in the middle, not at the back as we often think. It is at that joint where your head meets the spine that the head floats forward and up. As this happens, tension is released from the neck and all of the musculature in the body follows suit.

Figure 10.2

The top of the spine as it joins the head (left and middle), and the hole in the cranium where the spine connects with the head (right), showing how the weight of the head rests centrally over the spine, not at the back of the head, as most people imagine

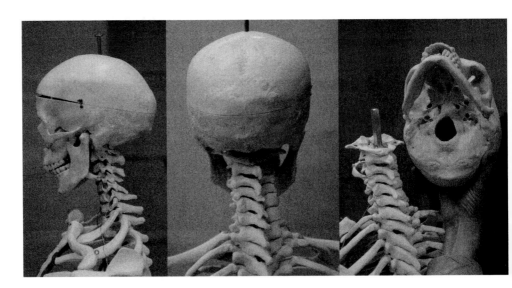

The joint where the spine and head connect—although it is not officially considered a joint—is the exact location where all movement in animals and humans begins—or at least should begin if our skeletons are being used correctly—and it is also the spot

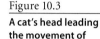

Figure 10.3

A cat's head leading the movement of the entire spine

that leads our movement. To help you visualize this, think about a cat and how it moves. When a cat is sleeping and then rises to stretch its spine and begin to walk, the motion always begins at the spot where the head meets the spine. The entire spine then follows the head, taking the limbs with it. If you don't have a cat to watch, note the head leading in Figure 10.3. Because the motion begins with the head, it creates free, easy, effortless movement.

Babies move like this as well. If you have the opportunity, observe a child learning how to crawl. You will see that the head is forward and up and that the joint where the head meets the spine is where the motion begins. As the baby moves forward and gains momentum, the entire spine follows the head. You will note the same motion as a child learns to stand and begins walking. Look at Figure 10.4 for an example. It is only as we grow older that we lose this natural movement.

In order for adults to regain this free and graceful ease, we must rediscover the alignment of the spine. True, Alexander training takes a lot of time and attention from a trained Alexander teacher who has spent at least three years working toward certification. For our purposes, however, we can begin to work on our bodies, and consequently our voices, through relaxation and the rediscovery of the spine.

Many relaxation exercises were discussed in the first chapter. Any of these techniques will help you begin to free the chronic muscular tensions that stop the spine from functioning properly. So to begin your work on the voice, return to Chapter 1 and try some of the relaxation exercises.

Then you want to work on finding the proper alignment of the spine. The floating up and dropping

Figure 10.4

A young child leading with his head

down the spine exercise in Chapter 1 will help you do just that. After you have done some relaxation exercises, float your fingers up to the ceiling and drop down the spine several times. When you get to the upright position, picture in your mind's eye the joint where your spine meets your head. Remember that it is almost right in the center of your skull. You can almost feel that joint if you take your tongue and run it over the roof of your mouth from the front to the back. When the tip of your tongue is on the roof of your mouth and pointing as far back as it can, it will be pointing at that joint.

Now allow your head to float forward and up from this joint. You will notice as you do this that your neck seems to lengthen and release from any muscular tension. As you get better at allowing your head to float forward and up, your neck will free and the entire spine will lengthen and free itself from muscular tension. This process takes time and cannot be forced to happen. If you try to force it, you will be adding tension into your body. Simply *allow* your head to float forward and up and your neck to free.

Next you want to try to move with your head leading the motion. After you have relaxed and aligned your spine, once again visualize the spot in your skeleton where the head floats on top of the spine. Think about walking forward and allow that joint to initiate the movement. Your entire spine will follow, taking your limbs with it. This also takes time and practice, but as it is the natural movement of our bodies, you should *allow* it to happen rather than making it happen.

Resonance and Power

After preparing your body for voice work with relaxation and alignment, you can begin to work on the resonance and power of the voice. The sound waves created by breath passing between the vocal folds resonate in hollow cavities. Although the voice can resonate almost anywhere in the body (or even in the floor surrounding the feet of a trained opera singer), there are five major resonating cavities: the chest, throat, mouth, nasal passages, and sinuses.

To work on power and resonance, you must essentially work to remove tension from these resonating areas so that they are free to vibrate fully—or in the case of character voices, so that you can easily "place" your voice in one of these areas to create a particular sound. As you free and open these resonating areas, your voice naturally gains power. You can gain additional power in your voice by working on your body so that it can expand more freely and thus take in larger volumes of air.

Chest, Throat, and Mouth Resonance

To work on the resonating cavities, begin by focusing on your chest, throat, and mouth. Relax and align your spine. Then allow your head to drop backward so that your throat is a wide open cavity, extending from your breathing center low in your body to your big open mouth. Your tongue should be relaxed, lying on the floor of your mouth.

Allow your head to hang backward for a short while (you don't want to strain your neck, which you have been allowing to lengthen and relax) and observe the big open space of your throat, chest, and mouth. Figure 10.5 shows an actor in this position. Then right your head and relax your neck by gently rolling your head across the front of your body from your right shoulder to your left shoulder several times.

Figure 10.5

An actor with her head dropped back

Drop your head back again, drop a big breath down low into your body, and send a wide open "hah" to a spot on the ceiling in a low but comfortable pitch. Place your hands on your chest and feel the vibrations there. Drop in a new breath and play around with different pitches until you find one that vibrates most strongly in your chest cavity. Right your head again and once more relax your neck by rolling your head back and forth across the front of your body.

Once more drop your head back and drop a big breath low into your body. Send the "hah" out to the ceiling on the pitch you found that vibrates the strongest. As you send out that sound, gently pound on your chest to awaken the vibrations living there. Right your head and relax your neck by rolling it.

Drop your head back one last time and once again picture the wide open cavity for breath and sound. Now think about using the muscles in the back of your neck to right your head. Allow your neck to be free as your head floats forward and up. It is important to keep focusing on the wide open cavity from your chest to your mouth. As your head moves into alignment, that cavity should remain just as large and open; the shape has simply changed. It is still open but at a different angle. Try dropping your head back and righting it several times, paying attention to the wide open cavity.

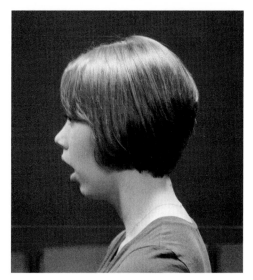

Now with your head aligned and floating forward and up, drop a breath down low into your body and send a "huh" to a spot on the wall in front of you, as seen in Figure 10.6. Place your hands on your cheeks and feel the vibrations in your upper throat and oral cavities. Do this several times, playing with different pitches until you feel the pitch that vibrates the most strongly in this area. It will be a slightly higher pitch than the one that vibrates most strongly in your chest cavity.

Finally, drop your head forward so that you are looking at a spot on the floor between your feet. Try to visualize the wide open channel for breath and sound as remaining

Figure 10.6

An actor with her head floating and sending a "huh" to the wall in front of her

Figure 10.7

An actor with her head dropped forward sending a "hee" to the floor between her feet

open. Once again, the shape of the channel has simply changed. Now drop a breath low into your body and send out a "heee" to the spot on the floor between your feet, as shown in Figure 10.7. The pitch should be slightly higher than the pitch that resonated most strongly in your oral cavity. Play around with different pitches until you find one that vibrates strongly on the back of your teeth and lips. Be careful that the sound is coming out of your mouth and does not jump to coming out of your nose.

Once you have found these three main resonating areas, move from one to the other. First, drop your head back and drop a breath in. Send out a low "hah" to the ceiling while you pound on your chest. Next, right your head as you drop a breath in and then send out a "huh" to the wall in front of you as you feel the vibrations in your mouth. Finally, drop your head forward as you drop a breath in and then send out a "heee" to the floor between your feet and feel the vibrations at the front of your mouth. The pitch should be moving slightly higher as your head moves from front to back. Now repeat the process in the reverse order, moving from your head dropped forward to your head dropped back. Your pitch should be moving slightly lower as your head moves from front to back.

After you have worked these three areas with one breath in between each area, connect them all. Drop your head back and drop a big breath low into your body. Send out a "hah" to the ceiling for a second or two, and then continuing with the sound, right your head, thus allowing the sound to shift to a "huh" going to a spot on the wall in front of you. Keep the sound going as you drop your head forward and the sound shifts to a "heee," going to a spot on the floor between your feet. Try to do this all on one breath. Then with your head dropped forward, drop in another breath and repeat the process moving from front to back. The pitch should always be at the lowest in the back and the highest in the front. Repeat this several times with one breath, moving from back to front and a new breath moving from front to back.

Nasal and Sinus Resonance

Often people think that if they work on their nasal and sinus resonances they will develop a nasal quality to their voice. Quite the opposite is true. A nasal quality occurs when a lazy soft palate that does not rise properly stops vibrations from freely going into the nose and sinuses.

The soft palate is at the back of the roof of the mouth. When running the tip of your tongue from front to back across the roof of your mouth, you will feel the soft palate in the rear. When the soft palate is functioning properly, it will easily lift up when your voice moves into higher pitches. If the soft palate is not functioning properly, it lies flat and doesn't rise, cutting off the passage for higher vibrations of sound to enter the nasal and sinus cavities. So the first step in developing the nasal and sinus resonance is to work on the soft palate.

First, make a "K" sound by placing the back of your tongue on your soft palate and then exhale air and explode the palate and tongue apart. Tucking the front of your tongue under your lower teeth helps with this motion. Now try making the spot where the tongue and palate meet a bit farther back in your mouth. You will have to drop your jaw, open your mouth wide, and raise your soft palate high up in the air. Now trying breathing in some air with the same "K" sound. Put the back of your tongue and your soft palate together a bit farther back than normal and inhale, exploding the two apart. "K" in and out air, stretching the soft palate high up. Keep the inhalation and the exhalation short and springy. Don't drag air into and out your mouth. Don't worry if you cough or gag a bit when you first do this exercise: that is common. After you do it for a while you will no longer have problems with this. This exercise helps to stretch and loosen the soft palate.

After you have your soft palate ready to rise for the higher pitches that resonate in the nasal and sinus cavities, work to awaken the vibrations in the those areas. First, work on the sinus cavities by rubbing the cavities on either side of the nose. Place your fingers on the bridge of your nose and run them down, following the line of your lower eye socket. You will encounter a small indentation, or divot, in the bone. These are your lower sinuses. Gently massage these sinuses with your fingers. They can be somewhat tender, especially if you have a cold, so be gentle. Now drop a breath in and send a "heee" out of your mouth while you continue to massage your sinuses. Figure 10.8 shows an actor doing this. Continue to do this while you are working up in pitch. Use a new breath for each new pitch. If you start to get tense, relax and breathe.

Now scrunch up your nose as if you smelled something awful or you were pushing up eyeglasses with the muscles on either side of your nose. Keeping this scrunched position, drop a breath down into your body and send out a "mee, mee, mee" through your nose on a higher but comfortable pitch. Really try to place that

Figure 10.8

An actor massaging her lower sinuses and sending a "hee" out of her mouth

sound in your nose. It will not be pretty. In fact, the more ugly and nasal it sounds, the better. Drop in a new breath and go up in pitch. Keep your nose scrunched up and go up in pitch as high as you can on the "mee, mee, mee." Figure 10.9 illustrates this. If you get tense, relax and breathe more.

Figure 10.9

An actor with a scrunched-up nose

After all of this, release your soft palate by "K"ing in and out some air. Drop down your spine and breathe into your lower back. This work builds a great energy in the voice and can translate to tension if you are not careful, so try to give in to gravity, breathe, and release. Then stack your spine back up and allow your neck to free and your head to move forward and up.

Breathing Power

Work on freeing the major resonating cavities from tension and awakening vibrations in those areas automatically increases your breathing power, but there are some additional exercises you can do to stimulate your breathing and expand your lung capacity. This will aid you in speaking those long sentences during your voice-over sessions and make sure you don't end up gasping for breath.

It is important to think of your body expanding in 360 degrees with your breath. Sometimes we think that only the front of our body expands, or if we are really tense only the chest, when we take in breath. Actually, our body moves in every direction. The pelvic floor will move down, the torso will expand all the way around from the pelvis up to the armpits, and the shoulder girdle will move higher.

To help you feel this expansion in your body, lie on your belly on the floor. Rest your forehead on your hands and relax. Notice where the breath seems to go in your body. You should feel your lower back rising and expanding as the breath drops in. Try to consciously breathe only into your back, thus expanding it even further.

Now roll over onto your right side so that the right side of your body is immobilized by the floor. Place your left hand onto your lower-left rib cage with your thumb in back and your fingers in the front. Feel your ribs on the left open and expand almost like a bellows as the breath enters your body. Now try to consciously breathe only into the left side of your body, expanding and opening your ribs even further.

Roll back onto your belly and once again breathe into your back. Then roll over onto your left side, immobilizing it on the floor. Place your right hand onto your lower-right ribs with the thumb in the back and the fingers in the front. Feel those right ribs open and expand as the breath drops in. Try to consciously breathe only into the right ribs to open them even further.

Now roll over onto your back. Place your right hand onto your belly so that your thumb is resting on your belly button and your pinky down toward your pubic bone. Place your left hand on your belly so that your left pinky is resting on your belly button and your thumb up toward your sternum. First breathe into your right hand and feel it rise. Then continue the breath into your left hand and feel it rise. Continue breathing, first raising your right hand and then your left.

Finally, allow your hands to fall off your belly. Comfortably lay in the "A" position (a relaxation pose from yoga). Lie on your back with your legs extended and uncrossed. Your feet should be relaxed so that they fall slightly to the sides. Your arms should be extended about 45 degrees from your torso with your palms facing the ceiling. Now think about breathing into every side of your body so that all sides of your body are moving and expanding outward. As you breathe in, your back should move toward the floor. The front of your body should move toward the ceiling. Your pelvic floor should move toward your feet. Your shoulder girdle should move toward your head, and the sides of your body should move toward the walls on your left and right sides. Lie on the floor and breathe for a while, allowing your body to expand in every direction.

Now slowly roll over onto your right side and lie there for a bit. Then push yourself over onto your feet and stack up your spine, allowing your head to float forward and up and your neck to free when you become upright. Since you have been taking in large amounts of oxygen, go slowly, or you may become lightheaded.

Kristin Linklater has a wonderful exercise in her book, *Freeing the Natural Voice*, called "vacuuming" the lungs. This exercise is designed to help the body take in large amounts of air very quickly, as can be necessary when you are speaking highly energetic pieces of text. Let's give it a try. Read the directions first, because they are far longer than the exercise itself, which only takes a few seconds.

First you want to exhale all of the air in your lungs as quickly as possible on an "S" sound. Really push out every last bit of air, but do it quickly. Then close your mouth and plug your nose. Now without opening your mouth or unplugging your nose, try to inhale. Obviously this won't work and you will set up a vacuum in your lungs. Then let go of your nose and let the breath rush in. If your nostrils happen to stick shut, which they do sometimes, don't panic. Simply open your mouth and breath will rush in. You can do this two or three times but not more. You may get lightheaded from all the oxygen flooding your system.

Speech Work

The final stage of working on your voice involves speech work. This requires perfecting your articulation and eliminating any regionalisms that you might have that limit the characters you can portray. Eliminating regionalisms is beyond the scope of this book; it usually takes assistance from a trained ear because often we can't tell exactly how

Figure 10.10

An actor massaging
her jaw open

we sound. If you have a distinct regionalism that you wish to get rid of, consult a voice teacher. Most major cities have professional vocal coaches who can help you with this or other vocal issues.

Working on your diction begins in the same manner as working on the rest of your voice: with relaxation of the articulators. If you are carrying any tensions in your articulators, just as with your breathing apparatus, your speech will be affected. So before doing your articulator work, we need to relax them.

Begin with the jaw, which is where many people carry their stress. Start by massaging the big jaw muscle on the back of your cheeks where the jaw hinges onto the skull. Massage it until it relaxes and drops down, leaving your mouth hanging open. Figure 10.10 shows an actor doing this. This may take some time. Then place the back of your hand under your jaw and raise it up to meet the skull so that your upper and lower teeth are gently touching. Try not to use your jaw muscles. Just allow your hand to raise the jaw. Then remove your hand and let your mouth drop open. If this doesn't happen, you are carrying tension in the jaw. Go back and massage the jaw down again, use the back of your hand to raise it, and then let it drop. A free jaw is an ideal and is often hard to obtain. Do this exercise throughout the day to release tension from your jaw.

Next, to release the lips, "buzz" them (like a horse does). Allow the wet parts of the lips to just flap together. Then place your finger between your lips and loosely move them up and down as if you were a baby playing with your lips. Buzz your lips again with a low motorboat kind of sound. Then purse your lips forward and pull the corners of your lips back quickly as if you were shooting a small pea across the room off of your pursed lips. Say "will you" as you do this. Use the "W" sound to shoot the pea across the room. Figure 10.11 demonstrates this. After that, buzz your lips a few more times to release any tension.

To release tension in your tongue, drop your jaw and hook the tip of your tongue on the back of your lower teeth. Now roll your tongue out of your mouth, thinking about rolling the middle of the tongue out of your mouth like a wave. An actor does this in Figure 10.12. Be careful not to push too hard with the tip of your tongue on the back of your lower teeth or you could push your jaw forward and out of alignment. Then let your tongue relax back flat. Do this several times. Then shake your tongue out by doing a smaller version of this movement quickly over and over again. The larger movement stretches the tongue and the shaking out releases the tension.

Figure 10.11

An actor pursing her lips forward and pulling the corners of her mouth back on a "W"

Figure 10.12

An actor stretching out her tongue

Earlier you learned how to stretch and release the soft palate by "K"ing in and out air. Try that again. Now that you have stretched, loosened, and released your articulators, you can move on to strengthening them.

One of the best ways to work on your articulators is by practicing tongue twisters or difficult phrases. We have listed some in the following section, but you likely have several favorites of your own. Try the ones we've listed or search for more on the Internet. When teaching voice class, we often require our students to purchase *Fox in Sox* by Dr. Seuss (Random House, 1965). It contains some of the best tongue twisters ever created, and it is just plain fun. Try saying your favorites over and over, exaggerating the movement of the articulators, and then relax and try them as quickly and easily as possible.

Vocal Warm-up

A vocal warm-up is necessary before any rehearsal, performance, or recording session. A good vocal warm-up will address all of the voice training areas listed earlier as well as any additional needs the actor might have for a specific role, including singing or dialects.

The following can easily be adapted to meet the actor's specific needs as well as the needs of the voice-over session, performance, or rehearsal. This warm-up should take about 20 minutes but can be adapted to almost any length of time.

On the floor:

1. Begin on the floor on your back in the "A" position, as described earlier.

2. Take a moment to relax your body and breathe.

3. Feed a big, open breath deep down in your abdomen and sigh out the sound as you exhale. Do this three times.

4. Pull your knees into your chest and roll out your lower back on the floor while you are humming gently in a comfortable register.

5. Drop your bent knees over to the right, keeping your left shoulder on the floor, and turn your head to the left for a nice long spine stretch, as shown in Figure 10.13. While you are in this position, feed a big sigh of relief down into your right hip socket, feeling the whole side of your body expand, and then sigh out the sound. Do this three times. Repeat this on the other side.

6. Roll onto your back, stretch your arms and legs out as far as they can go, and yawn. Let the yawn be heard; you can't be nervous about making sound during the warm-up. If you are still feeling tense, repeat this process a couple of times.

7. Roll over onto your stomach and rest your forehead on your hands. Feel your lower back expand as your breath drops in. Start humming gently in a comfortable register, trying to feel your lips vibrating. Keep humming on different pitches, continuing to feel your lips vibrate. Do this for several minutes on different pitches but don't push your voice too high or low so that you feel any strain.

Figure 10.13

**A twisting
spine stretch**

8. From here, push yourself up onto your hands and knees so that your hands are under your shoulders and your knees are under your hips. Inhale as you arch your back so that the top of your head and tailbone drop to the floor while the center of your spine reaches to the ceiling. You will need to relax your abdominal muscles for this to work. Then let your back sway so that the top of your head and your tailbone reach to the ceiling, your mid-back arching downward, as you sigh out a sound. Repeat this three times. Figure 10.14 shows you how.

Figure 10.14

Stretching the spine like a cat and arching it

9. Now push back onto your feet so you are standing but your body is released and hanging over from the tailbone. Don't lock your knees. Shake your shoulders to further release tension while you shake some sound out of your head. Relax your facial muscles and try to shake the skin and muscle off your face while you shake sound out of the top of your head. The sounds you are making here are loose and uncontrolled. Don't worry if they sound silly.

10. Roll your spine up as you did in Chapter 1, stacking each vertebra on top of the next. Allow your arms to float up as in Chapter 1, and stretch through the whole body. Let your arms and spine release so that you are once again hanging over. While upside down, once more shake some sound out of the top of your head while you shake the skin and muscle off your face. Stack your vertebrae back up.

Standing:

1. Imagine there are springs under your feet and that you are a rag doll. Bounce and shake, letting all of your joints go and your muscles relax. As you do this, bounce sound out of your body. You are shaking and bouncing sound around as you are bouncing your body.

2. Stand on your left foot and shake some sound out of your right foot. Repeat while standing on the right and shaking sound out of the left foot.

3. Shake out your right arm and then throw it away. When you loosely throw it away, say "hey" in a relaxed manner. Throw your arm away several times with the "hey," and then shake out your left arm and throw it away on the "hey" as well.

4. Stand centered, paying attention to your alignment. Next, drop down your spine, letting each vertebra bend over, one at a time, starting with your neck and moving down to your tailbone. As you relax over, run your voice up your vocal range, lowest to highest. Starting standing, sing your lowest pitch that you can comfortably hit without pushing. Then drop down your spine and let your voice travel through its range. When you have completely dropped over, your highest notes (without pushing) will be almost flying out of the top of your head. Then stack your vertebrae back up while you drop down your range. Start bent over in your highest pitch and roll up your spine as you sing from your highest to your lowest pitch. You will end standing aligned, upright, and singing your lowest pitch. Do this several times very loosely and freely. Do not become tense or self-conscious by the word "sing": you are just letting sound swoop out of your body. It does not have to be very pretty. The idea is to warm up the range of your voice in a free and easy manner. If you notice a "break" in your voice (a skip as you move from low to high or high to low), focus on running the range over this breaking point, smoothing it out as you roll up and down.

5. Imagine that you see your friend out a window and you have a need to call out to them on a "hey." See your friend. Feel the need to communicate. Drop a big breath in

and let out a long extended "hey." Do this several times and let your knees bounce as you call out on the "hey."

6. Standing upright and paying attention to your alignment, drop your head forward and roll it loosely around to the left. Repeat to the right. Now do this with a hum. Hum a comfortable pitch and roll your head to the left. Hum a new pitch and roll it to the right. Continue rolling your head in different directions on different pitches.

7. Drop your head back and imagine a big open cavern from low in your belly to the front of your mouth. Drop a big breath in and sigh out a "hah" to the ceiling. Pound on your chest a bit as you do this to awaken and loosen up the chest vibrations. Try this on several different lower pitches.

8. Right your head again so it is aligned. Massage your jaw and let it relax so it is dropped and your mouth is open. Hook the tip of your tongue on the back of your lower teeth. Keeping the tip of your tongue behind your lower teeth, roll the center of your tongue out of your mouth like a wave. Be careful not to push your lower jaw forward with the force from your tongue. Now gently shake your tongue forward and back as you say "hi-yah-hi-yah-hi-yah." Drop in a new breath and shake your tongue out with sound on a different pitch. Repeat several times on different pitches.

9. Scrunch up your nose as if you were smelling something really nasty and say "mee, mee, mee," sending the sound up into your nose. It should not be a pretty sound— in fact, it should sound nasally and nasty—so don't worry about it. Do this several times on higher pitches.

10. Once again, drop down your spine while you run up your range and then run down your range as you roll up your spine several times. Finally, call out on a long extended "hey" several more times.

For the articulators:

1. Warm your hands by rubbing them quickly together and then place them over your face. Give your face a massage. Pay particular attention to your forehead, temples, the bridge of your nose into your lower eye sockets, the area on the cheeks just outside each nostril, and your jaw. Try to let the tension drain out of the muscles on your face.

2. Buzz your lips like a horse. Keep the lips really loose with the wet parts of the lips flapping together. Continue to loosely buzz your lips as you sing low, then high notes.

3. Now that your lips are loose, hum an "M" sound. Try to feel the vibrations on your lips. (It can help to feel the vibration to curl the lips in just a bit over your teeth, but be sure your mouth and lips stay open and relaxed.) Now slowly say "mmmeee, mmmeee, mmmeee, mmmay, mmmmay, mmmay, maaah." Feel the vibrations on the lips on all of the "M" sounds.

4. Pucker your lips far forward and then pull the corners of your mouth back quickly as if there were a small pea resting in your pursed lips and you are shooting it across the room when you pull the corners of your mouth back. Now repeat this motion as you say "will you." Repeat several times quickly. Now say "will you wait for Willie and Winnie Williams" making sure that you purse your lips far forward and pull them back on every "W" sound.

5. Touch the tip of your tongue to the outside of your upper lip and move the tip to the outside of your lower lip as you say "la." Repeat this several times on different pitches. Then quickly flick your tongue inside your mouth saying "la" on different pitches.

6. "K" in and out some air, as practiced earlier, to stretch and loosen the soft palate. Make sure that the breath is quick and springy.

7. Keeping your lips loose, bounce a "B" sound on your lips. Say "buh, buh, buh, buh, buh, buh, bah." Then bounce a "D" sound. Say "duh, duh, duh, duh, duh, duh, dah." Then bounce a "G" sound. Say "guh, guh, guh, guh, guh, guh, gah." Next put it all together. Say "buh, duh, guh, guh, duh, buh." Repeat this over and over as quickly as you can (you can start slowly, then speed up). It might help you to think that you are moving from the front of your mouth to the back and then from the back to the front. Once you get good at this, sing it with your range. Be sure to keep your lips and tongue very loose while doing this.

8. Do the previous step, but only with breath and no sound. You will be practicing "B," "T," and "K." With just breath, run the consonants from front to back and back to front. Try to stay loose and don't add any tension.

9. Now do some tongue twisters. Repeat each phrase, going as fast as you can while enunciating very clearly—you should exaggerate the lip, tongue, and mouth motions while saying the phrases. Be sure you don't mispronounce words; if you do, start again and go slower. Following are some good ones, but do any that you know or like.

   - The big, black bug bled blue, black blood.
   - Sushi chef
   - Rubber baby buggy bumpers
   - I slit a sheet, a sheet I slit. Upon the slitted sheet I sit.
   - She stood at the window inexplicably mimicking him hiccoughing and amicably welcoming him in.
   - The guest's breasts are the best.
   - Eleven benevolent elephants

10. Run any difficult lines that you have to say for the session or show. Practice enunciating clearly and quickly, exaggerating the motion of your mouth, lips, and tongue.

Developing Your Character Voices

Whether or not you realize it, you have already begun to develop your own personal character voices. In fact, you probably have some already established voices that you do. Think about how you sound when you talk to your pets or children. Chances are that you talk in a different voice. Or how do you sound when you talk or sing in the shower? Or do you have some funny voices or accents that you use to entertain your family at Thanksgiving or your friends at the office? Do you voice any inanimate objects such as a coffee maker or your computer when they don't work properly? These voices, that are just a part of who you are, can become your first character voices.

Start by identifying any of these voices that you do as part of your life; then you want to codify them into a character. To do so, give your voices names so you can identify them. Try to have a key line or phrase that you say as this character, which will throw you into the voice. For example, maybe you do a great leprechaun voice; if you do, name him Blarney and attach the phrase "They're wonderfully delicious" to this voice. Then any time you say, "They're wonderfully delicious," you will automatically jump into that voice. Or maybe when you talk with your nephew who is only one year old, you do this really funny baby voice. So give the baby a name like Itsy Bitsy and a phrase like "Gotta love baby." Then if you want to assume the character of Itsy Bitsy, you can simply say, "Gotta love baby," and you are instantly talking in your character voice.

You might also be able to do impersonations. If so, find a key phrase for each of your impersonations that allows you to jump immediately into that person's voice. Can you do any dialects, a skill that is always useful in the voice-over industry? If so, create a character for each of the different dialects. Name your character and find a key phrase that throws you into the character and the dialect. Already you will discover that you have many different character voices right at your fingertips—or rather, vocal cords.

In addition, while you may not have realized it, by doing the exercises in this book you have started to create other character voices. You have found that your voice sounds different when you are doing the essence of a cloud or a thunderstorm. The bioenergetic body of the masochist creates a different voice from that of the oral. Different psychological gestures and Laban essences create different variations of voice. Even the different Alba breath patterns cause your voice to work in different ways. Thus, all of the various acting explorations that you have done have started to develop your character voices.

Go back through the exercises and/or your journal notes and rediscover the voices you found. Now give each voice a name and find a key phrase to speak that can help you find the voice and character in an instant. You could also use any of the techniques you have learned to create a new character voice. Say you need to voice a refrigerator or a coffee maker: you could use the essence exploration technique to discover a voice for your character. Or what if you are voicing an evil controlling villain? Perhaps the bioenergetic body of a psychopath will provide a good voice for your character. Even the different Commedia masks, gestures, and bodies will create different character voices.

As you develop and codify your character voices, make a written list of them so you can remember all of the choices you have. To help you strengthen these voices, talk in them. Spend a few minutes each day talking in your voices. You don't have to talk to other people. Talk to your plants, pets, or computer. Talk to other drivers as you commute. Talk to imaginary people in the shower. Improvise a conversation between one of your characters and another one of them, flipping back and forth between your character voices as you go. The possibilities are endless. Playing with your "silly" voices can be great fun, so enjoy all of your new personalities.

The Voice-Over Session

In many ways a voice-over session is no different than acting before the camera. The actor still needs to prepare for the role by scoring the script and doing research. He needs to create a living, breathing character that is fully vocally and physically realized. However, although he needs to rehearse his lines, he doesn't need to memorize them or learn blocking. Before the work begins, he needs to warm up, just as he would before a performance. But instead of acting with another person or to the camera, he is acting alone in a small, soundproof booth in front of a microphone. These conditions can be difficult for some actors to work within, but they do not need to be intimidating. After you come to understand the protocol and methods that best suit this type of acting, voice-over work can become quite liberating and fun.

When you enter the recording studio for your voice-over session, you will find that it is divided into two parts: the control room and the soundproof recording room. There are usually double-paned windows or a glass door between the two areas so you can see into the other area. When you are in the recording room, you cannot hear into the control booth unless the director pushes a talk-back button, and the director and sound engineer cannot hear you unless the microphone is turned on. You never know when that microphone might be turned on, so be careful what you say.

In the recording room is a music stand with a light on it, the microphone, and sometimes a stool or chair for sitting. You must *never* touch the microphone. It can cost thousands of dollars, and you don't want to be responsible for breaking one. It is the sound engineer's job to adjust the microphone to the proper height for your recording, so let her do it. You may adjust the music stand but never the microphone.

You will always want to remain the same distance away from the mic. Approximately 12 to 14 inches is good for a standard cardioid mic. Never blow into the mic because this can damage it. Keep some bottled water with you so that you can keep your mouth wet. When the mouth dries out, it can make some clicking or smacking sounds. If you have a particular problem with popping your plosive sounds such as "P" and "B," you might want to stand off center and talk slightly across the mic instead of straight into it. This will lessen some of the harsher articulation sounds. Remember to stay in the same place each time though, for consistency in recorded sound.

Position your music stand so you can easily see your script without having to turn your head from the mic. You should also arrange your script so you do not have to turn a page mid-sentence. This could cause a paper sound to be picked up on the recording. Only turn a page or adjust the script when you are silent. Figure 10.15 shows an actor with a properly placed music stand and standing the correct distance from the microphone.

Figure 10.15

An actor standing the correct distance from the microphone with a properly placed music stand

Treat the microphone as if it were someone's ear. Speak into it as if you were talking into someone's ear a foot away. You don't need to worry about projection at all with the microphone. If you have some lines that are very loud, you don't want to scream them into someone's ear. So take a step or two back from the mic to speak those loud lines. Be sure to step back during a period of quiet speech, though, or it could create a fade-out effect. If you want to sound as if you are leaving the room, you can step back as you speak to purposely create the fade-out effect.

In most professional sound studios, you will use earphones, or "cans," while you record. You will hear your voice through the earphones as it sounds in the recording instead of how you normally hear it rolling around in your head. At first this might seem odd to you, but it is necessary in order for you to adjust your voice and keep the sound level even with crazy characters. Earphones are also often the means by which the director will speak with you if there are no speakers in the recording booth. And if you are acting with another actor in a separate isolation booth, this is how you will hear her. Working with earphones allows you to hear what everyone else hears, so even though it sounds different to you, you should get used to it.

It is almost always best for you to remain standing when doing your recording. Standing helps your acting and thus recording in many ways. First you have more room to breathe properly when standing and so will have more control over you voice. You also generally have more energy when standing so your recording won't become too low key or uninspired. Finally, standing affords you more ease with gesturing. This is very important. In a recording, you need to gesture and act just as you would if you were in front of the camera. The physicalization of a character shows up in your voice. So don't think you can simply stand behind the microphone and read the lines. Gesture with your face and whole body. Be the character. It will be evident in your recording.

CHAPTER 11

Creating Lip Sync and Facial Performance for Voiced Characters

In Chapter 10, we discussed how to warm up and use your voice to create character voices for use with animation. In this chapter, we focus on the complementary aspect of taking a vocal performance and generating animation from it. Certainly knowledge of how to create a voice-over translates into a better understanding of how an actor works, and thus how to capture their performance when animating voice-over tracks. In addition, you need to understand the technicalities of creating lip sync efficiently, as well as how to translate what an actor does into the world of animation. So, we will discuss not only how to take recorded tracks and create proper lip sync, but also strong facial character acting while animating to a voice-over track.

This chapter discusses:

- **Understanding audio performances**
- **Fundamentals of lip sync**
- **Basic technical requirements for capturing voice**
- **Breaking down an audio/video voice-over shot**
- **Animating lip sync**
- **Capturing an actor's performance while animating lip sync**

"Reading" Audio Performances

Chapter 10 discussed concerns and solutions for vocal acting, whereas in this chapter we will deal with the question of how to take a solid vocal performance and use it as a basis for your animation work. The first thing most animators think about when given a script is how an actor will perform the lines, and how the animator will then match the words so that the character appears to be saying the lines. Second, and just as importantly, is how the character will perform the lines: Lip sync is only half the task that needs to be addressed when vocally scripted scenes are animated. A neutral, or "dead"-looking, character merely opening and closing its mouth at the right time is not sufficient to create a well-acted, interesting character for a given scene. Thus, as with the previous chapters, we will focus on the performance we can give, not just the technical elements of matching lips to lines of dialogue. On the other hand, lip sync is crucial to any scene where lines are spoken: if you don't do the lip sync properly, it distracts your audience from the performance you are trying to give. Fortunately, most proper voice-over recording sessions include video footage of the actors recording the lines of dialogue, and this footage can be a wonderful resource when distorting your character's face as they perform those same words.

> Lip sync is one of those thankless "invisible" animation tasks: the goal of lip sync is for it to be as unnoticed as possible. Like a goalie in soccer, if you do your job right no one even notices that you've spent a great deal of time syncing your character's mouth; it's only when you "let one slip by" and something calls attention to itself that people notice—and complain.

The first thing that you need to do when dealing with voice-over recordings is learn to "read" sound. Essentially, you want to look at the visual reference your 3D package or audio software provides for you and understand how the words are translated visually. Most audio and 3D software packages provide a visualization of the changing amplitude of the recorded sound over time, as shown in Figure 11.1. As is evident from the figure, while each interface is different the waveform is pretty much the same, so once you can read the waveform in one package, you can read it anywhere.

> If you use Maya, the process for importing sound is not particularly intuitive, because it involves two steps. First, choose to import a file (File ➤ Import); then, once you have imported your sound file, right-click on the time slider and choose Sound ➤ *YourSoundName* (where *YourSoundName* is the name of the sound file you just imported) from the pop-up menu. To make the audio file more visible, you can alter the Sound and Time Slider settings in your preferences. Choose Window ➤ Settings/Preferences ➤ Preferences, and under Settings/Time Slider set the Time Slider height to 2X or 4X to make the time slider taller so it's easier to see the sound. If you prefer to see only the top half (or bottom half) of the audio waveform (which is often easier to see on the time slider), select Settings/Sound and choose Top (or Bottom) from the Waveform display options.

Figure 11.1

From top to bottom, visualization of the phrase "You're pretty" in Amadeus Pro, Final Cut Pro, Logic Pro, and Maya's time slider

Let's look at the phrase "You're pretty," setting video stills against the waveform in Figure 11.2. Note how there are two distinct "humps" to the sound. As you might expect, the first is "you're" and the second is "pretty." "You're" starts with a "y" sound, revealed by the slow ramp-up of sound (at frames 21 through 24 of the included yourePretty.mb file on the DVD). Next, the "ou" sound joins with the "y" on frames 24 through 26. Then comes the "re" on frames 26 through 28, a very slight pause on frame 29, followed by the "p," split between frames 30 and 31. (You can see the spike on the sound form where the plosive "p" is spoken.) Also, as indicated in Figure 11.2, note how the actor prepares for the "p" sound by pursing his lips even before saying the "p." You can also see from the video sequence how the "p" visual actually precedes the sound by a frame or two; this is due to the fact that the plosive comes on the release of the lips, rather than the pursing. The "r" comes on frames 31 and 32, then the "e" on 33, the "t" (where there is a slight bump in the waveform) on 34, and the final "y" sound trailing off from frames 35 through 40. Something to notice, even here in a "straight," neutral, or emotionless reading of the line, is how sounds join together, and how lazy we are at pronouncing words. The actor doesn't say "you're (pause) pretty," nor does he actually enunciate the "t" sound properly. Instead, the sounds run together as the actor speaks the words, and what we hear is closer to "Yorpredee" than "You're pretty." Understanding just how little we articulate, as well as how much we run sounds together, is very important as you move toward breaking sounds down into "lip-syncable" chunks, especially when an actor is doing a character voice.

Figure 11.2

Analyzing the waveform for "You're pretty," using video reference to help

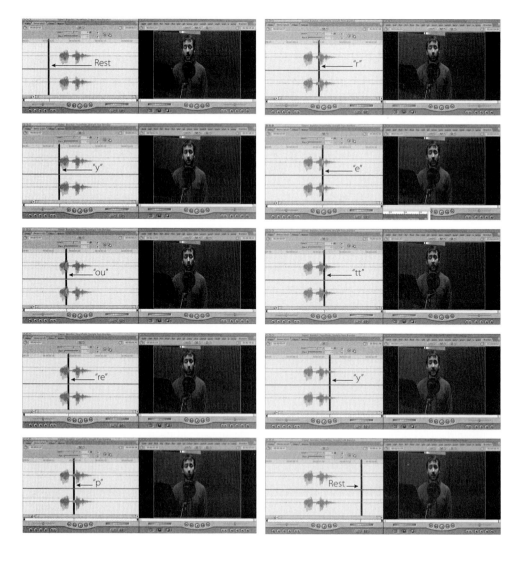

Remember that you can scrub the time slider back and forth in Maya (and most other 3D software) to hear the sound. This is a useful feature when working on any clip that contains sound, especially voice-over tracks.

One other important aspect of the video footage that will come into play when animating the lip sync is how little the mouth moves, visually, during much of the phrase. (Refer to Figure 11.2, or the `Brandon_YourePretty_Neutral.mov` file on the accompanying DVD.) While saying "you're," the actor opens his mouth a little to make the "y" sound, then purses them a bit for the "ou're." His mouth then closes (with the lips still pursed) to make the "p" sound, his mouth opening on the plosive into the "r" sound. For the rest of the word, "etty," his mouth remains almost immobile, only opening slightly wider on the final "y" sound. The tongue, which makes the "t" (or, more accurately, "d"), is invisible behind the actor's teeth, and thus is unimportant to the visual delivery of the line.

Looking at video like this example is very important in learning how much to do (and how much *not* to do) when creating lip sync, as creating too much action visually when animating lip sync is actually worse—more distracting—to audiences than creating too little action. The accompanying DVD includes two sets of video with audio (`Amy_VoiceOvers.mov` and `Brandon_VoiceOvers.mov`) that have the actors saying several words and phrases both "straight" (or neutrally spoken) and with various character incarnations. The DVD also has several snippets from these longer movies broken out to make it easier for you to grab a phrase and work with it. The actors speak the following lines, which go from a very simple sound to complete sentences.

- "Ahh"
- "Why?"
- "You're pretty."
- "I'm looking at you."
- "The quick brown fox jumped over the lazy dog."
- "Whoever you are…you will pay for this."
- "Try new Bromo-cola: good for your tongue—and your tummy."

These phrases provide you with a range of lip-sync challenges, from extremely easy ("Ahh" being a simple mouth open-closed action) to complex with the final sentences. As you watch and listen to the actors reading these lines, note how varied even the simplest words or phrases can be as the actor performs the line. Even the simple word "Ahh" can be performed numerous ways, as Figure 11.3 shows. Thus, lip sync becomes only part of the process of capturing facial performance; capturing the character and intention behind the words is just as important and will be more noticed by your audience (unless you do a poor job with the basic lip-sync process, which will distract the audience from your character's performance).

Figure 11.3

Various ways to say the simple word "Ahh"

Capturing Audio (and Video) for Voice-overs

Although we don't have space in this book to delve into all of the intricacies of capturing audio (and video) for lip sync, in this section we lay out the basic technical elements you need to know to get some good sound for your temp track—or even your final capture track—and to sync up your video with your audio capture.

First, if you have access to a real recording booth, by all means use it, especially for your final audio capture. Any large market city will have recording facilities for rent—just search the Web for something like "audio recording" or "recording studio" and the name of your city—and since you just need a tiny space to capture vocals only, you can probably rent the space inexpensively for a couple of hours. A recording studio will have equipment properly set up, along with a technician to help you, so you can get your recordings done efficiently—and, of course, the sound quality will be high.

Short of renting a space, there are some fairly inexpensive ways to capture audio, rising in quality (and complexity and expense) from very low quality temp track sound up to something that can approach dedicated studio recording sound.

First, there is your trusty video camera's built-in microphone. While you will certainly not want to use what you record via the built-in mic for your final dubbing, it can be great for exercises and project work, or as a temp track to work on. As a bonus, you get audio and video synced properly by default, since they're both captured to the videotape (or hard drive) on the camera. All you need then is a tripod to set the camera on, and some software on your computer—anything from iMovie to Premiere to Final Cut or Avid will do—to get the audio and video feed from your camera to your computer.

For the other recording methods, you will need a good microphone. While there are many mics you can purchase, ranging from $5 all the way up to $10,000 or more, the general rule that "you get what you pay for" is very much true of mics, whatever their brand. We have found that once you cross about the $150 line, most microphones will start to deliver good sound. Obviously if you can afford to purchase (or borrow) a Neumann U87 studio mic (which runs a bit more than $3,500), that will be substantially better than a $200 mic; however, unless you are planning to release your animation on the big screen, you can probably get away with the sound quality from a less expensive mic just fine.

Figure 11.4

An Audio-Technica AT4040 microphone

For our recordings, we used an Audio-Technica AT4040 mic, shown in Figure 11.4, which costs $300. In general, you are better off purchasing a condenser mic—either a studio mic with a cardioid pattern, or a "shotgun" mic (that usually mounts on a pole) with a super or hyper cardioid pattern. Shotgun mics often have a battery to provide power to the mic itself, while studio mics normally need "phantom" power (most modern ones expect +48 volts). So if you purchase a mic, be sure you understand its power needs: if the mic requires phantom power, you must have either a video camera that provides this power or a mixing board that provides the power and from which you can then output a line level signal to your camera or other recording device.

The second way to capture sound is to run a microphone into your computer, either directly or via a mixing board where the signal can be adjusted prior to arriving at your computer. From free audio programs like Audacity, to inexpensive programs like Amadeus Pro, to high-end tools like Logic and Pro Tools, there are myriad ways to get your audio into your computer. While the more advanced tools provide cleaner signal input and better sound manipulation tools, even a free program like Audacity does perfectly fine recording your actors.

The caveat to this method is that you do not get video with your audio. If you wish to include video for performance matching later on, be sure you use a clapper board or something like it—something that makes a sound and visual signal at the same time—so that you can go back and match your audio files to your video recordings at a later date. This matching obviously requires extra work, but that work can be relatively easy as long as you created a visual/sound "mark" at the beginning of each recording session.

The third way to capture audio and video is to run your mic output to your camera, either directly or via a mixing board. (This is the method we used to capture our voice-over audio sessions on the accompanying DVD.) If you have a high-end video camera that has XLR mic inputs and provides phantom power (the Sony HVR-V1U that we used to record our actors has this), you can simply run an XLR cable from your microphone to the input jack of the camera, as shown in Figure 11.5, and record away. If your camera has a "mini" 1/8-inch mic input jack, you will need to either use an independently powered shotgun mic and convert the output cable from XLR to 1/8 inch, or run your mic's output to a mixing board, then take the output of the mixing board and run it into your camera. In either case, you get audio and video matched automatically since both sound and visuals are recorded to the tape (or hard drive) together. In addition, as most cameras record 16-bit sound at 48KHz, you get high-quality sound that you can extract from your video source for use in your projects.

The one other thing you need to be aware of when capturing sound is that you hear *everything* when recording. Therefore, you need to find the quietest place you can, turn off all heating or air-conditioning units, turn off all fluorescent lights (that make a 50Hz or 60Hz buzzing sound), and if at all possible, line the walls with foam, egg cartons, yoga mats, or some other sound-absorbing material. Setting up a quiet environment means you won't waste that expensive microphone recording background noise and room reverberations!

Figure 11.5

Attaching an XLR mic cable directly to a Sony HVR-V1U camera, which has XLR mic inputs and provides +48-volt phantom power

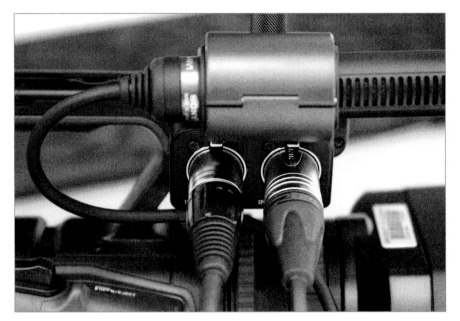

Creating Lip Sync

Now that we have looked at the basics of facial performance, reading a sound file, and recording your own audio/video tracks for your projects, let's consider breaking a sound down into "visemes," or visual phonemes, which will be used to animate a character's mouth when actual lip syncing takes place. You might initially wonder why you would go through the trouble of reworking sounds into visemes rather than simply using the phonemes that make up the words, but as we saw in Figure 11.2, the mouth often does not change visibly when creating sounds like "L," "T," "D," "K," and "G," and it also often elides sounds. Consequently, creating a mouth shape for every single phoneme sound only ends up creating extra work for you as an animator, and can produce an overanimated mouth, which is distracting. Humans are lazy, at least when it comes to speaking: we like to move our mouths as little as possible to say what we're saying. And while animated characters are obviously more exaggerated and move their mouths more than people would in normal speech, we as audiences still judge them based on our experience with people, so overanimating the mouth for lip sync often leads to problems.

There are two basic ways the mouth can move when creating sounds: lips wider or narrower, and jaw open or closed. (Obviously this is a simplification, but it works remarkably well to get the basic sync work done.) Thus for a sound like "Ahh," which can be represented by something like AH, the jaw opens with the lips remaining in place, width-wise, while for the EE sound in "bee," the lips widen while the jaw remains generally neutral (mostly closed).

> For an excellent, full study of facial modeling and performance, see Jason Osipa's *Stop Staring: Facial Modeling and Animation Done Right*, 2nd edition (Sybex, 2007). Much of our work breaking sounds down into visemes owes a debt of gratitude to Jason's book.

Let's take the phrases recorded on the DVD and break them down into their visual references, which we can use later when animating a character with those lines. Note that we are going to break down the sounds here for a "straight" (neutral) reading of the line. When an actor gives you a character voice, it will often change the visual references somewhat, so you will want to listen to the way the actual line is said when you create lip sync for exaggerated character voice readings. For the first sounds, we present a breakdown of how the sound is made visually. For the later sounds, we present the end result of the sounds in a more abstracted way.

Ahh. Ahh is about as simple as it gets, and here the phoneme and visemes pretty much line up. The mouth will start in a neutral position (usually with lips slightly parted) for the in-breath. Then the jaw will drop to create the AH sound, the lips remaining in a neutral position, neither wider nor narrower than their default position.

Why? Here we have two distinct shapes (not counting the rest position at the beginning and end): the "W" is made with pursed, or narrowed, lips, while the "y" draws the lips back into a wide position. There is very little jaw open/closed motion with this word. Although the W viseme is simple, the "y" sound here is actually a diphthong, comprised of the AH and EE shapes elided. Thus we could write out "why" as W-AH-EE. However, since the AH and EE sounds are similar in shape, and they run together quickly, over just a frame or two, we can instead simplify the word to W-EE visually. If it turns out that we need to go back and put the AH shape back in, we can later, but it is highly unlikely in normal speech that the AH will be missed. (Consider how little your mouth moves on "why" in a sentence like "hey, why are you here?") By breaking the sound down to W-EE, we simplify the shapes we need to animate, making our lives easier and representing the visuals better at the same time.

You're pretty.   A first pass on this phrase yields EE-OO-(R)-P-(R)-EE. The "t" is invisible as it's only a tongue inflection inside the mouth, so the final visual is a drawn-out EE after the P-R sounds. The Rs are in parentheses as they might or might not be necessary shapes since they form in between other sounds. In addition, depending on how the mouth starts, we can probably also eliminate the EE sound at the beginning, yielding OO-P-EE as our final visual for this phrase. Three shapes for the whole phrase (at least on a first pass): not bad! As a reference, Figure 11.6 shows an actor speaking this phrase, showing off the three mouth shapes she makes to create the phrase.

I'm looking at you.   A first pass gives us AH-M-(L)-OO-AH-(EE)-OO. Once again, we can eliminate "k," "ing," and "t" sounds, as they're internal. In addition, unless we are very close to the face, we won't be able to see the tongue create the "l" sound, and the EE at the beginning of "you" is a passing position, so we can probably eliminate it, at least until the finessing stage. The final shapes are: AH-M-OO-AH-OO. Five shapes for the phrase.

The quick brown fox jumped over the lazy dog.   The "th" at the beginning of this phrase will actually need a mouth shape, because the tongue needs to rest between the teeth (visibly) to make that sound. After working through the phrase, we get: TH-AH-EE-B-AH-F-AH-AH (more closed)-(J)-AH-P-AH-V-AH-TH-AH-(L)-AA-EE-AH. The final AH sound for "fox" becomes more closed as the "x" sound is made (using the tongue against the roof of the mouth), and so needs a separate shape. Removing the J and L sounds (which are not visible) and substituting F for V (since they are the same shape visibly), we end up with 18 shapes for a fairly long phrase: TH-AH-EE-B-AH-F-AH-AH (more closed)-AH-P-AH-F-AH-TH-AH-AA-EE-AH. You can see how much time this will save in the animation stage—and as we'll see when we animate our character, we don't lose anything noticeable when doing so!

Whoever you are…you will pay for this.   Our first pass on this sentence produces (W)-OO-EE-V-AH-EE-OO-AH-EE-OO-IH-P-AA-F-AH-TH-IH. The W is just an extra out-breath at the beginning of the OO sound, so we can strike that sound. The EE at the beginning (the first "e" in "ever") is written out as an EE sound, though it will be narrower than a full EE (the first "e" in "even," for example). The V is the same shape as an F, so to simplify our shapes, we can substitute an F there. The EE that starts "you" can probably be removed both times since it passes very quickly (again, we can always add it back later if it looks bad in a particular case). So the final viseme breakdown becomes: OO-EE-F-AH-OO-AH-OO-IH-P-AA-F-AH-TH-IH.

Try new Bromo-cola: good for your tongue—and your tummy. The beginning of this sentence has both a "t" and an "r," neither of which is a distinct viseme. Thus if we start from a neutral mouth shape, we can probably get away with making the first viseme shape an AH, and just look at the final product to be sure that this "cheat" works. Our first pass gives us AH-(N)-OO-B-OH-M-OH-OH-AH-OO-F-AH-EE-OO-(T)-AH-AH (more closed)-AH-EE-OO-(R)-AH-M-EE. The two AH-AH sounds together that make up the shapes for "tongue" need to be differentiated since there is a slight collapse of the mouth as the "ngu" sounds are made. We can also reduce the OH shapes to OO shapes, keeping in mind that the mouth will be somewhat wider when making these shapes (for "Bromo," for example) than they will when making a more pure OO shape (for "you"). Thus our simplified set of visemes for this phrase becomes: AH-OO-P-OO-M-OO-OO-AH-OO-F-AH-OO-AH-AH (more closed)-AH-OO-AH-M-EE. Nineteen shapes for the retro product pitch!

Figure 11.6

Creating the mouth visemes for the phrase "You're pretty": from left to right, OO-P-EE

Once you have studied how these words and phrases are created visually, try working through some lines you write (or read) yourself. Practice "seeing" the visual position of the mouth as it creates each sound, as well as how the sounds join with one another. Keeping a mirror or video camera with you to help you see the shapes you (or someone else) make as you speak is crucial to practicing your lip-sync technique. Either speak while watching yourself in the mirror or videotape yourself or a friend saying lines, then go back and watch them as you figure out how the words become visual sound cues. Above all, don't overenunciate when you speak; you want to speak at a normal pace so you can see just how little your mouth moves between sounds. Overenunciating will make your speech sound strange, and it won't give you the proper mouth shapes either.

Sync Step 1: Basic Lip Sync

Now that you have a good idea how to break down a phrase into its constituent visemes, or mouth shapes, let's determine how to animate a mouth based on these visemes. Once you have a good idea of how to do the basic lip-sync technique, we will move on to creating character performance based on the work our voice-over actor is doing.

The first thing we need to do is consider how the mouth moves. For our purposes, we can simplify things by breaking up the mouth motion into "horizontal" and "vertical" motions. The horizontal motions are any place the mouth gets wider or narrower, and the vertical is where the jaw opens or closes. For the word "you"—here assuming you over-enunciate it—the jaw never opens or closes; instead, the mouth goes from EE to OO, or from wide to narrow. (Of course at normal speech pace, the EE will probably get lost in the surrounding sounds, but for here, consider how the mouth looks when you overenunciate.) The opposite happens for a word like "I'm," where we get a mouth open-closed sequence for the AH-M visemes. Go back and look at the phrases we just analyzed and note which viseme sounds involve the jaw opening and closing, and which involve the mouth becoming wider and narrower.

As an example, let's take the phrase "The quick brown fox jumped over the lazy dog," and see how our two passes would look. The shapes we ended up with from our earlier analysis are TH-AH-EE-B-AH-F-AH-AH (more closed)-AH-P-AH-F-AH-TH-AH-AA-EE-AH. We can write out the open-closed shapes for each viseme as follows, with C for Closed and O for Open: C-O-C-C-O-C-O-O (more closed)-O-C-O-C-O-C-O-O-C-O (the final open covering the last "g" in "dog"). Obviously there are variations of the O and C shapes, and you can animate them as you go, but the point here is to think of your character as if it were a simple puppet whose mouth can only open and close. If you do this step only and stop there, you will be surprised how decent the animation will look—not great, but decent, especially for a simple character.

Now let's go back through the phrase, this time focusing on Wide (W) and Narrow (N) lip shapes (with U for neUtral distance—not wide or narrow): U-U-W-N (lips closed)-U-U (F shape)-U-U-U-N (lips closed)-U-N (F shape)-U-U-U-W-W (wider)-U. Once again the wide-narrow-neutral shapes will vary based on what is around them, but this gives you a basic starting point from which to animate the mouth. Also note that we have parenthetically noted where lip closed shapes—for "b," "p," "f," or "v"—are so that we can create those shapes as we do the lip motion.

After this analysis, the basic (first pass) lip-syncing process is best broken down into two parts. First, focus on the jaw open-close motions, thinking of your character as something of a simple puppet that you put your hand inside: you can only open the mouth and close it as you sync to the voice-over sounds. After this step, go back over the same phrase and focus on the narrow-wide aspect of the sync, creating all the sounds that need the lips to stretch or contract. Finally, if you wish to, you can add in the complex shapes like TH that visibly involve the tongue—we say if you wish because at normal speech pace it is often not noticed when the tongue isn't animated at all; creating tongue shapes then becomes something of a choice based on your desires for the scene and the realism required for the particular project.

EARLY IS ON TIME

Remember that annoying teacher who always said, "Early is on time, on time is late, and late... don't be late!"? Well, maybe she was thinking about lip syncing rather than your classroom tardiness when she told you that. When lip syncing, visuals should always precede sound. If you match your visemes up perfectly to each frame of the sound file you have, the sync will look slightly late, or "off." We are much more forgiving of sound that is too late than sound that is too early, as compared to the visuals we see.

One theory as to why this is the case is that we must form our words with our mouth before releasing the sound that people hear. Thus we form our lips to make a "b" sound before the sound is actually made. Another theory relates to the physics of sound: while light travels almost instantaneously over dozens or hundreds of meters, sound is much slower, traveling at about 343 meters/second (or around 700 mph). Human hearing can distinguish two sounds as separate when they are separated by about 50 milliseconds (0.05 seconds)—think of how a jackhammer sounds like one sound whereas tapping your pencil on a desk makes distinguishably different sounds—which is about the time it takes sound to travel 18 meters. If we assume our visual and auditory complexes are associated, then when we see anyone speak at a distance of greater than 18 meters, we will hear the sound enough after the visual information from the person speaking that we will note the sound as separate (and late) from the visual. While we normally speak to others over shorter distances, in a movie theater, we will often be about 18 meters from the nearest speaker, so the time lag will become noticeable.

Although it is debatable why perfectly synced visuals look bad, the fact is that they do. So, when creating lip sync, always tend toward the early side. One or two frames earlier than perfectly matched up will make your audience believe that the sound is, in fact, synced with the visuals.

Once you have finished, you should have a pretty good lip sync lined up with your voice-over track. Now watch your character's performance critically, noting any areas that are causing problems, and work through those problem spots to clean up the lip-sync animation. During this finessing stage, be careful not to add in so many shapes that you overanimate the mouth. Your mantra should always be "Is this enough?" and if it is, don't add anything else—more shapes will just make the lip sync get murkier instead of cleaner.

Sync Step 2: Facial Performance

At this point lip sync gives way to performance, and the animation should get more fun, because you are creating character rather than simply making a mouth move. If you have video of your actor creating the lines, watch that video and see what they do with their body and face to make the sounds they do. Normally the more exaggerated the character voice, the more distorted the actor will get to create it. Also listen to the audio over and over. What do you imagine when you hear the lines? Can you "see" the character voicing them? If so, how does it move its body and face when saying the lines?

If you wish to use the video reference to match your character's performance, bring in the video file and be sure it is matched to your audio; in fact, be sure to check that the audio and video match before beginning work. It is hard to tell, as you go through your animation one frame at a time, whether or not your audio and video frames are matching up, and it can create a real mess if you end up animating the face and lips at differing times. Whether or not you use video, be sure to keep the sound track visible in your time slider so you have a visual reference of where the sound is being made. Also be sure to create quick renders (playblasts in Maya) of your scene as you go, so that you can hear and see the performance going on as you animate.

Beyond the basics, when creating facial performance for your character, use all the tricks you have in your bag, including anything from the earlier chapters in this book. Consider how the bioenergetics character type will help determine the way the character looks when speaking the lines, or how the Alba breath pattern will adjust facial tensions, or how a given essence will affect the way your character looks. And rather than try to force something on your character here, look at the video of the actor (or at least listen to the audio) and imagine what bioenergetics character, Alba breath, stock Commedia character, and so on, your actor is giving you when reading the lines. Not only will this analysis help you for your lip-syncing scenes, but it will also help you create an overall character who is distinct and who matches the vocal qualities of the lines you are given.

We have laid out lip-sync animation doing the lip syncing first and then creating performance as this is normally simpler to do. It can become difficult to lip sync when your character is moving around and smiling while saying its lines. However, if you prefer to work backward—creating the performance and then lip syncing—by all means feel free to try it. You won't be breaking any laws (that we know of at least!), so do what works best for you when creating voice-based animation.

Exercises in Lip-Synced Facial Animation

Let's put theory into practice now and create some animations with lip syncing in them. First we will create a "straight" lip sync of a neutral line, focusing solely on the lip-syncing aspect of the animation. Then we will create a full-fledged character animation with lip sync and facial performance.

Creating Lip Sync for a Neutral Character

Let's take the phrase "I'm looking at you" and create a solid lip sync for it. First we need to break down the sounds into open-closed and narrow-wide sets so we can do our two lip-sync passes on the phrase. Open the Amy_LookingAtYou_Neutral.wav file from the accompanying DVD and listen to how the actor speaks the line. From our earlier analysis, we have AH-M-OO-AH-OO for our viseme shapes. For open-close, we have O-C-C-O-C. Given that the actor breathes before speaking, we should add one more open shape at the beginning, so we end up with O-O (more open)-C-C-O-C. On the wide-narrow-neutral front, we end up with W (slightly)-U (lips together)-N-U-N. Adding in the in-breath shape to the beginning, we get U-W (slightly)-U (lips together)-N-U-N. Adding both sets together, we get O/U-O/U (more open)-C/U (lips together)-C/N-O/U-C/N. Although it isn't necessary to place the shapes together like this, it can be helpful (especially if you're not used to working with visemes yet) to see how the shapes combine.

Now let's do the lip sync. Open a new scene in your 3D software package and import a character (if you're using Maya, feel free to use the Genna or Marcel rigs on the accompanying DVD). Now import the sound clip, Amy_LookingAtYou_Neutral.wav, into your software and enable its visibility in the time slider so you can see it as you scrub through the scene. (In Maya, after importing the sound file, you have to right-click on the time slider and choose Sound → Amy_LookingAtYou_Neutral from the list of sounds available.) Upon importing the sound and character, your scene should look like Figure 11.7. Our scene is set to 30 frames per second; if yours is set to something different, the frame basis of the timing of the sound file will be different.

> If you are using the included models (Genna and Marcel), which include built-in character/
> subcharacter hierarchies, you can have Maya automatically select the characters as you go.
> First, place the autoCharacterSelection.mel file in your home scripts directory (~Autodesk/
> maya/scripts on your home directory); then copy the line of code from ACSEnable.mel into
> the Script Editor input pane and drag it up onto your shelf. When you start up Maya, simply
> click the ACSEnable button, and from then on, Maya will automatically select whichever sub-
> character it needs based on what is selected in the scene. This makes selecting and keyfram-
> ing characters far easier than having to remember to do so yourself.

Looking at the time slider you will notice that the first 21 frames look blank; however, if you listen to the file you will hear that the actor is breathing in at that point, readying herself for speaking, and thus we should animate those frames as well. If you do a quick playblast render (using QuickTime as the output medium) you can hear the line spoken—and of course by scrubbing back and forth in the time slider you can hear the line frame by frame if you wish.

Figure 11.7

Importing a character and sound into a new scene

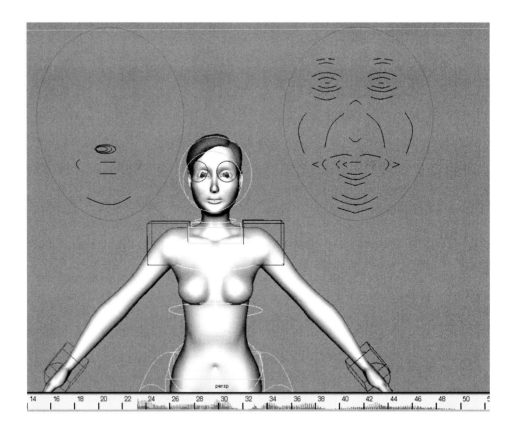

LIP-SYNC FACIAL CONTROLS

If you are using Maya, the included Marcel and Genna rigs have one more feature that we have not discussed until now: they include a lip sync–specific control setup, which is enabled when the lipSyncL layer is visible. To the model's right (our left), this face control, shown here, is similar to the main facial control, but focuses only on creating mouth shapes for speech. By breaking the controls into two separate setups, we have tried to simplify and clarify each step of the process of vocal animation.

As shown, the control setup is intentionally simple to use: there is a Narrow/Wide control (with a dummy control, for symmetry, on the other side); a Jaw Open control, which simply opens and closes the jaw; and symmetrical controls for the top and bottom lip, each of which can either raise (or lower) the lip, or pull it down (up) and in, as if the character were making an "F" or "V" sound. Finally, there are three tongue controls that provide basic rotation and scaling of the tongue for creating sounds like "Th" and, if needed, shapes like "L" as well.

LIP-SYNC FACIAL CONTROLS *(continued)*

One important thing to note is that the main facial controls and the lip-sync controls can (and should) be combined. In other words, if the character is smiling while saying a line, use the lip-sync controls to create the speech and the facial controls to create the smile.

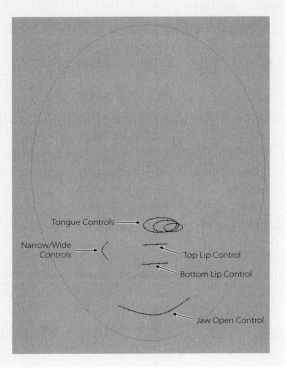

Tongue Controls

Narrow/Wide Controls

Top Lip Control

Bottom Lip Control

Jaw Open Control

Now let's break the lip sync down into two pieces—the jaw open/close and the lips narrow/wide—and, using our earlier analysis, match shapes up to the sound file. The first step is to create the "sock puppet" lip sync by opening and closing the jaw control *only*. (Don't give in to the temptation to start keying other controls yet!) For this portion of the lip sync, the waveform is very helpful: in general, where the waveform gets biggest, the mouth is open (thus generating more sound and therefore a bigger amplitude). Where the waveform is smaller, the mouth is generally more closed. This is by no means a hard and fast rule, but it can help you get oriented as you start keying in the jaw shapes.

We start with the mouth closed at frame 1, and then open it some by frame 4 for the "breathing in" frames, creating a moving hold (changing the shape very slightly) from frame 4 to 20, the mouth slightly closing over these frames so that the reopening will get more pop to it. The jaw then opens wider from frames 20 to 22, anticipating the creation of the AH sound, widening slightly to frame 24 as the AH sound is created. The mouth then closes to frame 26 to make the M shape. Since the entire word "looking" is created with a closed jaw, the jaw stays shut until frame 34, where it opens to anticipate the AH sound for the word "at." After staying open over frames 36 and 37, the jaw shuts again for the remainder of the phrase.

Figure 11.8

Creating the jaw Open/Close shapes for "I'm looking at you"

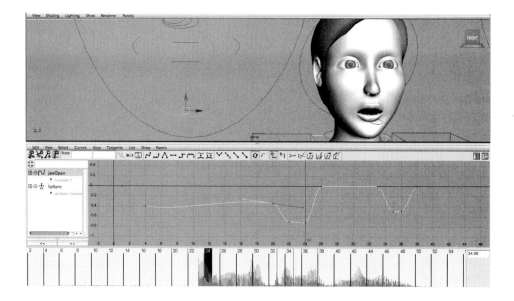

Figure 11.8 shows the curve for creating these mouth open/shut shapes. Although this animation certainly looks like a sock puppet talking, it communicates the basic nature of the phrase. For edification, we have included a playblast of the animation at this stage on the DVD: lookingAtYou_jawOnly.mov. As you can see, the work thus far is far from adequate, but once we add in the wide-narrow lip motions things will look much better.

> While we present the final results of our lip sync work, the actual work involves a good deal of trial and error and adjusting shapes backward and forward (usually forward) over a frame or two to create animation that appears correct with the sound. You, of course, might find that you prefer the shapes to arise at different times or to be larger or smaller than our results—and of course you should use what you think is best. Just remember to keep experimenting and tweaking until you are satisfied with your own results.

Now let's add in the lip motions, focusing on the narrow/wide dichotomy that we outlined previously. We have a slight widening at the beginning of "I'm," a closed mouth (as it is already) for the M shape, then narrow for the two OO shapes that come on "looking" and "you," separated by the more neutral lip shape for "at." As the "y" sound starts the word "you," we will pay attention to that area while working, and add in a slight widening of the mouth if necessary there. To make things clearer at this stage, we will only use the Narrow_Wide control for this pass. Once again, it is best to avoid the temptation to key in several controls at once, because correcting something that doesn't look right becomes more complex at that point.

After working through this pass, we end up with the animation curve shown in Figure 11.9. The lips stay neutral until frame 20, then widen slightly to frame 22 for the AH shape. The lips then move toward a neutral shape by frame 26, for the M shape. By frame 28, we get to the narrow OO shape for "look," then soften that shape back toward neutral as we get to the "ing" of "looking." There is a moving hold between frames 35 and 38 as the vocal line moves from "looking" to "at" (which has a neutral wide/narrow shape). For a little extra pop in the narrow shape, we create a slightly wider shape (relatively speaking) on frame 39, then move to the narrow OO shape on frame 41—once again anticipating the sound itself, which is about one frame behind the shape. We then back this shape off slightly to frame 49 as the word "you" is drawn out. Finally, we trail off to a neutral, "rest" shape on frame 55 (and go back and add a key for the jaw open/close control at frame 55 to create a mouth that is slightly open for the next sentence). The file lookingAtYou_jawPlusLips.mov shows a playblast of the animation at this stage, before final corrections.

Now for the final tweaking, which actually isn't much. The most egregious error that we see when playing back the animation at this stage is that the teeth are pressed together during the words "looking" and "you." We obviously need to open the jaw a bit at these points so that there is some room between the teeth. Aside from this problem, the rest of our fixes are just tweaks to the animation curves; as it turns out, we don't really need to involve the lip up and down controls at all for this phrase, so we'll save the effort of keying them. Though not absolutely necessary, we wanted to see the tongue move a little on the "l" of "looking," so we animated that as well. The final animation, lookingAtYou_lipSyncFinal .mov, is on the DVD. For your reference, the Maya project itself, lookingAtYou.mb, is also on the DVD.

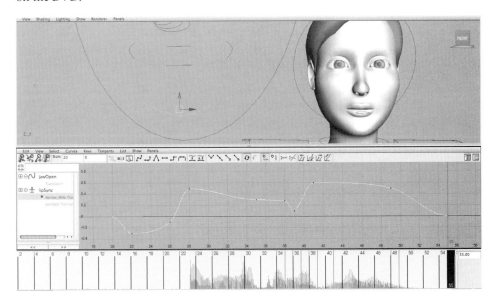

Figure 11.9

Adding in the lips Wide/Narrow shapes for "I'm looking at you"

Creating Facial Performance with Words

Now that you have learned the technical aspects of matching mouth shapes to words in a voice track, let's move on to matching character performance in addition to lip sync-ing. Open a new scene and import your model. (If you're using Maya and want to follow along, import the Genna rig.) Now we need to import both the audio and video files, separately. (In Maya, the image sequence will not provide sound, so you need to cut the sound from your video file to import separately.) First, create a new camera, then create an image plane and load the `Amy_PayForThis_Happy.mov` file from the DVD. Adjust your camera until your model is about the same size, but offset from the video so you can see both the actor and the model at the same time. Now import the sound file into your scene and select it from the pop-up list available when right-clicking on the time slider. When you finish these steps, your scene should look like Figure 11.10.

Figure 11.10

Importing video and audio files into a new scene in Maya

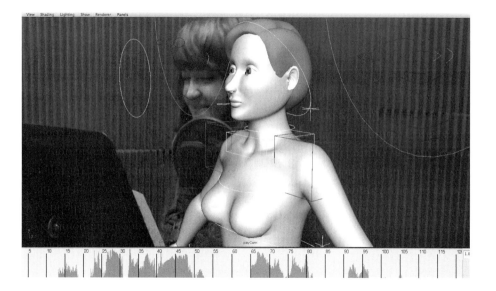

Please see Chapter 4 for more information on importing images and using the book's included rigs in Autodesk Maya. See the previous exercise for more on importing and showing sound files in Maya.

We break down our animation work into two steps: the first is matching lip sync only, which will be similar to the previous exercise; the second step will be to match our char-acter's animation (with lip sync in place) to the actor's performance. The reason we do lip sync first is that once the body is moving around and facial performance is animated, it is difficult to focus just on the syncing process.

To begin, we need to reanalyze the phrase, because this time the actor is performing the phrase rather than speaking it neutrally. We can use the video footage here to look at the shapes created to form the words, but be forewarned that it is sometimes difficult to separate the lip-sync expression from other things going on that will need to be animated in the following step. Recall that the basic phrase's visemes are OO-EE-F-AH-OO-AH-OO-IH-P-AA-F-AH-TH-IH. Listening (and watching) the clip, we get OO-EE-F-AH(very short)-OO-AH-R (the closed/wide R shape is clearly visible in this performance)-EE (no word here, but a very open shape)-OO-IH-P-AA-F-TH-IH. Thus the shapes are similar, though exaggerated (as you can see by looking at the video), and we have a few extra shapes thrown in due to the performance. Breaking down the mouth shapes into the Open-Closed and Wide-Narrow-neUtral sets—one for each viseme listed earlier—we get the following: O (this is previous to the words, but the mouth is open at this point)-C-C-C-O-C-O-C (mostly for R)-O (no sound)-C-C-C-O-C-O-C(mostly, but with enough room for the TH)-C. And W (previous to words, but the mouth is wide at this point)-N-W-U-U-N-U-N (slightly for R)-W (no sound)-N-W (slightly)-U-U-U-U-U-W (slightly).

Now we can begin animating, starting with the jaw Open-Closed curve, then the lips Wide-Narrow, and finally adding in the lower lip roll for the F/V sounds, and the tongue motion for the TH. Figure 11.11 shows the jaw Open/Close portion of the animation. Note how, after examining the video and watching the playback, we have added a good deal more jaw action than we originally had set out, and that the jaw is almost never closed completely due to the way the actor speaks her lines.

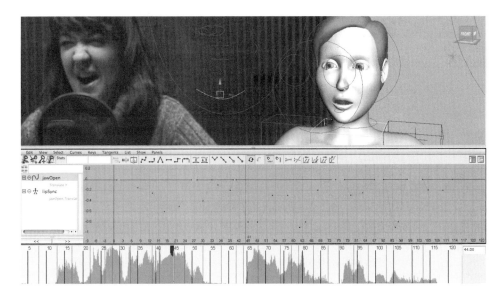

Figure 11.11

The jaw Open/Close curve for the phrase "Whoever you are... you will pay for this"

After adding in the lips Narrow/Wide curve, our animation is looking better, as shown in Figure 11.12. However, we still have some work to do creating the F/V and TH shapes, as well as some tweaks to the overall size and shape of the lip sync. In this particular phrase, the F/V and TH shapes help to sell the lip sync, getting the sync from barely adequate to looking correct (at least as much as possible with a nonanimated face).

Figure 11.12

The lips Wide/Narrow curve for the phrase "Whoever you are…you will pay for this"

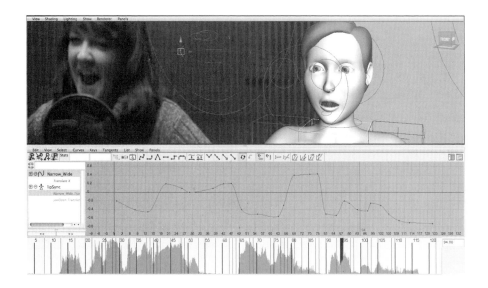

Tweaks mostly include moving keyframes around by one or two frames, and adjusting animation curves to match the actor's performance in the video. The "big ticket" fix, however, is pulling the upper lip up during most of the animation and, to some extent, pulling the lower lip down; while we want to save the expression work until the next section, the actor clearly has her upper lip up during most of the sequence, and pulling it up on the character sells the "happy" state of the line delivery. The lower lip is also important but is not as exaggerated as the upper lip. Upon completion we end up with a nonanimated face speaking the lines without much expression, as shown in Figure 11.13. This intermediate version of the animation is on the DVD: `payForThis_lipSyncComplete.mov`.

Figure 11.13

Completing the lip sync portion of the animation

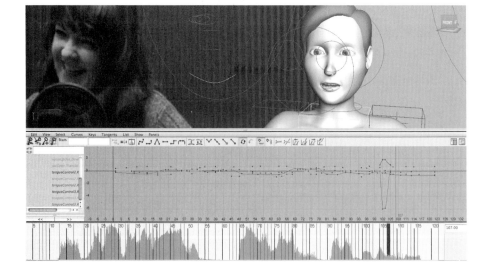

At this point, while the lip sync matches fairly well, the lack of facial and body animation is all too obvious. To correct this problem, we first tackle the general body and head motions, following the actor's motions. Once we have these blocked out, we turn to the facial expressions and add them in.

Generally, the actor's body is hunched slightly back with her head held forward, her hands at her hips (while her hands are out of view, this alters the way the arms hang), so we first adjust the model to fit this overall pose, exaggerating it slightly for the animated character. During the sequence, the actor is very mobile, rocking back and forth, slumping and raising her shoulders, and turning her head and even thrusting her neck forward at times for effect. Of particular importance is her finger wag, accentuating the word "will": this motion enhances the audio, making that moment the emotional capper for the phrase. Using the actor footage as a guide, we end up with an animation that is starting to look like a real performance. Figure 11.14 shows a still from the movie, payForThis_bodyAnimation.mov, on the DVD.

Figure 11.14

Creating the body animation to match the lip sync

Now all that's left is to use the video's facial motion as a guide for creating the facial animation. The actor has a wide smile during most of the sequence, her eyes are squinted (so that it is difficult to see them for almost all of the animation), her lower lids are drawn up significantly, and the lines between her nose and mouth (nasolabial lines) are accentuated. We use this as a basis for creating the character's overall facial look, then animate the individual moments from there.

As is obvious, the actor has a very mobile face, and her facial performance is marvelous fodder for animated character work. One interesting aspect of this "happy" line delivery is that the actor uses a great deal of the Nose Wrinkler Action Unit (AU 9), which is usually associated with either disgust or some anger. This is particularly interesting as it reveals something about the way the line is being delivered: while ostensibly happy in its delivery, the line is certainly not happy—in fact it is accusatory—and we discover a hidden nastiness to the line in the way it is being delivered. While the actor is smiling, she is doing this to cover a deeper anger, and this becomes evident when doing the nitty-gritty of the facial animation. Discoveries like this are a wonderful reason to have video reference footage when animating characters for dialogue.

When finished, we end up with the completed movie, payForThis_complete.mov, on the DVD. Figure 11.15 shows a frame from the completed animation. The complete project, payForThis.mb, is available for reference on the accompanying DVD.

Figure 11.15

The completed animation for the phrase "Whoever you are…you will pay for this"

After working through this example, you should have a solid methodology for creating voice-based animation performance using video reference footage. There are audio and audio/video files on the accompanying DVD, including two long takes of two actors creating the phrases we discussed earlier using several characters; feel free to cut out sections for more practice. We have already cut out several and placed them on the DVD for your convenience. And you should create your own voice-over recordings and use them for practice as well. Not only will you get faster as you work through more examples, you will also get better at reading what's going on internally with the actors, and then be able to translate that into your character animation, which will improve the impact of your work.

While lip-sync animation can be tedious, it is a necessary animation skill to have, and if you think of it in the context of creating a full-body performance by your character, then the lines serve to drive the animation, making them more fun to work on. With practice and patience you will be creating dialogue performances that will wow your audience and make emotional connections between your characters and those watching.

About the Companion DVD

Topics in this appendix include:

- ■ **What You'll Find on the DVD**
- ■ **System Requirements**
- ■ **Using the DVD**
- ■ **Troubleshooting**

What You'll Find on the DVD

If you need help installing the items provided on the DVD, refer to the installation instructions in the "Using the DVD" section.

Support Files

The DVD is organized into chapter folders, plus a General Files directory, which contains scripts and character rigs that are used throughout the book. Each folder contains files that support concepts and projects in the book: Maya character rigs, sample Maya projects, video reference footage of actors performing exercises (which can be studied or used as reference footage for animation work), video of completed animation projects, and still frames of reference footage for use with animation projects. Most chapters have Maya projects, so you can copy them to your hard drive and then work directly from them. We don't encourage you to work with files directly from the DVD.

System Requirements

You will need to be running Maya 2008 or higher to fully use all of the Maya files on the DVD. With a QuickTime-compatible player (anything that supports H.264 video and AAC audio), you will be able to view all of the video reference footage, and any image viewer can view the still photos on the DVD. Make sure your computer meets the minimum system requirements shown in the following list. If your computer doesn't meet these requirements, you may have problems using the files on the companion DVD. For the latest information, please refer to the ReadMe file located at the root of the DVD.

- A PC running Microsoft Windows XP (SP2 or higher) or Windows Vista
- A Macintosh running Apple OS X 10.5.2 or higher
- An Internet connection
- A DVD-ROM drive

For the latest information on system requirements for Maya, go to www.autodesk.com/maya. Although you can find specific hardware recommendations on these web pages, there is some general information that will help you determine if you're already set up to run Maya. For best results, you need a fast processor, a minimum 1GB of RAM, and a separate video card (rather than one with integrated graphics). For the video and still image reference files, any computer of recent vintage should be adequate.

To best view the video reference footage, download the free QuickTime player software from www.apple.com. If you have a Mac, this will be included. If you have a Windows PC, QuickTime will be included if you have downloaded a product like iTunes; if not, go to www.apple.com/quicktime to download the free player.

Using the DVD

To install the items from the DVD to your hard drive, follow these steps:

1. Insert the DVD into your computer's DVD-ROM drive. The license agreement appears.

> **Windows users:** The interface won't launch if Autorun is disabled. In that case, click Start → Run (for Windows Vista, Start → All Programs → Accessories → Run). In the dialog box that appears, type **D:\Start.exe**. (Replace **D** with the proper letter if your DVD drive uses a different letter. If you don't know the letter, see how your DVD drive is listed under My Computer.) Click OK.

> **Mac users:** The DVD icon will appear on your desktop; double-click the icon to open the DVD, then navigate to any files you wish to on the DVD.

2. Read through the license agreement, and then click the Accept button if you want to use the DVD.

The DVD interface appears. The interface allows you to access the content with just one or two clicks.

Troubleshooting

Wiley has attempted to provide programs that work on most computers with the minimum system requirements. Alas, your computer may differ, and some programs may not work properly for some reason.

The two likeliest problems are that you don't have enough memory (RAM) for the programs you want to use or you have other programs running that are affecting installation or running of a program. If you get an error message such as "Not enough memory" or "Setup cannot continue," try one or more of the following suggestions, and then try using the software again:

Turn off any antivirus software running on your computer. Installation programs sometimes mimic virus activity and may make your computer incorrectly believe that it's being infected by a virus.

Close all running programs. The more programs you have running, the less memory is available to other programs. Installation programs typically update files and programs, so if you keep other programs running, installation may not work properly.

Have your local computer store add more RAM to your computer. This is, admittedly, a drastic and somewhat expensive step. However, adding more memory can really help the speed of your computer and allow more programs to run at the same time.

Customer Care

If you have trouble with the book's companion DVD, please call the Wiley Product Technical Support phone number at (800) 762-2974. Outside the United States, call +1(317) 572-3994. You can also contact Wiley Product Technical Support at http://sybex.custhelp.com. John Wiley & Sons will provide technical support only for installation and other general quality control items. For technical support on the applications themselves, consult the program's vendor or author.

To place additional orders or to request information about other Wiley products, please call (877) 762-2974.

Index

Note to the Reader: Throughout this index **boldfaced** page numbers indicate primary discussions of a topic. *Italicized* page numbers indicate illustrations.

E